Twayne's English Authors Series

Sylvia E. Bowman, *Editor*

INDIANA UNIVERSITY

Louis MacNeice

(TEAS) 99

Louis MacNeice

By ELTON EDWARD SMITH

University of South Florida

Twayne Publishers, Inc. :: New York

To my wife Esther
Who makes everything possible

Preface

"In retrospect, the characteristic poetry of the thirties in Britain seems to have been doomed to expire in a dead end. Only two of the poets who seemed typical of their time, during the decade itself, survived into the sixties with anything like their early promise fulfilled: W. H. Auden and Louis MacNeice. For many years, MacNeice's survival seemed more problematic than Auden's, but survive he did, to end as he began, as one of the most original and significant poets of his time, and also, as a representative man of his time."

In this single paragraph, taken from the advertisement of a series of topics for the Columbia Lecture Bureau, Walter Allen introduces three of the themes developed in this study: MacNeice as representative man of his time; a poet who ended as he began; and one who fulfilled his early literary promise. This study is more concerned with the significance of his poetry than with the representative quality of his life. Yet the division of his work into chronological periods tends to fall into a calendar of the international currents and events of the era; and the budding, then disillusioned, liberalism of his personal experience mirrors the rather repentant liberalism of our time.

Thus it seemed quite natural to think of MacNeice first as a brilliant and talented youth in his college years and immediately after—and to call the first chapter "The Bright Young Man." The second chapter, "Member of the Group," shows the young poet amidst the froth of idea and creativity of his association with Wystan Hugh Auden, Stephen Spender, Cecil Day Lewis, and Christopher Isherwood. Along with the whole of the British Left, MacNeice detested fascism and sympathized with the Spanish Republicans in their fateful civil war—thus the third chapter is entitled "Left of Center." Like many of the other intellectuals of the 1930's, he was shocked by the Moscow-Berlin concordat and rather thoroughly disillusioned about the idealism of international socialism—thus the fourth chapter is called "The Disillusioned Liberal." But, at the end of his life and his poetic career, the poet who loved cycles and began as a brilliant student of the Classics, returned to a warm and deep Classical humanism which justifies the title of Chapter 5, "The Classical Humanist." Thus this work agrees with Professor Allen in viewing Louis MacNeice both as a man representative of his time—and as a poet who ended where he began.

In tracing the pattern of fulfillment of his early promise, I made the most exciting discovery in the preparation of this volume. Other critics had noted the signs of a crisis as a creative writer. They had recognized an imitative, Yeatsian beginning, the development along with a group of friends of a new prosodic diction and rhythm, as well as its issue into a kind of cretive "dead end." I believe that this study is the only one to date which traces MacNeice's long leap to a new style and a new tone by which to express new thoughts.

Although the poet died in 1963, his literary executor, Dr. E. R. Dodds, Regius Professor of Greek at Oxford University, has published a number of posthumous volumes, each requiring a revision and rethinking of the central thesis of this book. Finally, I had to take refuge in the briefest of comments in the Bibliography concerning the growing bulk of exhumed MacNeice relics. Obviously, the required brevity of the English Authors Series makes it impossible to deal with the totality of an author's works, just as the annotated bibliography limits the number of items that enthusiasm would admit. I am deeply grateful to Dr. Dodds for subjecting this manuscript to particular scrutiny, embodied in four pages of "Errata and Queries," in addition to penciled corrections throughout. Of course he is not to be held responsible for my own critical eccentricities or for the times I stubbornly chose to go my own way.

One particular bit of stubbornness (not in reference to Prof. Dodd's suggestion) was my rejection of the old advice to speakers: "tell 'em what you're going to tell 'em; tell 'em; tell 'em what you've told 'em." I preferred the more organic, and I think permissive approach of starting right in, cold, with the *juvenilia*, and letting the characteristics emerge, recede, and change as the poet changed and grew. In addition to partial summaries along the way, the Conclusion delineates the fully emerged pattern of development.

I especially appreciate the help and encouragement of my colleagues as I forsook the safe shelters of Victorian letters and steered into the whirling chaos of twentieth-century poetry. Dr. Jack Moore, who read the first two chapters, was most meticulous in his marginal commentary. Dr. Rainulf Stelzmann took Mac-Neice's translation of Goethe into German classes in which he was teaching *Faust,* and produced a detailed analysis of the strengths and weaknesses of the Irish poet's interpretation. Dr. Mildred Adams has been helpful with Latin titles, and Dr. Virgil Milani with Italian references.

I am indebted to the following publishers for their gracious permission to quote from Louis MacNeice's poetry and prose: Appleton, Century, and Crofts, Publishing; B. A. Blackwell and Mott, Ltd.; The Clarendon Press; Curtis Brown, Ltd.; Faber and Faber, Ltd.; Harcourt, Brace and World, Inc.; Longmans, Green and Co.; Oxford University Press; Random House; Victor Gollancz, Ltd.; and to the Literary Executor of the Estate of Louis MacNeice.

The work would have been impossible, of course, without the cooperation of Dean Elliott Hardaway and the library staff of the University of South Florida, and in particular, the skill of Dennis Robison in gathering MacNeice editions from university libraries all across the country. The South Florida Library and the New York City Library were most gracious in providing quiet places for research and typing. Dean Russell Cooper, Dr. Robert Zetler (then Divisional Director), and Departmental Chairman James Parrish graciously made financially possible several hurried dashes to New York City for last-minute bibliographic checks.

ELTON SMITH

Lakeland, Florida

Contents

Contents

Chronology

1907   Louis MacNeice born September 12, in Belfast, Ireland, son of Elizabeth Margaret (nee Clesham) and the Reverend John Frederick MacNeice, later Anglican Bishop of Down, Connor, and Dromore, Ireland.

1908   Father became rector of St. Nicholas Church, Carrickfergus (cf. "Carrickfergus").

1914   December, mother's death of tuberculosis in Dublin nursing home (cf. "Autobiography").

1917–   Attended Sherbourne Preparatory School for Boys, Dorset,
1921   England; Headmaster Littleton Charles Powys (cf. Owen in "The Kingdom," and *Autumn Sequel*, Canto XXII).

1921–   Marlborough College, Wiltshire (cf. *Autumn Journal*,
1926   XIII). Close friends included Bernard Spencer, John Betjeman, Graham Shepard (also at Oxford), John Hilton (cf. *The Strings Are False*), Anthony Blunt.

1926–   Studied at Merton College, Oxford University. Read Clas-
1930   sics and philosophy; took "double first" in Honour Moderations and "Greats."

1929   *Oxford Poetry: 1929*, edited by Louis MacNeice and Stephen Spender. *Blind Fireworks*, poems.

1930   ". . . junior member of the Auden-Isherwood-Spender literary axis" in the 1930's. June 21, married Giovanna Marie Thérèse Babette Ezra (cf. "Mayfly"). Appointed lecturer in Classics at Birmingham University.

1932   *Roundabout Way* (Louis Malone, pseudonym), first and only published novel.

1934   May, birth of son, Dan (cf. "Ode").

1935   *Poems.*

1936   November 2, divorce from first wife who later married American graduate student at Oxford, Charles Katzman. Louis MacNeice vacationed in Spain with Anthony Blunt, and spent summer in Iceland (cf. *Autumn Journal*, VI).

Appointed lecturer in Greek, Bedford College for Women, University of London. Aeschylus' *Agamemnon* translated by Louis MacNeice; produced in November by Group Theatre Company, Westminster Theatre, London; directed by Rupert Doone, and music by Benjamin Britten.

1937　Visited Iceland with Wystan Hugh Auden. W. H. Auden and Louis MacNeice, *Letters from Iceland,* travel diary in prose and poetry. *Out of the Picture,* play in two acts; produced in December by Group Theatre.

1938　*Zoo,* prose. October 18, MacNeice, Auden, Spender, and Day Lewis in Manchester to broadcast poems on the Northern B.B.C. Met Dylan Thomas. *The Earth Compels: Poems. I Crossed the Minch,* travel diary in prose with occasional poems. *Modern Poetry: A Personal Essay,* prose criticism. Visited Barcelona, Spain, in December and January, 1939.

1939　*Autumn Journal: A Poem.* April, lectured at Pennsylvania State University; met in New York City by Charles and Mariette Katzman (cf. "The Old Story"). Probably met Eleanor Clark, to whom he dedicated *Last Ditch* and *Plant and Phantom* (cf. "Cradle Song for Eleanor," "Meeting Point"). July, trip to Ireland with Ernst Stahl, collaborator in translation of *Faust* (cf. "The Coming of War").

1940　January, special lecturer in English, spring semester, Cornell University, Ithaca, New York. July, in Portsmouth, New Hampshire hospital with peritonitis (cf. "Jigsaws," "The Messiah"). October, visited Katzman poultry farm in New Jersey. Volunteered for Royal Navy; rejected because of poor eyesight. Served as London firewatcher in House Guard (cf. "The Trolls," "Brother Fire," "Homage to Wren"). *The Last Ditch: Poems. Selected Poems.*

1941　Joined British Broadcasting Corporation as scriptwriter and producer. Remained in that dual capacity until 1954, with exception of eighteen-month period, 1950–1951, as Director of the British Institute in Athens, Greece. *Plant and Phantom: Poems. The Poetry of W. B. Yeats,* critical study.

1942　April, Father resigned bishopric; died shortly after (cf. "The Truisms," "The Kingdom"). MacNeice married singer Hedli Anderson; one daughter, Corinna, born the following year.

1943 Graham Shepard drowned in action on Atlantic (Gavin in "The Kingdom"; cf. "The Casualty (in memoriam G.H.S.)" and *Autumn Sequel*, II).

1944 *Christopher Columbus*, a radio drama. *Springboard: Poems 1941–1944.*

1947 *The Dark Tower and Other Radio Scripts. Holes in the Sky: Poems, 1944–1947.* Visit to India (cf. "The Crash Landing," "Mahabalipuram") with Wynford Vaughan Thomas (Evans in "The Kingdom").

1949 *Collected Poems: 1925–1948.* MacNeice and Stahl's translation of Goethe's *Faust* broadcast October and November.

1950 Spent eighteen months with British Council as Director of British Institute, Athens, Greece.

1951 Goethe's *Faust* (Parts I and II) translated by Louis Mac-Neice with the assistance of E. L. Stahl.

1952 *Ten Burnt Offerings*, poems.

1953 Attended Dylan Thomas' funeral, Laugharne, Wales.

1954 Poetry readings and song recitals (Mrs. MacNeice) in America. Premio Italiano award for radio play *Prisoner's Progress. Autumn Sequel: A Rhetorical Poem in XXVI Cantos. The Penny That Rolled Away*, juvenile.

1955 Traveled in Africa and Asia.

1956 In Rouen, France, for the fifth centenary of the Rehabilitation of Joan of Arc (cf. "Visit to Rouen").

1957 Unpublished drama *Traitors in Our Way*, staged by Group Theatre, Belfast. Hon. D. Litt. conferred by Belfast University. *Visitations: Poems.*

1958 Became Commander of the British Empire, January 1. Judith E. Wilson Lectureship, Cambridge University.

1959 *Eighty-Five Poems: Selected by the Author. Solstices: Poems.*

1960 Third Prize in Guinness Poetry Award, for "Reflections."

1962 Moved thirty miles from London to village of Aldbury, Hertfordshire.

1963 Spring, delivered Clark Lectures, "Varieties of Parable," at Cambridge University. September 3, died of pneumonia, St. Leonard's Hospital, Shoreditch, London. Survived by widow, Mrs. Louis MacNeice (Hedli Anderson); daughter, Miss Corinna B. MacNeice; son by first marriage, Dan MacNeice; brother-in-law and sister, Sir John and Lady

Elizabeth Nicholson. October 17, Memorial Service at All Souls, Langham Place, London. *The Burning Perch: Poems* (posthumous).

1964 *Astrology*, prose. Two radio plays, *The Administrator* (written and broadcast in 1961) and *The Mad Islands* (written and broadcast in 1962).

1965 *Varieties of Parable: Cambridge University Clark Lectures*, delivered at Trinity College in 1963. *The Strings Are False: An Unfinished Autobiography*.

1966 *Collected Poems*, edited by E. R. Dodds.

CHAPTER 1

The Bright Young Man

LOUIS MacNEICE appears to have suffered more than most poets through identification with another poet—Wystan Hugh Auden, and with the poetry of a particular period—the 1930's. In the former identification he is barely visible standing in the deep shadow cast by his colorful friend and fellow poet. This study follows through the crises of his poetic development in order to show his originality and his continuing significance. In the latter identification, MacNeice has been lumped in the group of the 1930's poets so soundly castigated by F. R. Leavis and his followers for their sin of being products of Oxford, Bloomsbury, and the literary Establishment—a series of historical accidents which to the critics made them more fashionable than capable and more popular than significant. Perhaps this study might best begin at the very period when MacNeice was exhibiting that undergraduate brilliance at which Leavis considered the whole group to have been permanently arrested.

Louis MacNeice clearly showed that he was a "bright young man" by placing in the First Class both in the First Public Examination (Classical Moderations) and in the Second (Greats) at Oxford University, where he read Classics and philosophy in Merton College. The annual undergraduate anthology, *Oxford Poetry: 1929*, edited by Louis MacNeice and his friend and classmate Stephen Spender,[1] offered tangible proof both of his talent and of his fellow students' recognition of it. With the bright egoism of creative youth, the editors each contributed four specimens of their poetic craft, while the twenty other contributors were represented by two or three selections each (with the exception of John Hilton, of Corpus Christi College, one of MacNeice's closest personal friends,[2] who had four poems included).

I   Oxford Poetry (1929)

"Cradle Song," with its ballad refrain "Sleep, sleep, Miriam,"
dates itself and MacNeice, its creator, as post-Freudian. Beneath
the troubled surface of the world, behind the dark wool of sleep,
there erupts something unsleeping, "something that whines and
scampers," something that will have to be fastened and muzzled
all of its life. Unity is achieved at the poem's beginning and ending by the image of flames in the bedroom hearth. They suggest
the simpering of faded ladies who were once the world's beauties
but who now posture, chatter, and die unheeded. "Spring Sunshine," also in celebration of sleep, asks if, instead of colonizing
"any more the already populous / Tree of knowledge," it would
not be better to "hide one's head in the warm sand of sleep" and
thus "be embalmed without hustle or bother"?

"Address from My Death-Bed" points to the reader in philosophy with its references to the concrete universals of the philosopher Giordano Bruno. The Italian philosopher's interest in the
new astronomical knowledge of the sixteenth century is symbol-
ized by the poet's description of his own birth, as he enters the
universe, catching with his infant fingers at the "nipple of stars."
The philosopher achieved unity through the concept of the universal immanence of God. He achieved individuality by a Stoic
monadology and an Aristotelianism in which form and discrete
matter are both real and eternal. The poet plays with the thought
that the net of individualism too much divides, but that, if the
dividing strings should break, the two personalities would merge
only "in lost togetherdom." With the wit which later becomes a
characteristic signature, the youthful poet depicts the philosopher
as a discursive cow, content to chew upon absolutes, phenomena,
and prolegomena, but, with all his weighty wordiness, "Playing a
joke you were, you are, you WERE"—Philosopher past tense; poet
very much present.

"Laburnum" strikes the same notes of time and death—the ab-
sorbing interest of those so very young that they feel personally
safe from both. The bells of the yellow blossoms are the motley
mockery of jesters, pealing one hundred and one times; under-
neath, a "cold bell murders" the jesters, and damns their souls
"with a smack of the metal lip at a hundred-and-one." Peeping
Tom peers and plays until Old Tom Time touches him with "fin-

gers of poisoned death." Time, death, sleep and wit of that variety
the literary necrologist of *Time* magazine called "cynically cheerful" [3]—these are the major themes and the characteristic manner
of these slender exhibits of *juvenilia*. The language and imagery
are both more elaborate and allusive than in his later poetry when
the sprung rhythms of Gerard Manley Hopkins gave him a "resilient conversational tone." [4]

II   Blind Fireworks (1929)

Blind Fireworks, published by Victor Gollancz in 1929, was
dedicated "To Giovanna" (Marie Therese Ezra) whom MacNeice
married in 1930. With his bright, light facility for the breezy explanation, he apologizes for his title on the grounds of his admiration of the Chinese who "invented gunpowder only to make fireworks with it." Like Chinese fireworks, the poems of this first
collection are "artificial and yet random; because they go quickly
through their antics against an important background, and fall
and go out quickly." [5] Herein, with precocious acumen, the young
poet avoids the vast, vague outlines of early poetry; he settles
down to what Thomas Stearns Eliot ascribed to William Blake:
"Quite mature and successful attempts to do something small." [6]
The humility and tight control of the impulse and the product are
praiseworthy; the smallness of compass raises the question of self-
limitation. Perhaps for a young poet to distrust the resounding
phrase and to dislike rhetoric represents a premature coming-to-
peace with small things well done.

The comatose emphasis upon sleep, already noted in the Oxford
poems, is noticeable in *Blind Fireworks* in the witty close of the
first poem, "Inaugural Rant": summer "pulls the cords of slumber"
and langorously "folds her drove of sheep." In "Bound in Stupid-
ity and Unbound," a boy grovels in his "nice comfy bed" interred
"in hugger-mugger." The treasure-ship of his dreams may sink—
"H.M.S. *Life* is reported lost at sea"—but the lost boy remains
dormant.

Contrary to the practice of rhetorical young poets who take
themselves more seriously than MacNeice, there are many poems
in this early collection which have their origin in childhood experiences. The second poem in *Blind Fireworks*, "Reminiscences of
Infancy," yawns with the recollection of childhood slumber interrupted by two metallic sounds: the soothing "metal murmur" of

trains, and the deep-toned menace of the "steel-bosomed siren calling bitterly" from the sea. The third poem, "Child's Terror," raises MacNeice's familiar figures of time, sleep, and death in a nightmare about a swing that was supposed to lift the lad "to meet the surpliced choir of clouds" (a natural enough image for the son of the Angelican Bishop of Down, Connor, and Dromore). But the swing breaks, letting him fall into a bottomless hole from which he cries to his nurse, "Turn a light on my snowy counterpane" so that he may know "it is linen . . . not rock."

In the sophisticatedly innocent tone of many of these poems about childhood, "Child's Unhappiness" introduces the new themes of the search for identity and the loss of faith. When the nursemaid asks "Where is yourself, my child," he seeks the key to personal identity in the existence of the Classical deities. But when, like Daphne, he spies the sleeping Apollo in the sun's great house, instead of her "half-enjoyed despair," he knows real despair as his search for identity ends in a "ghastly cul-de-sac," from which all he can see of the god is a "stark stranded wreck," the "bones of dead divinity." The rectory child began early to question the household gods through the mild substitution of the Classical divinities.

In "ΓΝΩΘΙ ΣΕΑΥΤΟΝ" [7] the childhood quest for identity leads Narcissus away from his motionless reflection in the still lake to his struggle with the changeable Proteus of reality. When he comes to the sea, he rejoices once again in his mirrored image, but the calm features are now all stormy and distorted. The flowery hours of childhood depart, and the Three Old Women of adulthood arrive. The stillness of the lake is exchanged for the waves of a sea that rush "to rend that beauty if they cannot end it." All that is left of the meditation upon the meaning of selfhood is "simulacra trailing in the void." Although not about childhood, this search for identity ending in simulacra probably needs to be capped by the witty shocker "Middle Age" which portrays the perfect conformist who walks "the parade of earth with confidence" and, when he searches for his identity, shops "in Heaven's Woolworth's for a soul."

In "Poussin," MacNeice reveals both the beginning of a life-long interest in modern art and an awareness of the personal idiom of the artist's vision. The clouds in the painting remind the poet of the golden tea he drank as a child, when he dipped his spoon and sweetened the cup with the sugar-like stones of a marble fountain. And in "A Serene Evening" the poet describes a garden as "all Renoir and Keats," probably more allusively than descriptively. Imitation of Keats may be almost a trademark for young poets of MacNeice's generation. Although they had Eliot in the foreground, they also surely had the Romantic poets in a not-very-distant background.

Childhood memories in "Happy Families (A Satirical Lyric)" offer no escape from the triviality of family surface respectability, the catching of buses and trains, the hiring of taxis, or the social decorum that keeps the family undisgraced. "Fossils in rock" and "crusted in sandstone," they live their mummified existences in the dry pattern of good manners. They listen to that beggar the wind who raps and knocks, blows and ruffles; but they know he extends no freedom to the locked inmates of their family.

"Harvest Thanksgiving," one of MacNeice's witty religious poems, arises out of the memory of the rectory child. The sun-flowers wave their heads in the wind out of doors, but Auntie gathers them for altar decorations for the Harvest Festival. Thus, once again, the poet compares the freedom of the outside, natural world to the rigid conformism of the life of home, church, and school. The stained-glass flowers in the windows look coldly at the live captives from outdoors; the choir "will pant the anthem for their funeral." The sexton turns down the gas; the brass plates on the pulpit gleam down the aisle; time crusts into a fossil; eternity tinkles "in stony droppings from the monuments." No more will a preacher's voice break the icy darkness, nor a "choir chip the egg of silence."

The poet, himself an undergraduate student, asks in "A Classi-cal Education" if time cannot have the decency to drown the rust-ing Greeks at their pier-heads and to bury the Romans who are goose-stepping beneath their crooked arches. There are moments, on a windy night, when he can hear once again their "frivolous phalaecians" and "stern hexameters." Perhaps on such a night the deadness of the past will lessen; and, if he looks and listens, he will hear a human heart beat, or find a poet guttering like a pale candle "on a worn window-sill in the wind."

In the Foreword, MacNeice called Thor "the Time-God," and defined his poet image of Pythagoras as "a grotesque, automatic Man-of-Science, who both explains and supports the universe by counting." However, MacNeice's use of both figures to measure time makes it clear that something more than ordinary time is indicated. This is final or end-time, what the Greeks called ἔσχατος. The theme of doom or finality, introduced in his early poems, comes to maturity in the radio drama *Out of the Picture,* through the form of a war to extinction after the last international peace conference has failed.

There are a number of Pythagoras, or Thor poems, in *Blind Fireworks,* all with the multiple or single themes of time, death, or doom. "This Tournament" expresses the absurdity of human arrogance, when, like moths in the sun, we joust and strive at mock-tournaments for unreal prizes. For over all the mock-heroics, the poet visualizes, with a rather savage glee, "the hammer of Thor descending." In "A Lame Idyll," even Pythagoras is warned that his time, too has come; he must make ready to join the "wan Adonis and Proserpine." The seven spheres sink out of sight; the "universe fades in the upper distance"; time, space, and matter are no more.

On the surface, the poem "Coal and Fire" discusses the discovery of the use of coal as the basis of the Industrial Revolution. But, by allusion, it may more perceptively be read as one of the eschatological Thor poems, pointing by analogy to a revolution-yet-to-be, in which there will be no "golden mean," no "damned middle." Similarly, "Falling Asleep" might be grouped with the poems on childhood or sleep; for the child's mind is alive with dreams of pygmies, dark dwellers, white kings, arrows, and wizards, but the central emptiness and hopelessness is far more like death than slumber: "Oversnowed is the mind, empty white, / Beneath the sheet there is no noise, no stir." There shall be twilight, but without light; night comes, but no footfall—and the poem ends on the dying cadence of "no call, no bird-call."

Death is a theme, also, of "Cynicism"; but, instead of the death of modern men, the demise is that of the Classic gods and goddesses, as in "A Lame Idyll," "Child's Unhappiness," and "ΓΝΩΘΙ ΣΕΑΥΤΟΝ." Arrayed as poppies, the deposed host of heaven smile toward the God in the sky Whom they would fain put to sleep forever. But He recognizes them even in their disguise and reaps their beauty with His scythe "because He is so wonderful and wise." In echoes of Charles Algernon Swinburne's "Hymn to Proserpine" and D. H. Lawrence's *The Man Who Died,*

the Classical scholar mourns the dead beauty of antiquity and de-
plores the moralistic authoritarianism of the Judeo-Christian
deity. It is clear, from the many references to god and hero from
Classical myth, that these poems might have been classified on the
basis of the strength of their echoes of ancient legend and learning. "Twilight of the Gods" repeats the thought of "A Lame Idyll"
as around the mulberry tree of a stark industrial chimney the dead
gods circle. Pythagoras has broken his abacus; and, because he is
no longer able to count, he cannot keep the world going. Down
fall the flakes of timeless nothingness "anything, everything, all
things covering."

A strange mingling of the Classical and Christian appears in
"Adam's Legacy." "Spoked" with pain that pierces the marrow of
his bones, Adam sleeps under the leaves, haunted by dreams
of eons of deferred doom. Then Anadyomene comes to him out of
the waves to share the forbidden fruit. Seconds—or is it centuries
later?—the cock crows from a sepulcher; and Adam turns in his
sleep, an inhabitant of Plato's cave, with shadows writhing "from
the mimicking hands without." The roll is called, the drum rolls,
and man waits in vain for either a "door that never opens," or the
trump of doom. Within the realm of the possible, the experiential,
there comes only the reply of a mocking nonsense-question, "have
you heard the mocking-bird, the mocking-bird, the mocking-
bird?" as MacNeice plays one of his favorite games: the juxtaposition of weighty issues and the non-solutions of trivial singsongs.

In "The Court Historian (A Satirical Composition)," MacNeice
treats the writer just as he treated Pythagoras. When the historian
is at his most godlike, he disposes of dates, kings, and nations; but
a figure is looking over his shoulder and waiting to ask, "but what
about the court historian?" In "Gardener Melancholy," the poet
returns to the theme of the twilight of the gods as he strikes the
doom-struck note of the seeds that grow while the gardener dies,
and Ganymede is hidden from the light forever by the "hawk-face
king" of the underworld.

Five poems printed consecutively are all variations on the
theme of death. The "Sailor's Funeral" is held at the bottom of the
sea, "his bright life dead and gone." But there are many more sail-
ors, so who will lament the passing of one? "A Cataract Conceived
as the March of Corpses" portrays uncoffined bodies blinking in the
rush of a river, "drowned and drunk with the cataract that carries

them and buries them" and which "lilts and chuckles over their bones." The generally pentametric rhymed couplets of "Corpse Carousal" imitate the hoofs of the sable steeds of death; then, with macabre humor, the couplets become clapper bones which "play cottabus on the heavenly roof/Till the dead will rise to dispose reproof." The busy and sinister wind of "A Night," after all its activities, finally passes on "to a larger emptiness." On the other hand, when the "bloodshot sails" described in the poem "The Sunset" are gone, everything will continue forever just as it has always been.

And in another, instead of the blood-red sails of galleons described in "The Sunset," "The Sunset Conceived as a Peal of Bells" plays a requiem for the day on "angry bells that shake back their manes," with blind bats hanging in the belfries, and spiders clicking "their knitting needles," while "Time beats time with a crooked stick." Two "Candle Poems" may appropriately be added to the previous six poems, for although they begin with a waning cylinder standing in an island of wax, they proceed to pronounce that an island of wax is an inadequate breakwater against the tides of an unquiet world. After all, candles can be used most appropriately to light the foot of a deathbed or the demise of a failing culture.

The theme of a dying culture is repeated in "Neurotics," as the poet asks if there is no way to escape a morbid, moribund culture just as Aeneas escaped from burning Troy. "Is there no escape/ From the weltering closet," he asks, of Bluebeard's chamber, the door of Menelaus left open by Helen, the shambles of the house of Atreus, Orestes in the darkness, and Attis and Hamlet and De-Sade and Origen flickering "in the blood-light." Aeneas fled his burning city; but Louis and "Sister Anne" of ballad fame are left to burn.

"Beginning of a Comic-Delirious Drama"—a fragmentary, thin model for the later more successful eclogues and verse plays—also combines the themes of doom and death that MacNeice uses so often in *Blind Fireworks,* along with the *décor* of T. S. Eliot, and his own fondness for expressing tragic meanings through the use of nursery rhymes and rhythms. The setting is the corner of any street, bordered by long, high, ugly houses with boarded-up windows. Two policemen, *A* and *B,* are walking their beat. Each begins his speeches with the rhyme "There was an old woman and she didn't know what to do," but A always ends on the insistent refrain of doom: "But all the time she throbbed like parchment,/ For she can't keep the crossbones off her skull."

Several of the poems have impinged upon the theme of the poet's task, but two take that theme as their chief topic. In "Homo Sum," the moon fishes in the human depths below. Now and then a single mortal fish, hooked by the moon, is lifted upward, "lisping poetry." But the rest of humanity neither stops, nor feels, nor thinks. People break "the meshes of the lunar net" only by clamant demands for another drink, or another cigarette. In "A Conventional Serenade"—the first published example of the dramatic-dialogue form that was to be used frequently and effectively in the later eclogues and radio verse plays—Amyas is the poet-lover "wrapped in a dewy cloak brooched with stars," waiting to sing his serenade beneath a "frayed and crumbling balcony." The Rustick has cattle to tend and a dinner bell to answer. The Owl wryly calls his serenade desperate, "amorous runes," and assures him that, in spite of all his ululation, "No guitar can save a damned fate." In two striking figures, the poet sketches a copulative landscape of "trees with vegetable desire" that "stretch themselves upon the yielding sky"; and all the while he listens to the note of doom struck by a "distant summer beating like a drum." The diction is decidedly old-fashioned and even melodramatic; so, too, is the rather conventional theatrical attitude struck by the serenader.

This first volume of MacNeice's poetry has little of what Geoffrey Grigson called T. S. Eliot's "cultural reference rock-jumping style," [8] although Eliot's *Waste Land* and James Joyce's *Ulysses* were considered by MacNeice to be the two standard test pieces of the twentieth century.[9] Of Eliot's three cardinal requirements for modern poetry—difficulty, intellectuality, and empiricism[10]—MacNeice seems to have accepted only the last two. Indeed, it is quite possible that his clarity of language and reference have harmed his reputation in an age which cherishes agonized ambiguity.[11] However that judgment may be, after observing that the "best poets of today belong to, and write for, cliques," [12] MacNeice proceeds to prophesy that it may be "possible to write 'popular' poetry again . . . because the poet will find that he can best express his newly found attitude in terms of a symbolism which happens to be of exceptionally wide validity. . . . The poems in this book [*New Signatures*, edited by Michael Roberts, 1932] represent a clear reaction against esoteric poetry in which it is necessary for the reader to catch each recondite allusion." [13]

In the same essay, the young philosopher-poet indulges in a bit of Sophistic reasoning: "Poetry at the moment is becoming narrower and less esoteric. The narrower it becomes, the wider the public it represents. It will not become so narrow as to be truly popular (representing the masses) but it seems at the moment in England to be reaching a stage where it will represent and be acceptable to a considerable minority." [14] Whatever the strength of the argument, the logic of choice is clear. Louis MacNeice judged poetry of the nineteenth century to be "doomed by its own pretentiousness." Early twentiety-century poetry was brilliant but highly esoteric writing for cliques. The youthful poet judges that this era, too, is past and that a poetry of straightforward comment on anything and everything, in the language of common speech, is once again possible.

III   Roundabout Way (*1932*)

In Louis MacNeice's fragmentary autobiography, published by his literary executor E. R. Dodds as *The Strings Are False*, the author makes offhand reference in Chapter XXVIII (of the A^2 manuscript) to two novels: "We had an old record of 'The Blue Room,' one of the most out-and-out jazz sentimentalisations of domestic felicity—far away upstairs but the blue began to suffocate. I wrote a novel which was basically dishonest and ended in a blue room as if that solved everything. I followed it up with a very different novel called *The F. Vet*, a purgation of my grudges against my family, after which I felt more kindly to them." [15] Of the second-mentioned novel, Dr. Dodds comments that, so far as he knows, it was never published; no manuscript of it exists; and even the title is problematical—perhaps *The Family Vet?* But the former novel was published in 1932 by Putnam, with the title *Roundabout Way*.

Although prose rather than poetry, the novel very aptly fits this period of MacNeice's life and work. Indeed, it is hard to resist the temptation to identify the friends of his youth with the characters of the novel. *Roundabout Way* starts appropriately with a dedication "to my wife who has the gift of enjoying and so will (I hope) enjoy this unheroic story." The dedication is appropriate because the title of the novel presumably refers to the roundabout way that led a youth, who got sick everytime he heard about sex, to a happy marriage, and a scholar who thought he wanted to be a gardener, to acceptance of an Oxford fellowship.

In this novel, Sir Randal Belcher, England's leading neurologist, has four daughters, Maude, Aileen, Janet, and Elaine. Thinking himself advanced, he is nevertheless a Victorian parent from whom Janet has to break free by smashing an enormous dining-room mirror with a port decanter. Thus she announces herself an emancipated spirit and prepares to meet and fall in love with Devlin Urquhart, the scholar who thinks he wants to be a gardener (note MacNeice's many poems about gardens and gardeners), and whom her father has branded as an acute psychotic and as just such a boy as those moral runaways who founded the Bolshevik form of government. Sir Randal has become a co-leader with the Reverend John Bilbatrox of a new crusade for sanity and purity among the youth of England. But when Devlin first sees Bilbatrox, who, after the gloomy Dean Inge, is the second most advanced cleric in England, he describes him as "the world's ugliest clergyman—filthy vulture-face, fleshy and pouched and foul, selfish and sensual, pig pike and serpent." [16]

Janet and Devlin get married and spend their first night together in his boarding-house room, whence the poet novelist offers this poetic-prose paragraph as a substitute for orgasm: "Graft fire on ice, let the flowers and stars go drunk, and the sky tilting take us back to its bosom; close and near now beneath the cold, gold grandiose quilt of essential being let your heart barge its way, let its red petals pelt, let the world's brim swim with the spilth of the blazing, crazy mount, the fount and font of flowers, let Ygdrasil and all other tall trees tug, and sleep so come down a long approach of trees, the air sweet with bee's trove and the sapphic of doves' calls." [17] Amidst the boyish effusiveness of the rhetorical prose, there bounces a refrain of sound-alikes that reminds us that the young scholar is not above singsong repetition which has nothing to recommend it intellectually but is very pleasant vocally.

The rather slender main plot line of a youth who must find himself by first taking wrong paths and only finally arriving at destination, is greatly enhanced by the wild humor and the excellent, sharp delineation of supporting characters. Cyril Hogley, the Oxford don who keeps trying to steer Devlin into his predestined academic career, is actually the chief influence toward making him feel he does not want to become a teaching scholar. Hogley, who is essentially cold and anti-creative, remembers all details but has no theory of coherence. He lives on golden gossip of the creators and the bright young men whom he can paw. Devlin recognizes that Hogley is the born critic because of his inability to be vulgar, crude, or creative, and thus he is essentially dead.

Hogley is the neuter link between the heterosexual world of Devlin and the homosexual world of Gabriel Crash, whom he describes as a character out of a Russian novel. Red-haired, gray-eyed, enormously tall, Gabriel is incapable of loving women, or of teaching the piano. His credo is that the only decent existence in the artist world is to compose or interpret music, but without the prostitution of teaching—and to recognize that music is without message, morals, or point. Gabriel, with his wild drunkenness, his passionate devotion to Devlin, his enormous sheepdog, and his disastrous attempts at social diplomacy, provides much the richest vein of humor in the novel. Gabriel's long-lost mother turns out to be Mella, mistress of Herzheimer, the Jewish aluminum king. Herzheimer is clearly the *deus ex machina* of the novel; warm and entirely unbelievable, he provides the few means and solutions that the novel stoops to offer. He hires Devlin to write weekly blurbs on aluminum kitchenware, provides a cottage for the honeymoon, urges and makes possible Devlin's return to the world of scholarship, and sends Gabriel to America, a place presumably wild enough to make even so wild a musician a crashing success.

The young author keeps shining through, but far less autobiographically than in most first novels. The setting is the fringe of that Marlborough-Oxford world that MacNeice knew best; the young men are clever, questioning, upper class, witty with their posh pub talk, their private vocabulary, and their essentially coterie jokes. In the newly established home, the novelist's picture of Janet's much-beloved kitten is a practice sketch for MacNeice's extraordinarily touching and eloquent late requiem for a cat in *Ten Burnt Offerings*. The hero, Devlin, does some broadcasting so well that he is tempted to remain in the field; but Herzheimer sends him scurrying back to his academic tasks by warning him that he would become a mere machine. MacNeice himself, in addition to rather pedestrian wartime broadcasting, was one of the first to attempt to use the new medium as the basis of the unique art form of radio verse drama. Devlin and MacNeice both took First Class in their examinations and were appointed to lectureships in London. Devlin's thesis topic—"on the reaction of the latest physical theories upon pure philosophy or metaphysics"— sounds much the type of topic MacNeice might have tackled, except that, like Devlin, he could not give his whole heart to philosophy. The comment of the fictitious critics on the publication of Devlin's thesis sounds like the kind of criticism MacNeice often received—"clarity and vigour." Devlin is anti-Zolaesque in literary allegiance for reasons that sound suspiciously MacNeicean—because natural life is rather dull, requiring the writer not so much to exaggerate life as to give it a coherence theory.

The brief (259 pages) first novel ends with a scene unmistakably modern in the Aldous Huxley tradition. Just as Gumbril, Jr., and Myra Viveash (*Antic Hay*) keep passing through Piccadilly Circus as they shuttle back and forth across London, so Devlin and Janet go to St. Giles's Fair and ride intoxicated on the carousel. Whirling about, they see the world as God must see it. Devlin slips his arm about Janet's waist; then, raising his hands, he cups her breasts while he kisses her; they ride out into the sky, laughing together at the world and all its prudery and prurience.

IV   Poems (*1935*)

Many years after, T. S. Eliot spoke of his pride in having published the "first volume he [MacNeice] had to offer after coming down from the university." When Faber and Faber published Louis MacNeice's *Poems*[18] in September, 1935, the new collection included no selections from *Blind Fireworks;* and it repeated only one of the four selections from *Oxford Poetry*, "Spring Sunshine." Dedicated to his wife (the Giovanna of the former volume of poems), the collection includes a number of poems which had first been published in *The Criterion, Life and Letters, The Listener, New Verse,* and *This Quarter.*[19]

A glance at the table of contents immediately suggests that MacNeice does indeed write poems about everything. The diction of the poetry is rather emphatically contemporary, with an insistence upon the wireless, factory chimneys, policemen, and buses that might have imparted a strident tone to the singing voice of many poets. But two qualities rescue MacNeice from overemphasis. First, although the circumference of diction, setting, and imagery

is always social, the center of mood and characterization is
warmly personal. Thus, the public manifesto is muted to a personal testament. The second redeeming quality is the remarkable
style which tosses off every choice of subject with equal *savoir-
faire*. The "rocking-chair rhythm" [20] produces a careful imitation
of doggerel, and the naiveté of tone is all the more effective because it is so contrived and adroit. Down the street, someone is
practicing scales: "the notes like little fishes vanish with a wink of
tails." Is this line from "Sunday Morning" a bit of verse to bring
home to try on the children; or is it a carefully designed pattern
which manages to hold in extraordinary juxtaposition extreme
clarity of image, explicit statement of meaning, the social inter-
play of neighborhood life, and a cool distancing of sentiment and
emotion? If juxtaposition is the case, the doggerel, rocking-chair
rhythms express MacNeice's own thesis that the poets of his generation had forsaken free verse for the sake of counterpoint, sheer
technical brilliance, and elegance of style.[21]

Poems begins with "An Eclogue for Christmas," much admired
by the critics, which represents a midway stage between the dialogue of "A Conventional Serenade" in *Blind Fireworks* and the
host of later radio verse plays. The pastoral poem is composed as
a dialogue between *A*, a city dweller, and *B*, who lives in the
country; the distinctly different speeches are only slightly blurred
by *B*'s description of *A* as an "analogue of me." Actually, each
characterization is sharply defined, although the speeches mesh
well into the interspersing of two fractured monologues. *A* be-
moans an evil time, the "excess sugar of a diabetic culture." He
listens wearily to the jazz of drums and Hawaiian guitars, not to
enjoy the music, but to cover the ache of his question of identity.
At the beginning of the twentieth century he was Harlequin,
"posed by Picasso beside an endless opaque sea." Since then he
has been sifted, splintered, and abstracted. With "endless liabili-
ties, no assets," he has never been allowed to be himself, never the
real soul and flesh, but always form, symbol, or pastiche. Now
everything draws near an ending, not a new beginning—a time of
the final crumbling of a moribund culture as "the Goths again
come swarming down the hill." He foresees a time when "the
sniggering machine-guns in the hands of the young men" will
mow down all the trivial flats, clubs, and beauty parlors, and civilization will be "like a long pent balloon." But there is no escape,

no new turning. He can only return to London and be anesthe-
tized by

> . . . the saxophones and the xylophones
> And the cult of every technical excellence, the miles of canvas in the
>   galleries
> And the canvas of the rich man's yacht snapping and tacking on the
>   seas
> And the perfection of a grilled steak—

B, who is as grim as Thomas Hardy, is somewhat less sensa-
tional than A. He assures A that the English countryside has no
solace or peace for the urban expatriate, for "One place is as bad
as another." Every situation is simply a place to die. The country
is inhabited by heavy drinkers and tweedy women bristling with
pride. They still hunt, although the prophetic smoke from factory
and mill hangs heavy over fields and forest. The country gentry
are incapable of change. They require that "flotsam of private
property, pekinese and polyanthus"—all good things "which in
the end turn to poison and pus." The state will remove the walls
of private manors, private shooting enclosures, and private ponds.
When this happens, the only people who will be able to keep their
places and "be reinstated in the new regime" will be the whores
and the buffoons; the dreamers will simply lose their dreams. But
there is nothing to do and no place to go, so as B walks around a
farmyard as replete with the smell of memories as of dung, he will
tell himself lies once more. He will say "What we think, we can."
He will stand on the bare, high places of England, with his face
burning in the wind, "and the sheep like grey stones all about him,
humbling his human pretensions with their unthinking permanence. B closes the eclogue by reminding A that this is Christmas
Day, that on this morn "they say, interpret it your own way,
Christ is born."

Some old themes and some new changes are immediately noticeable. Declining culture, the desire to escape, the triviality of
modern life, the references to modern art, and the witty statement
of the hopeless truth are all present and familiar. There is a new
emphasis upon the use of rhyme to make lines sound singsong and
parodic. The vocabulary has roughened and coarsened, and the
words for material things tend to replace the words of philosophic

abstraction and poetic musing. This "tough toff talk" [22] is easy to parody and easily arouses a sneer when the Oxford accent peers through, but the total effect is in the direction of strength as a new masculinity supports the poetic structure.

The third selection in *Poems*, "Eclogue by a Five-Barred Gate," is far more literary and derivative in style: it is reminiscent of the fourteenth-century shepherds' plays and of Geoffrey Chaucer's "Pardoner's Tale." In the eclogue two shepherds attempt to feed and water their flock in Death's country. Death promises to open his gate to the one who sings more truly of his last night's dream. The first dreamed of God's face swinging on the neck of a snake; the second forsook marching men to couple with a water nymph. Suddenly she was gone, and "the sky was full of ladders" with "angels ascending and descending, with a shine like mackerel." The gate is opened, and both shepherds enter to live in the new land where "there is no life as there is no land," and death is left standing by "a gate the facade of a mirage." Well done though this poem is, in comparison to "An Eclogue for Christmas" it seems strangely irrelevant to modern life and even precious in its deliberate antiqueness.

The second poem, "Valediction," is one of a group of poems scattered through the volume which clearly arise out of the poet's Irish boyhood and youth. Louis MacNeice said a "poem, like the idol, is a kind of Alter Ego. . . . As Ego it is self-expression; as Alter it is escape from self. Hence the dangers of explaining a poem through its author." [23] Although we may respect the impulse that leads a writer to post his private life with a "no trespassing" sign, we can scarcely avoid the assumption that the Belfast-born youth has something distinctly personal to say about the Dublin he visited both as boy and man.

In Dublin, writes the Irish poet, history never dies; "arson and murder are legacies" like rings hollow-eyed without their precious stones. Belfast, MacNeice's birthplace, is "devout and profane and hard." Its legacy to the poet has been indifference, sentimentality, a metallic giggle, a fumbling hand, and "a heart that leaps to a fife band." Ireland is "hooey," a gallery of "fake tapestries," yet the poet cannot curse his mother nor deny his past. But he will do his best to exorcise Ireland from his blood, to become a mere visitor, to bid "Good-bye" to Irish "drums and . . . dolled-up virgins, and . . . ignorant dead." In fact, after his college years, Louis MacNeice never returned to Ireland for any length of time.

In "Turf Stacks," which continues the poetry about Ireland (obviously not completely "exorcised" from the poet's blood), the peasant, protected by "the tawny mountain," is not exposed to the "shuddering insidious shock of the theory-vendors." Those who prefer the unmechanized, simple life need to retreat to Asia or, like the screaming gulls, to "rip the edge off any ideal or dream." In "The Individualist Speaks," a lad and his dog who live in a quiet rural valley, go together to the Fair (which is the way the boy refers to the outside world). Even amidst the innocence of a valley which cannot remember an enemy, a prophet might tell of wars and rumors of war—in particular, the war of youth unmasking lying age. But the boy will have no part in either the masking or the stripping of masks; he will escape, with his dog, "on the far side of the Fair."

The "Train to Dublin" is full of passengers who are idols of painted wood, set up and operated by God, carried about by the trains. For only a tiny portion of time does the idol live and walk freely. All over the world men are drinking a toast to the King, but the poet chooses to toast "the incidental things" as they move "outward through space exactly as each was." Among other things, he toasts the laughter of the Galway sea, the "toy Liffey and the vast gulls," the smell of Norman stone, the squelch of "bog beneath your boots," faces that are not masks, the sea's thunder. As he holds all these images together on the moving train, he knows that such a synthesis makes the holder rich indeed. The poem "Belfast," with its opening reference to the "hard cold fire of the northerner," returns once again to the anomalous Protestant segment of the older Catholic island. There the Romish minority walks with "cowled and haunted faces"; each male murders his woman; and no Madonna replies to the woman's prayer for oblivion.

Many of the poems which are occasional in subject matter have the unity of the eschatological vision so vividly presented in *Blind Fireworks*. In "Morning Sun," the poet sees the radiant sight of a city "kissed and reticulated with sun." But, when the sun goes down, the streets turn cold, the women hurry and falter with dead faces, and the fountain in the square, instead of the rainbow water it formerly splashed, seems to dust gray powder, turning everything ugly and dead. In "Perseus," the Classical scholar depicts the "gay hero swinging the Gorgon's head" turning everything into stony death, so that an empty earth is left spinning like a mad moth around the blackening sun.

MacNeice commented that his poems occasionally record facts which belong to dreams rather than to the waking world. Thus in "Perseus," to look in a looking glass is to find it full of eyes, as if "the ancient smiles of men" had been "cut out with scissors and kept in mirrors." This waking-dream experience was characterized by terror of petrified unreality, hence the dominance in the poem of the Gorgon's head: "In such a mood, both when a child and when grown-up, I remember looking in mirrors and (a) thinking that my own face looked like a strange face, especially in the eyes, and (b) being fascinated and alarmed by the mysterious gleams of light *glancing* off the mirror. And, lastly, a mirror is a symbol of nihilism via solipsism." [24]

Even a doctrinaire poem like "To a Communist" carries the eschatological threat. A sudden snowfall can make the earth fair overnight. But before the Communist plumes himself on his solution of all society's woes, he should remember that the snow lasts but a day and that, before one proclaims the millennium, it is well to "consult the barometer." The "Wolves" of the poem by that title are the enemies that howl along England's coast. The only defense men offer is to form a circle, join hands and make believe, build castles of sand, and assume that no one hears the wolves' howl above the "talk and laughter."

In "Aubade," the poet asks what we have to look forward to after the happiness of youth. Not as we once thought—a liberal and enlightened "twilight of the gods"—but "a precise dawn / Of sallow and gray bricks, and newsboys crying war." In "Spring Voices," the season may lure the householder out to putter in the garden, gamble on a horse, or buy a cigar. Memory breathes on his neck, reminding him that all this has happened before. Let him not try to board Spring's car nor ride the wind, for he may "loiter into a suddenly howling crater" or fall over backward "garrotted by the sun." In the poem "Trapeze," MacNeice strikes that precarious balance which John Crowe Ransom described in "The Equilibrists." No longer is the laboring man obedient. An "end is set to respectability"; we "only live on sufferance"; and the "rope is wearing through." This "star-seat world" serves as our trapeze, and we know full well that circus jobs mean death sooner or later.

In this section of eschatological poems, we note the preliminary sketches of earlier poems (cf. the "Hammer of Thor" poems in *Blind Fireworks*) being filled in and made solid with the reiteration of the theme of coming danger and death to men who only dance and look the other way. Perseus and Circe are the chief representatives of the poet's Classical interests. Picasso in "An Eclogue for Christmas," Chardin in "Nature Morte," and Poussin in "August" underline the poet's interest in modern art.

The last poem in the volume, "Ode," is in some ways the most significant and certainly the most personal. The second stanza insists that, although God is boundless, only a little "segment of His infinite extension" is enough for the poet. The third stanza assures his wife that he does not desire a hundred wives or lives, to be too well read, to have money or ability like Hydra's heads. He wants just the "sufficient sample," the "islanded hour." From that point on, the poet prays for his son in his own individual diction but with themes reminiscent of William Butler Yeats's "A Prayer for My Daughter": let him not have too great a love for the infinite or the Absolute; let him corroborate the blessedness of fact. Give him five good senses, a feeling for symmetry, a mind deft and unflustered, not easily deceived by words. May he strike that golden mean which includes seasonal extremes. And then the poet jumbles similes in a ridiculous jargon:

> May his good deeds flung forth
> Like boomerangs return
> To wear around his neck
> As beads of definite worth.

Let him ride two horses at once and pay his debt to each. Let him make the strange discovery that people are lovable (a bit of bathos perhaps excusable on this sentimental occasion). Keep him from brooding too much on the "forking paths."

The father-poet has no scarab or compass to guide his son's journey—no decalogue, no chemical formula; only images and symbols: fly on the pane, tulips in a hearse, cock crowing in the dark, airplane in June. But a warning: the sound of the fly buzzing on the pane is the sound of a plane buzzing in the sky, and its

drone may become "augury of war" and "calmly draw our death
. . . on the graph of Europe . . . over the hairy flatnesses of
Russia." May his son not attempt to falsify the world by taking it
to pieces, divorcing cause and effect, form and content. Let him
live more freely than those conformists who are remembered by
horseshoe wreaths in the Birmingham Market Hall. But the poet
must put away this code, too, with its many qualifications, aster-
isks, asides, crosses in the margins. He, as a father, must become
the "migrating bird following felt routes." With this final invocation to Sidney Lanier's marsh-hen, the poet concludes that only
by learning the pride of humble acceptance may father and son
come at last to their own true home.

Poems clearly represents the working out of many themes and
experiments begun in the preceding volumes, such as: modern art,
the witty statement of philosophical problems, poems on death
and doom, the poet's boyhood, the search for identity, and the
initiation of the innocent child into a dangerous world. But, in
addition, it also points toward new developments. The toughness
of language, the jargon of science, the interest in dialogue, the
accent of speech, the constant social reference and political criticism, the new urgency of the eschatological warning, the sense of
the incorrigible plurality of everything, the counterpoint of Communist dialectic—these are all notable elements in *Poems* that
grow and develop in later work.

V *Aeschylus*, Agamemnon, a Translation (1937)

Louis MacNeice revealed both his Classical interests and his
considerable Classical scholarship by his translation of Aeschylus'
Agamemnon,[25] published in Great Britain, May 24, 1937. In the
preface, he states his central insight into the nature of ancient
drama: "Here we have a chain of crimes, one leading on to another from generation to generation by a logic immanent in the
blood and working through it. But the cause of the crimes, not
only of the first link, the first crime, but present in every one of
them, is the principle of Evil which logic cannot comprehend."
Since this version was to be produced in the autumn of 1936 by
Mr. Rupert Doone and the Group Theatre, MacNeice designed
the translation primarily for the stage: "It is my hope that the play
emerges as a play and not as a museum piece."[26] In order to

achieve dramatic effectiveness, he sacrificed the liturgical flavor of the diction and the metrical complexity of the choruses.

The closeness of the translation to the Greek original may be seen even by those unable to read the play in Greek. Herbert Weir Smyth, in the Loeb Classical Library, offers the following literal translation of the first seven lines of the play:

Release from this weary task of mine has been my cry unto the gods throughout my long year's watch, wherein, couchant upon the palace roof of the Atreidae, upon my bended arm, like a hound, I have learned to know aright the conclave of the stars of night, yea those radiant potentates conspicuous in the firmament, bringers of winter and summer—the constellations, what time they wane and rise.[27]

We may note the closeness of MacNeice's version to the literal, unliterary translation given above:

> WATCHMAN. The gods it is I ask to release me from this watch
> A year's length now, spending my nights like a dog,
> Watching on my elbow on the roof of the sons of Atreus
> So that I have come to know the assembly of the nightly stars
> Those which bring storm and those which bring summer to men,
> The shining Masters riveted in the sky—
> I know the decline and rising of those stars.[28]

The Greek original of this passage uses forty-three words; Smyth translates them into a minimal seventy-one words, MacNeice uses only seventy-four words in his dramatic-verse version. Thus it is clear that he avoids the temptation to embroider and enlarge the text, and he also avoids the Latinate diction of the literal translation. Perhaps MacNeice's dictum on contemporary verse—"Economy is the key-word to the best modern poetry"[29]— proved to be equally useful for the modern translation of ancient drama. Terse, careful, and strong, MacNeice's is a good, non-idiosyncratic translation.

VI   Out of the Picture (1937)

In 1937 Louis MacNeice wrote the play *Out of the Picture*[30] for which his earlier eclogues and serenades might be considered the technical preparation. Dedicated to Graham and Anne Shepard, the play was produced during the summer of 1937 by the Group Theatre and Rupert Doone, with music by Benjamin Britten, and sets and costumes by Robert Medley. Early in the two-act play, the Radio Announcer warns:

> We wish to remind you that upon this stage
> Slapstick may turn to swordplay,
> The cottage flowers may give a sudden hiss
> The trees curve down their hands in heavy gloves—
> A malediction on the nape of the neck.[31]

The theme of the play is the attitude of men who face annihilation in an impending war, and the principal exhibits are Portright, a young man who plays with art quite seriously and happily, and Moll O'Hara, who because she loves him, must kill him before he is either conscripted or forced to acknowledge his failure as artist, lover, and man. These two, plus a charwoman, represent the real people who "will hold the world together" [32] (an unacknowledged quotation from the Patristic *Epistle to Diognetus*) because they have kept the courage of their limbs, their animal instincts, and their human souls.

At the other end of the social spectrum, the persons who are in charge of the world are Two Framer's Men; a Bailiff; Dr. Spielmann, a psychiatrist; Sir Sholto Spielmann, minister of peace; an Auctioneer; Collectors; and Clara de Groot, a movie star. The connection between these two worlds is made by the only painting Portright has ever completed, "Rising Venus, or Botticelli with a Difference." Moll, who could give the artist the warm love of a real woman, plans to buy the painting to return to Portright after it has been seized by the Bailiff and put up for auction. But he falls in love with the frigid Clara de Groot, who buys the canvas for three guineas and an autograph.

Portright describes himself, early in the play, as a non-political man who never gets mixed up in world movements or embarks on rotten crusades. He exults in his private failure, his neuroses and psychoses, "the delight of defeat . . . the haunted sleep of the emphatically lost." [33] But now that he has been dragged out of the seclusion of acknowledged failure, Portright shoots the minister of peace as his great and heroic service to the world, and Moll slips the poison in his cup of celebration.

The London *Times* commented that the weakness of the play

"lies not in dealing in abstractions, but in trying to crowd in far more concrete and present matters than even so loose a form can hold and remain a form." [34] There is no question but that this tragic farce runs the gamut of the genres. There are elements of French *revue* in the sophisticated and singable little songs set to becoming music. There is the frequent and ominous interruption of the Radio Announcer to show the desperate state of a world on the brink of global war. Portright introduces a kind of "epic catalogue" of travel agency posters and mottoes.[35] The fourth scene of Act I is an auction in the form of a travesty on a church service.

The room is a neo-Gothic hall; a commissionaire ushers guests to pewlike seats; the auctioneer wears a surplice; the organ plays softly in the background; the auctioneer interlards his remarks with such phrases as: "silent prayer," "solemn duty," "I only pray," "this congregation," "this is holy ground," "communion," "an offering to God," "altar of human aspirations." And the collectors respond with a hymn.

An offstage chorus chants that the golden cycle is over; fire will consume everything: Troy, Babylon, Nineveh, London; and the "buckets are empty of water . . . the holy well is dry." [36] Special news bulletins are introduced from an international peace conference at Geneva which adjourns without any satisfactory solution having been reached. The announcer sings a song which elucidates the title of the play: it is the individual modern man who is "out of the picture," [37] a picture which needs only men in the mass, bombs, and gas.

At the close of the play, the auctioneer tries to auction off the world for a song, next to nothing, for nothing, to no one. "One two three four. Going Going Gone." [38] The last, best hope is offered by Moll in her exit line: "I will give you sons. Good luck go with them." [39] Biological continuity and luck are all the playwright has to offer, for Louis MacNeice is far too honest to offer a specious solution in which he does not wholly believe. When MacNeice was concluding an essay on "Poetry Today," he moved from the consideration of levels of ambiguity, the a priori background (tradition), and the a posteriori foreground (life), to a final, bald banality: "To write poetry needs industry and honesty and a good deal of luck." [40] Thus the dilemma of modern man receives no more, no less a prescription than the task of writing a modern poem.

The "long-rhymed, lithe verse"[41] is strong and resilient in the drama, and the clear and precise imagery adds a wry dryness to the language. MacNeice is clearly indebted to musical comedy, radio, and perhaps to W. H. Auden, to the Sweeney poems of T. S. Eliot, and also to Gilbert and Sullivan. There must be something to laugh at, if one is also to cry. Auden and Isherwood's *The Dog Beneath the Skin* had its madhouse scene, and *Out of the Picture* presents a milder comic relief in the auction scene. MacNeice, who considered his friend Auden's greatest literary asset to be his curiosity, spoke of him as a man who was never tired, as Eliot always was. Auden's gusto came from people, politics, science, journalism, and a sense of humor. He had a strong tendency toward satire and burlesque.[42] Perhaps this same assessment may be applied in a lesser degree to MacNeice. The very multiplicity of effects to which critics objected may well be a strong intention of the author. If modern man is barraged by noise, drowned in crowds, and plucked at from every point of view, the very distraction of announcer, chorus, auctioneer, songs, and peace-conference news may be essential to that total effect. Certainly, the play never lags; it leaps from laughter to despair— and the hopelessness of the end is all the stronger because the playwright did not weep all through the beginning.

In this first period of publication, 1929–37, Louis MacNeice published four poems in the annual undergraduate anthology, *Oxford Poetry: 1929*. Two of the poems ("Cradle Song," "Spring Sunshine") celebrate the security and danger of sleep. The third, "Address from My Death-Bed," raises the philosophical problems of the relationship between form and matter, and between universal and particular, but discusses these weighty issues in a lightly humorous manner. The fourth poem, "Laburnum," picks up the recessive notes of time and death from the previous three poems, and adds the element of inescapable judgment and doom.

Blind Fireworks, 1929, underlines the characteristic elements of the *Oxford Poems* and adds to them. It includes poems on modern art; it celebrates sleep as beneficent retreat and Freudian danger; and it often deals with philosophical problems in witty tones. It develops the early themes of the poet's boyhood, the search for identity, the passage from childhood innocence into the experience of puberty, and it has much to say about the favorite topics of time, death, and doom. The melodies are less mellifluous and the diction fits the rhythm of common speech as the poet emerges from Yeatsian imitation into contemporary jargon.

Poems, 1935, repeats all the stylistic and topical gains of *Blind Fireworks* but adds new developments as well. The language which had already moved from the poetic diction of the late Romantics toward the common speech of twentieth-century men, now takes on a harsher, tougher quality, with emphasis upon the language of science, the vulgar artifacts of the Industrial Revolution, and the patterns of speech dialogue. Topically, there is a constant reference to social relationships and a dialectic of political criticism that often reveals the influence of Socialist and Communist thought. The old attempt to classify everything into a neat Platonic pattern seems to have spilled over into a helpless sense of burgeoning plurality. The eschatological warning of doom which tolled from the earliest poems now knells with new and powerful urgency.

The translation of Greek drama (*Agamemnon*) in 1937 acts as a reminder of Louis MacNeice's considerable Classical scholarship and fits in with the frequent references in the poems to the mythology and history of ancient Greece and Rome. His novel (*Roundabout Way*), 1932, makes unmistakable if oblique reference to MacNeice's altogether natural interest in the achievement of personal identity, the tension between philosophy and life, and the longing for the most perfect possible union of love. His verse drama (*Out of the Picture*), 1937, shifts to his concern about the relationship between art and life, and reiterates the recurrent warning of his occasional poems that the old order is moribund and the emergence of the new is yet entirely hypothetical.

CHAPTER 2

Member of the Group

IN A newspaper article entitled "Modern Poetry Should be Subtle and Tough," [1] Louis MacNeice referred to the accidents of birth and schooling that made him one of a group of young British writers, later called "the Thirties' Poets." [2] Another of those writers was Stephen Spender, co-editor with MacNeice of *Oxford Poetry: 1929*. The echoes of Wystan Hugh Auden, a member of the same group, were quite audible in MacNeice's play *Out of the Picture*. Two other names frequently mentioned as "members of the group" were Christopher Isherwood and C. Day Lewis.

These poets knew each other very well, lived in the froth and ferment of the same ideas, and shared the sense of bringing new life, new ideas, and a new diction into modern poetry. Perhaps it would be impossible to trace which of these writers originated each image or idea that was used in their verse and drama, yet no one would suggest that these four men were exactly alike in temperament, emotion, or talent. Of the group, the dominant figure seems to have been Auden, with his overwhelming interest in every aspect of life, his vast and fertile creativity, and what seemed to MacNeice the vulgar, peasant-like zest and drive of the man.[3] Because of this dominance, the other three members of the group are not likely to be confused with one another; they are to be seen standing in the shadow of Auden, glimpsed as through a glass darkly. MacNeice laughingly confessed that Day Lewis wrote at his worst when he attempted a slapdash Audenesque satire; "while I myself—in so far as one can judge one's self—suffered, I should say, when I forced myself to feel things that in fact I merely thought; feelings are one's own, but thoughts come from the group." [4]

Of their similarities of thought, there can be no doubt; but the more perceptive critics have recognized the individual temperaments and talents within the group, even to the point of deploring an occasional warping of a man's own particular message by the current thrust of the group ideology. F. O. Matthiessen pointed out as early as 1938 that MacNeice's course has been fairly independent. His poetry is not so likely to be either dogmatic or doctrinaire. He has not joined Stephen Spender in his "romantic proclamations of faith." [5] Nor has he included the wide subject matter of economics and science which Auden's curiosity has explored; nor has he insisted quite so mechanically upon the culverts and pistons of Day Lewis' contemporaneity. Matthiessen concludes that there is a very distinct difference between the easy conversational style of MacNeice and the public voice of Auden's exciting rhetoric.

MacNeice permitted himself the vulgarity of comparative judgment when he attempted to explain why Day Lewis was an "inferior poet to Auden." [6] Day Lewis' vision was both purer and more consistent than Auden's, and this quality tended to make his voice declamatory and strident as he preached for the causes in which he so completely and singleheartedly believed. He played upon a kind of one-stringed instrument alongside the full-chorded richness of Auden's exuberance and MacNeice's two-stringed awareness that life is "incorrigibly plural." Perhaps a more objective explanation would not have dealt in comparisons at all, but would simply have indicated the kind of diversity in unity which develops when quite different but highly talented young men share the same experiences in the same social milieu. Perhaps all four poets owed at least as much to William Butler Yeats, T. S. Eliot, and Gerard Manley Hopkins as they did to each other.

I Letters from Iceland (1937)

That strange travel book *Letters from Iceland,*[7] written by Auden and MacNeice in collaboration following a trip to Iceland in 1936, should have first place in this chapter in which the poet is related to his contemporaries. The strangeness of the book arises from the multiplicity of genres that seems to be characteristic of work in which W. H. Auden has a hand. He was drawn to Iceland rather than the too-hospitable South by his Scandinavian ancestry and his boyhood interest in the Norse saga.[8] Having contracted with Faber and Faber to do a travel book, he arrived in the country before the others, and then was joined later on in the summer by MacNeice and other friends. Resisting the temptation to brood over *ultima Thule,* he arrived armed with a volume of Lord Byron's poetry.

From this "vacation reading" Auden developed five chapters of the book (I, V, VIII, XIII, XVI) as the five racy installments of a *terza rima* letter to the nineteenth-century Romantic poet, from the twentieth-century British poet isolated at the tip of Europe. Always a remarkable tour de force technically, richly illustrating Auden's talent for parodies of anybody from John Skelton to Alfred Tennyson and Rudyard Kipling, it describes the thoughts and a portion of the life of an English poet of twenty-nine to a youthful poet of an earlier century who might well sympathize and understand. The seven lines of pentameter, rhyming *ababbcc,* work remarkably well to produce a lighthearted, casual touch which conveys now the brilliant insight, now the scrupulous triviality. MacNeice, Auden's companion and co-author, points out that "Byron's lighter stanzas . . . are a . . . more elastic form, able to carry the discursive comments of a Don Juan on a world of flux and contradictions. Auden, who holds strongly that chat belongs to poetry as well as incantation or lyrical statement, uses it easily and lucidly to give with point and humor a memorable summary of his position. . . ." [9]

Auden, in bed with a cold, recalls Housman's dictum that "many a flawless lyric may be due" not so much to the broken heart of the lover, "but 'flu." [10] He had considered, of all unlikely things, writing his poetic letter to Jane Austen; but he decided not to, because novel writing is "a higher art than poetry altogether" and because the realism of the grim little spinster frightened him. It was painful to a romantic youth to think that a middle-class, unmarried virgin should "reveal so frankly and with such sobriety/The economic basis of society." [11] The twentieth and twenty-first stanzas of "Letter to Byron" [12] indicate the self-conscious collage the book will be: photographs, press clippings, gossip, maps, statistics, graphs, natural scenery, men and women, the arts, the European news—and, above all else, Auden himself.

The second chapter is a light, prose account of the journey to Iceland, followed in Chapter III by a delightful poetic letter from Louis MacNeice to Graham and Ann Shepard (to whom *Out of the Picture* was dedicated), written from Reykjavik on August 16, 1936. The heroic couplets start out with the hope that "Pauli [a dog] is rid of worms" and that "the new cook is a success." But the lines move quickly from such urban banalities to the reasons for coming to the North instead of the usual trip to the more-frequented South. In his century William Morris exchanged the frills and fuss of Tristram and Theseus for rugged poetry about rocks and sagas. Earlier Irish hermits came to Iceland to mortify their flesh, but modern men need the silence there to mortify their "blowsy intellects" [13] before they die. Chatting, self-pity, noise, and crowds are not to be found here—reason enough to come to Iceland. This is not an escape trip; the travelers have come to find facts and to simplify the complex. They recognize that new sights and new faces will aid young men in the old Aristotelian task of "realizing their own nature." The letter is interrupted by Auden, who drags MacNeice out into the rain "to see a man about a horse" or, more properly, two horses for a ten days' ride around the Langjökull.

The fourth chapter is directed to the general tourist with a list of sights to be seen, clothing to be packed, and foods to be sampled. The suggested food includes dried fish, tough or tender: tough, "tastes like toe-nails"; tender, "like the skin off the soles of one's feet." [14] In Part II (Chapter V) of the letter to Byron, Auden confronts the aristocratic lord with the contemporary critical canard that the "Teutonic Führer-Prinzip" would have appealed to his concern for social status—"Lord Byron at the head of his storm-troopers!" [15] By far the most extravagantly funny contribution comes from neither of the collaborators. If MacNeice's introduction can be trusted, the letter from Hetty to Nancy (Chapter XII) is a bona fide personal item here published and preserved. The exploits of a woman teacher reluctantly accompanying a group of girls to Iceland, as confessed with utmost frankness to a friend who is safely and wisely back in London, it has all the charm of stolen mail and overheard conversation. When the male humor sags and the little collectors' items sound more and more like a mail-order catalogue, we wish Hetty and Nancy had written more letters.

In many ways the best things in this collage of a volume—besides the Byron letter—are Auden and MacNeice's "Last Will and Testament," MacNeice's "Eclogue from Iceland" and his "Epilogue." With boyish high spirits, the two friends settle down to write "Their Last Will and Testament" (Chapter XVII). The irregular iambic triplets, rhyming *aba*, spiral upward through sheer brilliance and journalistic contemporaneity into an incomprehensible world of the little coterie of Oxford and London friends, their private peccadilloes, and their very private manner of speech.

MacNeice begins with grateful thanks for his ancestry and the country of his birth. He sings of whitewashed rooms overlooking the Atlantic and of air softened by peat smoke. He is thankful for what is left in him of peasant vitality, peasant sense of humor, and a peasant instinct to find his way through the forking paths of "briars and mud." [16] He expresses his admiration for his father, who has kept "his pulpit out of the reach of party slogans," [17] and has never offered the help of religious authority to those who seek to "silence moderation and free speech." [18] Sincere spiritual bequests are made to his stepmother, his sister Elizabeth, his son Dan, and to an unidentified Mary. From stanza thirty-two on, the beneficiaries shift to the public world and become as current and breezy as the personal items in the local newspaper. Stanley Baldwin is bequeathed the false front of Lincoln Cathedral; the Cheshire soapworks go to Ramsay MacDonald; the pick of one hundred converts from the social register for Frank Buchman; a little Christian joy to gloomy Dean Inge; life in an English boarding house to I. A. Richards; and a belief in God to Bertrand Russell. Moving into a more personal, but still well-known grouping, the friends assign their minor talents to Cecil Day Lewis and Stephen Spender, a passionate romance to Benjamin Britten, an even more inclusive death roll for a novel by E. M. Forster, a little accurate information for St. John Ervine, and a box of toy soldiers and the Martyr's Stake at Abergwilly to Wyndham Lewis.

"Eclogue from Iceland" (Chapter X), set on the Arnarvatn Heath, consists of a conversation between Craven (presumably Auden), Ryan (MacNeice), the ghost of Grettir (hero of one of the last of the Icelandic sagas), and the Voice of Europe. In irregular iambic tetrameter closed couplets, the travelers decide to hobble their horses and settle down for the night. The entrance of Grettir Asmundson is heralded by the rhythm of his limping walk in the mist. Sentenced to eternal wandering by the curse of a foe, he wonders if there are men in this age whose compass always leads them down forbidden roads. He addresses the question to the one with "crowsfeet" around his eyes, and Craven (Auden) replies; then Grettir turns to the man "with the burglar's under-lip," and Ryan (MacNeice) responds. When Grettir asks if they, too, live on islands "where the Lowest Common labels will not stick," Ryan replies that he comes from an island named Ireland, built upon "violence and morose vendettas," where his "diehard countrymen . . . drag their ruin behind them," and shoot "straight in the cause of crooked thinking." Craven admits they are all three exiles; he was in Spain at Easter, "gobbling the trip-per's treats," soaking up the local color, and running away from his own household gods "with no intention of finding gods else-where." Now, in Iceland, their latest joyride, they have simply found "more copy, more surface."

Grettir describes himself as the "doomed tough," exalted by hard blows; he is an outlaw, never stopping to rest, always mov-ing on. In life, he wore his fatal sense of doom without the air of martyrdom, preferring to death the daily goods of horses, fighting, women, and food. Craven describes the heroes of his era as facing death with a blasé face; they risk their lives, too, but in order to divert ennui, not to fill their stomachs, avenge an affront, or win a prize. The war hero with the empty sleeve stands in front of the neighborhood delicatessen and cadges small change from former comrades-at-arms, while girls with "silken legs and swinging but-tocks" sell little cardboard flags on pins. Grettir agrees that in his day also heroes were sold cheap by the women and the "men with many sheep."

Craven interrupts because he hears music in the air, music like the Wurlitzer organ in the Gaiety. Soon enough the travelers will be back in London to stand in queues for tickets, browse around counters of dead books, and reinterpret the words of "obsolete interpreters," collating, deleting, and preening themselves on the goodness of the life of art. Ryan thanks God for those who dare to go on their own way, who do not kiss "the arse of law and order" and thereby purchase physical comfort at the price of pride.

The distant sound of music now becomes the blues-singing Voice of Europe, chanting the bright, brittle little ditties both MacNeice and Auden became famous for:

> I don't care always in the air
> Give my hips a shake always on the make
> Always on the mend coming around the bend

Always on the dance with an eye to the main
Chance . . .

Craven replies that there have been many heroes, even in the
modern era, who made their way through the complex maze by
common sense, a sense of humor, or the sheer "desire for self-
assertion." They won the battle but did not gain happiness. The
Voice continues to sing the blues; self-pity swells with the music,
and the refrain insists "I don't care." Grettir urges Ryan and Craven to give the Voice the lie and go their own way. They must go
back where they came from. He could have fled to the Orkney
Islands or the Hebrides, but he preferred to assert his rights in his
own land. It may be a small gesture, but it must be made. They
must face their hazard, make their act of defiance, and sing their
hymn of hate; "it is your only duty. / And, it may be added, it is
your only chance."
    The long catalogues of the modern malaise are handled with
superlative ease; the characterization remains constant throughout the sustained eclogue; the mingling of past and present and of
near and far is technically superb. But there are some curious iro-
nies about the final advice of Grettir. Earlier, the youthful poet
had resolved in the poem "Valediction" [19] to exorcise Ireland from
his blood, to say a resolute good-bye to all his homeland meant,
and to turn away from his own country in the manner which
James Joyce's *Portrait of the Artist as a Young Man* had made
intellectually respectable. Now the two young intellectuals are
being counseled by the heroic voice from the past to return to the
contemporary culture they have fled and, in the midst of all that is
commonplace, narcotic, and spurious, to make their defiant gestures and live out their individual destinies.
    This advice may be very good, and it is perhaps a little bit more
in the mood of Auden than MacNeice; but the itinerary which
issued from the experience is disillusioning, to say the least. Grettir claims that he might have run away from Iceland and become
rich and famous in the Orkneys or the Hebrides. MacNeice, having realized on the Iceland trip that additional travel would produce only more surface souvenirs and literary copy, nevertheless
is found in the very next year, 1937, in the very islands Grettir had
mentioned as his own possible escape, the Hebrides, from which

the poet writes more detached and sensitive descriptive poems about one more group of islands.

Appropriately at the close of *Letters from Iceland,* which gathered in so many styles and genres, Louis MacNeice wrote an "Epilogue for W. H. Auden." In quatrains of rhymed open couplets of trochaic tetrameter, the poet rehearses the Icelandic trip "before the memory slip." It was a "fancy turn" in a world which was engaged in producing a "graver show": Seville fell in southwest Spain, the Olympic games were held, and Hitler spouted Aryan philosophy. The Oxford "don" in MacNeice had pointed out that the landscape of the north produced the plodding miles of the saga style. The "don" in Auden had replied that "the north begins inside." They had been happy watching ravens, walls of shale, rotting whales, and the boiling sulphur basins transforming the domestic valley into a "sketch of Judgment Day." It was a relaxed holiday with no overemphasis, vision, conversion, or great happening at all. Now in Hampstead, in a book-lined room, the poet sits alone and waits for the telephone to ring. A "litany of doubt" comes breathing out of the walls, and the room becomes a pit humming with fear of loneliness, of inability to communicate with others, and of life itself. So MacNeice writes these lines to Auden, who occasionally experiences the same death wish as MacNeice, but whose lust for life always prevails. The two men will drink coffee and tell tales, aware that their "prerogatives as men" could be canceled at any moment. He drinks Auden's health before a "gun-butt raps upon the door."

It is easy to dismiss this rather insignificant-looking poem as a casual beginning, a trivial middle, and a melodramatic close. But to do so would be to miss the clues the poet has hidden deftly and meaningfully. The room in Hampstead is a lonely place, humming with the fear that no one will call or come. But earlier in the poem, the poet suggests that the rugs, the cushions, and the long mirror are not true comforts; they are a kind of disguise to cover the real desert that lies beneath. Bare, empty Northern skies were more honest than this room with its pretense of social warmth and security. A health is drunk to a friend before a gun butt raps on the door. The dizzy descent from the domestic to the catastrophic is not confined to the last two lines; for, amid the pleasant sights and sounds which made up the vignettes of their holiday jaunt, there

is the ominous transformation of a domestic valley, by boiling sulphur basins, into the vale of Armageddon on Judgment Day. The
gun butt is simply the precise particular which brings that Judgment Day from the sulphur basins of Iceland to the bachelor
apartment of Hampstead Heath.

II   I Crossed the Minch (1938)

The year 1938 was Louis MacNeice's *annus mirabilis* in which
he had four volumes published: *I Crossed the Minch*,[20] a book of
travel; *Zoo*, chatty comments on captive animals and zoos in general; *The Earth Compels*, a volume of poetry; and *Modern Poetry*,
his major book of poetic criticism in prose. *I Crossed the Minch*
was illustrated rather ineffectively by Nancy Sharp and dedicated
to Hector MacIver, a native of Lewis, the chief island of the Hebrides. "I looked up and saw Hector MacIver in a mackintosh and
a black hat. 'Where in God's name have you come from?' " [21] But it
was not important where he had come from; it was important that
he was returning home to Shawbost on holiday and that the poet
would have the pleasure of the company of a native.

At the very beginning of the book, MacNeice mourns his ignorance of Gaelic. Somehow he had not realized that nearly all the
islanders speak Gaelic and that the language is an integral part of
their lives. Because of this language barrier, the book is condemned to be "a tripper's book written by someone who was disappointed and tantalized by the islands and seduced by them only
to be reminded that on the soil he will always be an outsider. I
doubt if I shall visit the Western Islands again." [22] Samuel Johnson
must have offered some consolation to such an outsider when he
was tempted to become sentimental about the Gaelic tongue. On
his trip in 1773 Dr. Johnson had classified Gaelic as "the rude
speech of a barbarous people, who had few thoughts to express,
and were content, as they conceived grossly, to be grossly understood." [23]

Although the trip to Iceland had taught MacNeice that such
journeys are outside the true center of the writer's life and experience, he nevertheless determined, the very next year, to travel to
the Hebrides. Anthony Blunt, a former Cambridge don with
whom he had recently traveled to Spain, said "You seem to have a
mania for going North"; and Auden, his companion of *Letters
from Iceland*, pontificated: "One goes North in order to escape

from sex." Apparently this statement was one of the bitter bits of wisdom Auden had accumulated that cold summer of 1936. Just as Auden brought Byron to Iceland, MacNeice revels in the possession of a very "un-Hebridean book," [25] *The Notebooks and Papers of Gerard Manley Hopkins,* which he was to review for a British periodical. But he "ought to have foreseen" that he would be unable to read it until his return to London. Even on the train to Edinburgh he found it very heavy and fell asleep with it in his hand.

But, while any tourist to the outer isles of the Hebrides might have shared quite the same experiences as the author, few could have produced a travel journal which included: a verse dialogue between the head and the foot; a life of the late Lord Leverhulme in ballad form; a dialogue with his guardian angel who was urging him to become an active member of the Communist party; a delightful bit of verse that imitates the wild squalling of the bagpipes; a chapter of brilliant parodies showing how the islands would have been described by Walter Pater, Ernest Hemingway, D. H. Lawrence, and W. B. Yeats; and some miscellaneous poems as good as anything he had yet produced. In addition, there are several interludes with absurd fictitious characters, Perceval and Crowder, who seem to represent fashionable friends of Oxford days and business acquaintances from London whom MacNeice has the misfortune to meet while he is abroad. And, quite astonishingly, the Hetty of *Letters from Iceland* appears in the Hebrides (we begin to suspect pursuit); and again she obligingly shares one of her inimitable letters to the novelist Maisie Reynolds.[26]

MacNeice actually chose to visit the Hebrides for a reason similar to Auden's nostalgia for his Icelandic forebears and the sagas of the North. MacNeice had hoped that the Celt in him would be drawn to the surface by the pull of persons and places, but this "was a sentimental and futile hope." [27] Barred from intimacy by the language difficulty, he found the islands had both an expected and an unexpected problem. Dr. Johnson had warned him of the wholesale emigration from the islands even back in the eighteenth century: "It may be thought that they are happier by the change; but they are not happy as a nation, for they are a nation no longer. As they contribute not to the prosperity of any community, they must want that security, that dignity, that happiness, whatever it be, which a prosperous community throws back upon

individuals." [28] MacNeice was quite unprepared to find that the
islands, instead of possessing that insularity which by very definition should characterize them, were the victims of cultural inva-
sion from the mainland. Their primitive culture was dead; the
succeeding culture was still foreign and not yet sophisticated:
"More than one generation is required before a man can be a
capitalist with grace." [29]

MacNeice muses that the Soviet Union encourages the mainte-
nance of local tradition and culture, although within and in sub-
servience to the new order. This pattern seems to him the proper
one for historical development; but, in England, so many of his
left-wing comrades "suffer from the masochism of the puritan." [30]
There must be no frills, comforts, or luxuries for the body or the
mind. No differences between persons or communities may be
permitted to impede economic cooperation or the united statement of the Marxist creed. So bleak a social philosophy looks to
MacNeice like a "future of Esperanto, Sunday School treats and
homage to the Highest Common Factor." But he takes comfort
when he reflects that Lenin recognized the necessary role of
differentiation. (At this point a previous reader pencilled in the
margin of my copy, "Poor Fish.")

Back in Edinburgh Hector MacIver had already told, with
splendid venom, how Lord Leverhulme the soap magnate had
wanted to turn the island of Lewis into "Port Sunlight" (named
after his soap), but had failed because of the noble obstinacy of
the islanders. Then in a rage at such unaccustomed economic failure, the Viscount gave part of Stornaway back to the islanders,
carved up the remainder of the island into hunting blocks, selling
them cheap to "the ragtag and bobtail of England." [31] In islands
where the great career is the dole and where the merchant service
comes second, the poet sets himself to extolling the economic bob-
ble of an economic baron. He begins with the rhythm of Gilbert
and Sullivan:

> Lord Leverhulme was a grocer's son,
> He learned to sell when he was young,
> And all the tunes that he could play
> Was "Advertising makes it pay"—
>   Over the hills and across the skies,
>   By God it pays to advertise. [32]

With other echoes of Gay's *Beggars' Opera* and "Over the Hills and Far Away," the rollicking stanzas proceed to retail the progress of Lever from Bolton, traveling for his father, to the patenting of "Sunlight Soap." With the expert advice of Monsieur Lavanchy-Clarke, Egyptologist and pioneer of the penny-in-the-slot machine, he advertises, expands, and buys up Vinolia and Monkey Brand. He runs unsuccessfully four times for the House of Commons from Birkenhead; then, after switching to the Liberal party, he is elected as member from Wirrall. He is libeled in the press controlled by Lord Northcliffe, but collects £50,000 in damages. He buys large patches of the tropics for production of vegetable oils, and he has his portrait painted by Sir William Orpen and Augustus John. When he is almost seventy, he decides to establish a branch of his mercantile empire in the Hebrides; but he finally has to confess that the Isle of Lewis is his Waterloo. So he gives back Stornaway Parish and sells Lewis to Englishmen for hunting lodges.

When he stands at last at the gate of Heaven and St. Peter asks if he has any failure to confess, he has to admit "the Western Islands had me beat!" But St. Peter, who admits that Celts are difficult to handle even in Heaven, promptly admits him to Heaven's "joint-stock" company:

> He began his business then and there
> And the stocks in Heaven rose like air;
> The Devil's business fell as flat
> As a nudist camp or an opera hat.

Now the moors are quiet once again in the Hebrides; the crofters continue their gossiping in Gaelic; the waves still creep over the lonely beaches.

A fragmentary bit of verse describes a dialogue between the head and the foot that occurs in the lounge of an island hotel. The head in the air demands that the foot firmly placed on the floor go both to a Gaelic poetry and music festival as well as for an evening stroll. The position of the head is loftier than his diction: "Get up, you lazy bastard, RUN." [33]

In a whimsical, but equally important interview with his Guardian Angel,[34] MacNeice is asked if he has read *Forward from Liberalism,* that nice book by his friend Stephen Spender, and if it isn't about time that he took some definite attitude on political subjects. MacNeice replies that his sympathies are Left, "on paper and in the soul," but not in his heart or his "guts." [35] "I would vote Left any day, sign manifestos, answer questionnaires. . . . My soul is all for moving towards the classless society." But in heart and "gut" he laments the passing of class, property, and snobbery: "A man for me is still largely characterised by what he buys. . . . I am both a money snob and a class snob." [36] As for women, it adds to his pleasure if they are rich and are called "Honourable." He prefers those "gestures of the hand, poise of the foot, intonations of the voice or eyebrows" which are "imitated from snobs by a snob and practiced for the seduction of snobs." [37] Claiming to belong irrevocably to the lost intelligentsia, MacNeice is thoroughly aroused by the Guardian Angel's penultimate speech: "Are you going to, partly out of pique, partly out of vanity, but mainly because you are just darn bone lazy, wilfully espouse a life of outmoded triviality and inaction—" to all of which, the poet can only reply profanely, "Oh, go to hell." [38]

Perhaps in conscious emulation of Auden's fabulous talent for writing poetic parodies, MacNeice includes prose parodies of the way several well-known authors would have described life in the Hebrides. The Walter Pater parody is one long undulating sentence weaving in and out the ideas of the "synopsis of the popular imagination," [39] the expression of beauty, the coherence theory of truth, a "flush upon the skin," a sudden "excitement not untempered by sadness"; ending with the mild snobbery of a Latin tag, "Terra Incognita." D. H. Lawrence would have described a woman at whom the crofters did not look, but "sensed her presence . . . deep down somewhere in the darkness below the diaphragm." She stands there, saying or doing nothing, "waiting like the peat for someone to bring me to the surface, with kind ferocious hands to cut me in blocks and lay me in a pile in the sun." [40] Ernest Hemingway's tight-lipped hero knocks at the door of a Black House. No one answers. He opens the door and enters. There are four men in the room and one woman. The room is full of smoke. He sits down. He gets up. He says he must go. No one answers. He puts his hands in his pockets and opens the door with his knee. He steps outside. The "rain was raining." " 'What the hell,' he said. 'What the hell.' " [41]

William Butler Yeats, waking from deep sleep in the reading

room of the British museum, wonders whether that old lady, when she went back into her sod hut, did not return to some more elemental abode than that simple room. After talking it over with an old man in Merrion Square, who had once had tea with Parnell, he decides that slipping from the material to the psychic is as easy as shifting gears on a car. After all, the yogis, Lady Flora Barsac, and he agreed that the universe is a series of Chinese boxes which we open from the inside out. When Lady Flora once showed him a poem written with a wild goose quill, his considered opinion was that that poem was more "profound, more exquisite, than the other poems of our century." [42]

Several brief poems imbedded in the often inconsequential prose are worthy of mention, even though not penned with the quill of a wild goose. "Leaving Barra" [43] is written in trimeter quatrains with the last word of each stanza repeated at the end of the first line of the next stanza. The poet, who is leaving Barra, one of the southernmost of the Hebrides Islands, writes to the woman to whom he is returning; he sees the dazzle on the sea as a brilliant carpet leading from the island, which he will never visit again, to the dazzle of the life in her. He wishes he could quell the restlessness that keeps him seeking for the lost Atlantis; then he would be happy like a fool, or a dog, or a buddha, giving not a damn for existence. But any philosophy on religion that alleges that life is a fiction is essentially alien to man, and the believers give only a token assent. He would like to wake up some morning understanding some of the facts that make life seem good: the beauty of music and the moon, the routine courage of workers, the "gay endurance of women," and, most of all, the life of his beloved who moves as surely and beautifully as a musical fugue.

In "Eclogue from Iceland," [44] Louis MacNeice confessed that travel contributed only copy and souvenirs to the traveler. In *I Crossed the Minch* he develops that disillusioning reflection. When he was a youth of nineteen or twenty he used to feel like a G. K. Chesterton character who expected some adventure around every corner. But in 1938, with the advanced wisdom of thirty-one years, he recognizes that the globe-trotter, the "wandering dilettante of sensations," [45] does not have adventures. An adventure must be important to the adventurer; it must be related to his work and his life. Even if he were to fall off a cliff or be robbed by a Hebridean thug, it would be merely an episode, not an adven-

ture integral to his life and work. So he simply wanders about the
Western Islands "with scissors and a pot of paste." "Leaving
Barra" suggests that his urge to travel is not simple forgetfulness
of his own hard-gained wisdom; his is the compulsive urge of a
man who is fretful for "different values." [46] Atlantis may be unseen, uncomprehended, or "dimly divined"; but it still bites him
with a keen and phantom hunger.

"Bagpipe Music" [47] sounds a brighter note as it swirls to the
swishing of kilts and music. In this fast-moving patter song of
barbaric diction and cheerful cynicism, modern man wants neither Yogi nor Madame Helen Blavatsky—the leader of the
Theosophists; man wants only bank balance and "a bit of skirt
in a taxi." The mood and the rhythm can be captured completely
from the rueful-glad last quatrain.

It's no go my honey love, it's no go my poppet;
Work your hands from day to day, the winds will blow the profit.
The glass is falling hour by hour, the glass will fall for ever.
But if you break the bloody glass you won't hold up the weather.

In a very different mood, after MacNeice wrote "The Heated
Minutes Climb," [48] he lay in bed and listened to the whirring
clock. Most good poems, he muses, seem to have been written by
the collaboration of Dr. Jekyll and Mr. Hyde. For himself, he sus-
pects his poems are mostly the work of Hyde: self-pity, greed, and
nostalgia. Yet two seven-line stanzas of a muted love lyric do not
sound like a very sensual or brutish Hyde. In this poem, the
heated minutes climb an anxious hill, cash registers fill with
money, clocks chime, and ashes pile up all over the world "from
fingers killing time." If his loved one were with him among the
rocks, he would not be dull, anxious, or fearful.

The last poem in *I Crossed the Minch* is "On Those Islands (A
Poem for Hector MacIver)," [49] retitled in later anthologies as "The
Hebrides." It celebrates the old ways of the unchanging island
breed: no one hurries; the fires are built of fragrant peat; the photographs in the parlors extol the successful sons who left the Hebrides and married wealth in Toronto or in New York. The young
men who remain have to be poachers to assert their ancestral
right to the salmon and the deer. The Gaelic tunes are preserved
unspoiled by the traveling tinkers, and women in blue calico press

the hand plow into the rocky soil. The men fish, the minister "points the tour of hell," and the unregenerate keep right on drinking. A girl marries a tenant on seven acres who must go south each year to work on the roads and earn his ground rent of forty shillings. A few surnames cover a host of people, and the islanders have not yet imported the "art of being a stranger with your neighbour." Elopement, birth, death, marriage are all family matters to the whole community. Where many live on the dole or on old-age pensions, there is peace for those who can live just as their fathers lived before them on those islands. But "not for me," says the poet—and means perhaps not for anyone for very much longer.

III Zoo (1938)

Does a collage represent such richness of creativity that no one style will do, and thus many styles and types must be crowded on the canvas? Or does it mean that the artist is beating the bushes very hard for a subject; and, in lieu of finding a single significant one, is substituting the insignificant many? *Letters from Iceland, I Crossed the Minch,* and *Zoo*[50] all raise this central question in spite of their verve of high, boyish spirits (how late in life are boyish spirits an asset?) and the undeniable quality of several individual ingredients.

Auden had suggested, in the fourth letter to Byron, "let me pretend that I'm the impersonal eye of the camera."[51] John Van Druten, who accepted the suggestion, wrote a play adapted from Isherwood's *Berlin Stories* (1946) and entitled it *I am a Camera* (1955). MacNeice calls *Zoo* "mainly a series of impressions,"[52] and he seems to feel uncertain enough of the value of such visual impressionism that the first chapter of the book is entitled, "In Self-Defense." His defense is essentially that Julian Huxley is *in* the zoo, whereas he, Louis MacNeice, is outside. This juxtaposition does not refer to Huxley as an animal to be kept in a cage but as the author of the excellent *Official Guide* to the London Zoo. If Huxley has done so well, why should MacNeice add his very slight two cents? He does so simply because he is an outsider, a layman, who is uncommitted to the official viewpoint about zoos in general and about the London Zoo in particular. MacNeice's is a weak defense; but he does make a few stimulating and entertaining comments—and the most lively bit of all is the personal digression of Chapter V which has absolutely nothing to do with the zoo. As part of his usual critique of the labor dilemma of modern man, he points out that for 90 per cent of the people, their job is hackwork; they come alive therefore, only on the weekends when some two million of them visit, among other places, the London Zoo.

Amid the blended smells of stables, saloons, urine, beer, tobacco, boiled sweets, horseflesh, and hay, MacNeice considers how much he likes the new conception of evolution advanced by Gerald Heard in *Science in the Making*.[55] Heard suggests that mankind has not evolved by superb specialization to its environment but precisely by avoiding specialization. (This idea is the same basic one that Loren Eiseley later explored in *The Immense Journey*.) But MacNeice reminds us that we could as easily trace literary relationships of the idea by going backward: Aristotle remarked that man was by nature a barefooted animal and that, far from being a liability, this state was an asset: " 'For other animals have each but one mode of defence, and this they can never change; so that they must perform all the offices of life and even, so to speak, sleep with sandals on, never laying aside whatever serves as a protection to their bodies, nor changing such single weapons as they may chance to possess.' " [54]

MacNeice's skepticism when he hears human beings envying the existence of animals leads him to reflect on Walt Whitman's famous lines in *Song of Myself*. Whitman says he could live with animals because they are placid and self-contained; they do not whine about their condition nor weep for their sins. Whitman is quite right, says MacNeice; animals do not do any of these things. But "how would Whitman have liked it if he had found himself an animal and deprived of the gift of gab? Man is an unhappy animal and one that can talk. If he was not unhappy he would have nothing to talk about. But if he had nothing to talk about, he would be unhappy." [55]

MacNeice flew to Paris for a bank holiday weekend with his South African friend, Ernst. The latter had suggested that they go to the Cotswolds to play golf; but MacNeice had decided that they would go to Paris to see the Zoo. Ernst was most adaptable. He simply said: " 'That will be very nice,' and put on his dark suit." [56] The *Album* of the Paris Zoo opens with a quotation from André Demaison: "Lorsque dans les parcs modèles, les bêtes, même privées de leur climat d'origine, sont entourées de confort, de soins, lorsqu'elles sont comprises dans leur conscience profonde, elles arrivent à préférer cette paix, cette sécurité, aux errances et aux terreurs militaires." [57]

MacNeice marvels how anyone can know whether or not the animals prefer the security of captivity to the dangers of freedom. And, if it were so, would it not be a vicious preference? Then, parodying Tennyson's "Locksley Hall," he insists that blood, hunger, and fear of the dark would be better for them than the comfort of a prison with the certainty of buns. After all, "Original Sin won for us a life of progress, pattern of dark and light, the necessity of winning our bread which builds our wits, the tension without which there is no music and the conflict without which there is no harmony." [58]

Other than these random comments, the only valuable part of the book is the highly autobiographical personal digression of Chapter V. The poet, with his son, returns to his native city of Belfast and is outraged by the continuous sunshine. In his recollection of Belfast, the city was gray, wet, and repellent; and the people were dour, rude, and callous. But, on the boat train from London, a Belfast man smiled at his little boy, saying, "A child should live a life like an animal till it's five." [59] Such a permissive comment did not seem true to type; a Belfast man ought to be a sadist whose stock joke is gruesome—"'D'ye know what I saw yesterday—a boot floating down the river?' . . . 'There's nothing much in that.' . . . 'Nothing much in it! There was a leg in it.'"

Probably MacNeice's disapproval of the North of Ireland stemmed from a nursemaid from County Armagh who led him to think of Ulster as a prison and of the South as a land of escape. His father's Home Rule sympathies amidst the ardent Unionism of his congregation linked to the music of his South Ireland brogue, bred in MacNeice a love of the South. In an English school, the boy had felt among his equals; at home in North Ireland, he felt he belonged nowhere: neither to the barefoot boys in the street, nor to the hostile gentry. Perhaps they seemed hostile because they idolized the military, whereas his father was a clergyman and a pacifist; or because they were ardent Unionists, and his father a Home Ruler. The North Ireland gentry, comparatively new to their class, had to keep proving that they are at home. As a consequence, they set out to be more English than the

English; all their sons go to English public schools, and any daughter is a failure who does not marry a soldier.

For some twenty years the MacNeice family had lived in an ordinary little house at Carrickfergus, ten miles down the lough from Belfast. Then followed three years in a Queen Anne house at Waterford, before the large, ugly, but comfortable bishop's mansion on the Malone Road. Built in the last century by a tea merchant, the house was large, with a greenhouse full of azaleas and geraniums; and it was kept and run by five maids who slept in a wing over the garage. On Sunday morning his father went to preach at Ballymena, while MacNeice attended morning worship in the cathedral with his stepmother. Sitting in church, he was forced to remember that religion is still a positive influence on the social and political life of Ireland. Religion and politics are so inextricably fused that, when Ulstermen look at the cross with half-closed eyes, they see it shoot out rays and blossom as a Union Jack while the Son of God goes forth to war beneath an orange banner. As a little boy, MacNeice would return from the city with his sister on the train, both swinging their legs and chanting "'Belfast! Belfast! The city of smoke and dust!'" [60] To MacNeice, who lived in a town of Norman remains, Belfast was *ipso facto* evil because it was raw, ugly, and industrial.

IV   The Earth Compels (*1938*)

The Earth Compels, a volume of poems published by Faber and Faber in London, April, 1938, contains very little new work. Dedicated to Nancy (presumably the Nancy Sharp who illustrated *I Crossed the Minch* and *Zoo*), seven of the selections had been previously published in MacNeice's two books about travels in Iceland and the Hebrides and in various periodicals: *The Criterion, The Listener, The London Mercury, New Verse,* and *New Writing*.[61] There are, therefore, only seventeen new poems in the collection.

In the title poem, "The Sunlight on the Garden," the earth's compulsion is toward death; sunlight, minutes, freedom, sonnets, birds, and dancers are irresistibly drawn toward its descent. But, even though this is so, the poet is grateful for the sunlight hours and for the person with whom he spent some of the best of them. Other poems which emphasize this same melancholy Romanticism are "June Thunder," the Horatian ode "*Solvitur Acris Hiems,*"

"Passage Steamer," "Books, Do Not Look at Me," and "Homage to Clichés."

"June Thunder" follows the pattern of Matthew Arnold's "Dover Beach" as it moves from scenery to the human predicament to the solution of interpersonal love. June is beautiful, with indigo sky and the garden hushed and still. Suddenly, the curtains are blown inward, and the rain falls. The downpour is a catharsis cleansing the world of "overdated fancies," "old sentimentality," the whimsical "loves of the morning." The sky is black before nightfall; the clouds are like falling masonry; the lightning flashes like the "sword of the mad archangel." What is left when the rain falls, when civilization falls, when the world ends? If only the loved one would come, the poet could be happy—even if only for now. The poignant, if banal, "if only you would come" is an echo in mood and language of "if you were here, my dear," from "The Heated Minutes Climb." [62]

"*Solvitur Acris Hiems,*" [63] a translation of a Horatian ode, celebrates the coming of spring with dances led by Venus of Cythera, the Nymphs, and the Graces; but the celebration is saddened by the recollection that the shack of the pauper and the towers of kings lie equally beneath the heel of white-faced Death. In such a world the beloved must not ravel out "lengthy hopes"; she must simply make the most of the present company in the present hour and of the wine on the table. In "Passage Steamer," the passengers sit at ease on the decks while the great cranks in the engine room rise and fall to the refrain of doom. Back from a journey, the poet needs a new focus for desire; but the open sea offers none, and the calling of the gulls insinuates that all beginnings were in the past. When he thinks of a dear one, who was once so near, the barren skies appall; the sea becomes a grave; gray are both world and day. In "Books, Do Not Look at Me" ("Sand in the Air" in later collections), the sand of memory is sifting down through the air: Where is she walking; why is she absent? Dial her number; she will not reply. Dear, go away and leave the crags of my memory.

"Homage to Clichés" is a much more intricately developed poem than the others in this group. F. O. Matthiessen believed that the complex harmonies of the architectural structure of Mac-Neice's longer poems were the chief index to his growing skill as a poet. [64] In "Homage to Clichés" the poet manages to interweave a complex pattern of familiar responses elicited from his female companion as if they were the purrs of a stroked cat, fish angling off from the main stream of conversation to swim into the net, or drinks swimming across the bar. Throughout the poem the images intermesh so intricately that the reader is delightfully surprised at each repetition and transformation of the individual image; but it is impossible to illustrate the process by a single example. In line 5, the cat's fur sparkles; in lines 15 and 16, "an old man momentously sharpens a pencil as though/He were not merely licking his fur like a cat—." In line 17, the cat's tongue curls to the back of its neck; but, in line 41, the domestic, purring cat is transformed into eight black panthers gathering their muscular tension for a spring.

In similar fashion the other major image of fish develops from the expected response, through drinks that swim across the bar, to a giant bell of doom. MacNeice commented on his own technique in this poem: "Sometimes, more fantastically, I take several images and ring the changes on them. Thus in a philosophical poem 'Homage to Clichés,' I think of the brute Other, the fate which we cannot influence: (a) as an Egyptian Rameses, (b) as a tenor bell (which we cannot peal but can only play chimes upon), (c) as a black panther (black because unknown and because the black panther is popularly said to be untamable). The movement of each of these three will be the movement of Fate. . . ." [65]

"Homage to Clichés" exhibits the familiar MacNeice pattern of thought and solution of problem. How pleasant it is to sit in relaxed friendship with an attractive woman in a bar, and there indulge in a game of cliché and response, each making the expected reply, with nothing to ripple the surface of mood. But pass through a door, climb up a belfry stair—and there within the womb of stone hang eight black bells. We have imagined that the jingling our fingers made on the bells was the final music. But the ringers are taking off their coats to toll rather than chime, and a timekeeper with watch and pistol stands ready to signal the end of the whole delightful world of cliché and refrain. What can be done to change or escape the doom? The male can only ask his charming female partner "What will you have, my dear? The same again?"

"Chess," in hexameter closed couplets, strikes a similar eschatological note as the old men play games and the young recruits die in battle. "Circus" gives a splendid example of that technical dexterity which has been admired even by critics who did not really like MacNeice's poetry. The poem is in four sections: 'I, *Trapezists;* II, *Horses;* III, *Clowns;* IV, *Elephants.* The dimeter, unrhymed quatrains have a delicate intricacy that trembles on the edge of disaster but never topples over. The Sitwells' technique of "transference of sense-epithets" [60] is used with studied and precise effect: "our fear their frame," "a disc of dreams," "drumsticks flower/In pink percussion," "metal petals," "the child's face pops/Like ginger beer." The first two lines of *Trapezists*—"Intricacy of engines,/Delicacy of darkness"—become the last two lines of *Elephants:* "Efficacy of engines,/Obstinacy of darkness."

"Eclogue Between the Motherless" represents MacNeice's favorite dialogue form. However, in his other eclogues, although they have distinct characterization, the characters tend to be representative types of humanity who are used for making a social criticism, rather than inidvidual personalities. But "Eclogue Between the Motherless" is essentially a mordant, mounting narrative arising out of a slow-moving, reminiscent start. Both *A* and *B* are men whose mothers have died some years before. *B*'s father has married a rich, thirty-year-old girl, and *B* has obtained a divorce from a wife who was beautiful but who had always seemed alien. *A* returns for the holidays to his father's home, now run by an unmarried sister. There, surrounded by memories of his childhood and of his mother, he sifts through the brittle recollection of his many mistresses and decides, at last, to marry. He has written a proposal to a woman in India who has only a single year to live, and he now awaits her reply. At this point *B* begins to interrupt, demanding to know the name of the woman, who is, of course, his own divorced wife.

Essentially dramatic, the poetic narrative bristles with energy and emotion; and even the long reminiscent passages are essentially dramatic monologues in the Robert Browning manner. This eclogue is one of the early poems that give the promise of a later characteristic—brevity of statement in sharp, precise wording, combined with a rich mulch of memory, desire-fantasy, and incalculable loneliness. Perhaps the beginning and the ending are too sharp and brisk in comparison with the deep, slow-moving middle for this poem to be an entirely successful experiment. But it does foreshadow a fusion more equitably made in later poems.

"Hidden Ice" and "Christmas Shopping" present opposite dangers to domesticity. The former begins bravely to celebrate the heroes of domestic life; routine workers who spend years in offices, planners with clock and calendar—they are to be praised for inconceivable stamina and for the "equilibrium of nerves and notions." But not all achieve this quiet heroism; some strike hidden ice and come to disaster. "Christmas Shopping" takes the reader on a buying spree, but its dangers do not arise from rocks beneath the surface, hidden ice, or unsuspected currents. The frightening reality is "blank momentum": the sense that, beneath all the scurrying crowds, there is the emptiness of vacuum.

MacNeice later used "Hidden Ice" as an example of concentration of language and imagery which could be destroyed by discursive, prose treatment. Because he was often told that the poem was obscure in meaning because of that condensation, he took the trouble to explicate it. This poem, says MacNeice, written in praise of the ordinary people who live faithfully by routine, also portrays some who fall away from their loyal allegiance; and their lives develop new and dangerous centers: "They are persons who become unable to keep their aesthetic sense or their outside interests or their erotic emotions pigeon-holed off into the hours when they are not on duty. They become obsessed by something which, on their system, should not be allowed to intrude into their eight-hour day. They kiss flowers and [become] like Judas because the act is treacherous to their whole system. . . ." As Judas betrayed Christ, so, in a sense, Christ destroyed Judas. As Judas kissed Christ, these persons kiss flowers; and both kisses are potentially fatal to their system of life. We may consider, for example, the routine worker who becomes an active Communist: "And some of these people become *fatally* addicted to what belongs, on their premises, to their pet hours only. Such people in everyday life may end in suicide or the asylum. Such a man is like Saint Sebastian because his collapse is brought about through the things he loved —the arrow in his body feathered from the birds which he himself reared." [67]

With the figure of a man between the clock and the sun, MacNeice poetically places man between the two great symbols of routine, one artificial and the other natural. "Further, both a clock ticking and a shaft of sun entering a room (the dust-motes dancing in it corresponding to the inevitable ticking of the clock) seem to me, at moments, sinister, hypnotic. And—a minor point— the sun enters the room at the time when the malingerer ought to be at his work." [68] The picture is concrete and factual as well as symbolic, for the poet explains that he had a clear picture in his mind of a particular man who was harboring suicidal thoughts, sitting in a room with a clock on the mantel behind him, and the sun creeping closer and closer on the floor from a window in front of him.

A group of six poems relate to the childhood and adolescence of the poet. "Carrickfergus" traces the boyhood years in Belfast and in Carrick in County Antrim. The lad, a rector's son, was born in the Anglican order, and thus cut off from the life and religion of the Irish poor. During World War I a huge army camp was established within sight of the boy's home. All day he could see the dummies hanging for bayonet practice and hear the sentries chanting their martial challenge. Even when the boy goes to school he travels in a camouflaged steamer. At school, in Dorset, he is separated once again from the real world of poor workers, singing soldiers, and German prisoners-of-war. The form of the poem is MacNeice's usual long, pentametric line in quatrains rhyming *abcb*.

"Taken for Granted" quite simply reviews the household blessings taken for granted until we reach the age of twenty. "Thank You"—written to a youthful friend, a head shorter than the poet— has a placid, sure touch and humor. The poet thanks him for his sensual poise, his gay assurance, for all the times of contact, but most of all for "the abandon of . . . giving,/For seeing in the dark, for making this life worth living." In "Only Let It Form," an obscure little stanza, the artist feels like the last diner in an empty hall that is filling up with clogging snow; and he begs for the creative moment to return, to be cradled like a brandy glass in his hand. But in "Now That the Shapes of Mist" the writer is glad that the night is dark and the roads are wet because he will the more easily slip quietly into sleep, the brother of Death. The "Rugby Football Excursion" is made by an adult, but one who is recalled to his adolescent years, back to Ireland, to Midland voices, and to Wicklow apricot jam. These memories are jostled by the swirl of the scoring, tea and toast with Fellows of the university, and bishops, friends of his father; and a walk through Dublin as the dusk bathes the children of the city streets. Reluc-

tantly he must tear himself away from the past and rejoin the
beery tourists who have to be drunk in order to bear the pressure
of memory.

Because *The Earth Compels* contains so little new work, the
collection cannot be expected to be very important. Probably the
two best poems of the period 1937–38 are "Bagpipe Music" and
"Eclogue from Iceland," neither one from this collection but included, respectively, in the prose travel volumes *I Crossed the
Minch* and *Letters from Iceland.* "Bagpipe Music" represents just
about the furthest a modern poet can go with a cheery jingle
about gloomy times. The closest MacNeice comes to the level of
this achievement in *The Earth Compels* is the virtuoso performance of "Homage to Clichés" with its themes of fate and doom
floating lightly in casual cocktail glasses.

The poem "Eclogue from Iceland" is important because it portrays the dialogue of representative men on the topic of the
world's ills, and thus is a shorter version of MacNeice's verse
dramas which might aptly be described in exactly the same way.
It is also important because of the struggle that takes place later
in *Plant and Phantom* and *Ten Burnt Offerings* between the sophisticated and despairing brief jingles (like "Bagpipe Music")
and the longer, more richly evocative, and also more hopeful
poems MacNeice was to write in his maturity. "Eclogue Between
the Motherless" (from *The Earth Compels*), although an exercise
in the same poetic form as the other eclogues, misses having the
same developmental significance as "Eclogue from Iceland" because it is more personal than typical and makes almost no social
or political reference. On the other hand, it is remarkably dramatic in its gradual enunciation of the clues to mystery, its mounting emotional tension, and the sense throughout of an obsessive
undercurrent that quite transcends the surface movement.

The Earth Compels contains the usual handful of nostalgic
echoes of the poet's childhood. In "June Thunder" MacNeice reiterates the Robert Browning ("Love Among the Ruins") and Matthew Arnold ("Dover Beach") theme of interpersonal love set
against the backdrop of a failing civilization and a dying world.
"Passage Steamer" chugs out his customary refrain of doom. "The
Sunlight on the Garden" expresses the old idea—both for Mac-
Neice and most other poets—that the sunlit hours are precious
because so few. But MacNeice adds the new and autobiographi-

cal postscript that they are precious because they were shared with the right person.

The concern for the poet's craft, the source of one or two poems in each collection, is represented in *The Earth Compels* in a manner reminiscent of Samuel Taylor Coleridge's "Dejection." In the poem "Only Let It Form," the hour is late, the other diners have departed, and only one remains in a hall silently filling up with snow. This diner wishes to cradle once again in his hand a glass of brandy; the poet wishes to recapture the creative mood and moment; but a hall filling up with snow offers slight prospect of the fulfillment of either desire.

V Modern Poetry: A Personal Essay (*1938*)

Louis MacNeice's most important body of literary criticism is to be found in *Modern Poetry*, published by Oxford University Press. The volume requires very little reference to his later periodical articles of literary criticism to caulk the seams of this most consistent of critics. The very first sentence of the Preface states the case succinctly: "This book is a plea for *impure* poetry, that is, for poetry conditioned by the poet's life and the world around him." The poet is visualized in this highly "personal essay" as both critic and entertainer. As entertainer, the poet may fall over into the writing of escape literature; as critic, he may become so deeply committed to a particular school of thought that his poems become propaganda. There must be a middle course in which the poet is not so much the echo in verse of the prose convictions of his community but "its conscience, its critical faculty, its generous instinct." [69] He will be plucked at by the constant emphasis upon specialization—the department of poetry in contemporary culture. The practical necessities of war and peace, prosperity and depression will press upon him to falsify his vision to fit the obvious needs and opportunities of the hour. Ideological organizations will clamor for him to "tell lies to order." But he must give poetic truth.

The eleven chapters of the essay move in an essentially personal rhythm, with an introductory and a concluding chapter which have wider, more general applications. Chapter I presents what MacNeice considers to be the evidence for "A Change of Attitude" on the part of modern poets. The self-consciousness of a poet ought to be a consciousness of himself as a man—not, as often in the preceding generations, as a poet. Beginning with the Romantic era, poets have thought of themselves as rebels, parasites, aliens. They practiced their art, not as criticism of life, but as art for art's sake. This led them into the extremes—and dead-ends —of Decadence, Imagism, Parnassianism, and Symbolism. In this regard, Matthew Arnold's hierarchy of poetic values is probably a better guide than Walter Pater's insistence that the most important thing about a work of art is its style. Arnold contended that of first importance was subject; second, construction; and only third, expression.

After a brief, corrective Georgian period of simple, healthy, back-to-nature poetry, T. S. Eliot and Ezra Pound began to write poetry that was more esoteric than any since the Metaphysical period of seventeenth century. Eliot pontificated that in an era of such complexity, poetry must also be difficult.[70] And his tendencies toward defeatism, pedantry, synopticism, and realism made it easy for him to fill his own prescription. But MacNeice agrees with Michael Roberts (editor of *New Signatures*) that their generation, although profoundly influenced by Eliot and Pound in their schooldays, has turned to the writing of a more popular poetry—"more popular" not in the sense that it is read by more people, but because it defines man as a political animal with strong physical instincts, needs, and affections.

Therefore the poetry of W. H. Auden, Stephen Spender, Cecil Day Lewis, John Lehmann, Julian Bell, and William Plomer (all included in the anthology *New Signatures*) sets as its appropriate subject matter the economic, material, social, and sexual factors that are common to the lives of all modern men. This significant linking of economics with physical instincts, bridged over by the sense of community, suggests that the architects of modern poetry, as of modern society, are Karl Marx and Sigmund Freud. Generally, MacNeice treats D. H. Lawrence as the introducer of Freudian psychology into literary usage. It is clear that Lawrence's use of the world Freud made provides a strong corrective to a culture which emasculates, sublimates, pushes the naked sexual urges into neurosis and psychosis, and tends to replace the healthy animal with the efficient machine. And the materialism of Marxian dialectic forces the poet to face the world of concrete things rather than the shadowy universe of Platonic forms or of Shelleyan ideas. It also forces the disinherited, disoriented artist to become emotionally partisan. With its certainty of the ultimate success of the proletarian revolution, Marxism gives a sense of direction to thinkers who feel themselves imprisoned in an ideological cul-de-sac.

After pointing out this significant shift from withdrawal to involvement in the common life of men, MacNeice writes three chapters, which he calls his "Case-Book," covering the periods of his childhood, public school, and Oxford. This section is an intensely interesting analysis of the impact of the history of English poetry upon a sensitive and creative youth. On the other hand, it is more biographical than critical, more random jottings than analytical structure. The poet is viewed as a specialist in what everybody practices—the use of language both for pleasure and communication. The poet has no different capacities or talents; "he merely has more highly developed muscles and better coordination. And he practises his activity according to a stricter set of rules." [71] After thus restoring the poet to the realm of normality, he performs the same office for the reader of poetry: ". . . the poet should imagine as his audience an ideal normal man who is an educated member of his own community and is basically at one with the poet in his attitude to life." [72]

As a child MacNeice preferred dolls and bears to machines; therefore as a youth he preferred language with style to strictly scientific prose. Since his father was a clergyman, he tells us that he was first fascinated by the cadences and imagery of the Bible. At the age of seven he wrote poems in which he was chiefly interested in the pattern of words. The recipe was simple: to use "thou" instead of "you" and to make the ends of the lines rhyme. One example of his early poetry has the merit of being taken from life and of having a personal application: "O parrot, thou hast grey feathers/Which thou peckest in all weathers./And thy curled beak/Could make me squeak. . . ." [73] He was impressed by Neoclassical poems in the grand manner of Dryden and Pope when they were read aloud magnificently by his headmaster: "A controlled flamboyance of diction has always moved me, so that I have never subscribed to the Wordsworthian exclusive crusade for homespun." [74] This statement of his taste may surprise the critics who complain of the flat MacNeice diction, the conversational tone, and the casual manner of statement.

At the age of eighteen, MacNeice read the early poems of Eliot and found them repellent. The subjects were ugly; the form, unpleasant; and the meaning, obscure. But then the budding technician discovered the principles of Eliot's technique; "the blend of conversation and incantation, the deliberate flatnesses, the quick cutting, the so-called free association." [75] Even at that early age, MacNeice had already been attempting to write with deliberate flatness when he described anything he considered commonplace or sordid. The example of a conversational style was clearly not lost on the younger poet; unfortunately, the incantatory manner was seldom found, so that MacNeice's poetry rarely dips to intensity or lifts in exaltation.

Chapter V begins the more detailed discussion of six areas of special concern in contemporary poetry: the personal factor, imagery, rhythm and rhyme, diction, obscurity, lighter poetry, and drama. This section also includes a curious and rather touching catalogue of the influences which have conditioned his own poetry: rearing in the North of Ireland, a clergyman for a father, mother's death while he was still a child, "repression from the age of 6 to 9," inferiority complex on the basis of physique and class-consciousness, lack of social life until he was an adult, late puberty, ignorance of music, inability at those sports which might foster a sense of rhythm, an adolescent fondness for the role of "enfant terrible," shyness with girls until twenty, a fondness (now dead) for metaphysics, marriage and subsequent divorce, Birmingham, a lazy pleasure in gardens and wild landscapes, enjoyment of animals, and an interest in dress.[76] Since MacNeice later refers to Auden's fondness for catalogues, this was evidently another quality the two poets shared.

MacNeice points out that imagery may be primarily cerebral, emotional, or sensuous; and he uses illustrations from the Greek, Roman, Renaissance English, Romantic, and modern poets to prove his point. The obscurity of Eliot's images is not always due to vagueness of suggestion, nor to the private vision of the poet; it arises from ellipses which omit the links between the object or action described and the literature which it suggests. These ellipses are even more characteristic of Pound, whose chief difficulty arises because he constantly uses other writers' images lifted out of their living context.

Auden often uses a dramatic imagery in which the meaning is absorbed in the image as an actor is absorbed in his part. A poet of great concretion, he also uses a dream technique as well as the rhetorical or Classical image and conceit. His later poems are full of popular wit arising from American folk-ballads, the blues, or Cole Porter's musicals (witness *Cocaine Lil*). MacNeice, himself, tends to use images "(a) to clarify a picture, (b) to express an idea with more concentration and more shock to the reader. . . ." He gives illustrations from his works of the sensuous image, the cerebral, a blend of cerebral and sensuous, and most complex, the use of several images which change and develop in the course of the poem ("Homage to Clichés").[77]

Modern poetry is often accused of lack of appeal to the ear. Louis MacNeice very much approves of the sound of modern poetry and describes himself as one who nearly always writes for the ear. His argument (Chapter VII, "Rhythm and Rhyme") points out the necessity of a great deal of expenditure of modern poetic energy on simply breaking away from the tyranny of the models of immediately preceding periods. But contemporary poets have not been content merely to break away; they have also been engaged in using the forgotten forms of Classical verse, Anglo-Saxon rhythms, Metaphysical wit, Skeltonic meter, and variations on old models such as Hopkins performed in his "sprung rhythm." MacNeice considers that the younger poets have now served an arduous technical apprenticeship which has brought them to the point at which they can let their subject dictate the choice among a great variety of techniques.

Modern poetic diction arises out of a similar process of rebellion, adoption, and adaptation. Aristotle advocates the conscious decoration of speech for poetic tragedies but limited by certain rules of decorum. Thus a noun may be the ordinary word for the thing, the foreign word, a metaphor, an ornamental word, a coined word; a word which is lengthened, curtailed, or altered in form.[78] Even with these precise limitations, the concept of diction as decoration is not acceptable to modern poetry. The point of view Wordsworth expressed in the Preface to the *Lyrical Ballads* and that Coleridge corrected in the *Biographia Literaria* is much closer to the modern mood. Modern "diction" must have vigour, be "familiar enough to be recognizable, new enough to be arresting." [79] After the feminine writing of most of the nineteenth century (with the exceptions of Byron, Wordsworth, Browning) and after the neuter writing of the Georgians, the vigor of contemporary poetry should be masculine but not exhibitionist. Hopkins called Dryden the most masculine of British poets, one whose style and rhythms were based soundly on the "naked thew and sinew of the English language. . . ." [80] MacNeice is convinced that the thew and sinew of language are now reappearing in new and vigorous verse.

The public is fond of complaining that modern poetry is obscure. Rejecting the position that poetry is purely music or the position of the Surrealist Manifesto that poetry gives absolutely no witness of the real world as it comes under judgment,[81] MacNeice turns for explanation to the cinematic technique of "cutting." [82] Modern poets tend to leave out the links between idea and idea or between image and image for the sake of speed and concentration, or because they wish to convey their sense of the broken patterns and the quick transitions of their own thoughts and lives and world. This technique, so integral to contemporary art, explains the collage or mosaic of Eliot as well as the "telegraphese" [83] of Auden. MacNeice, in examining his own poems, finds that any obscurity is likely to arise because the meaning is complex in its very nature, or because he chose to compromise lucid expression for the sake of speed, concentration, color, or music of the verse.

Chapter X is a plea for lighter poetry and poetic drama: "The lighter sides of the human animal should be represented in verse as well as his 'high seriousness.' " [84] Even a passing acquaintance with the poems of Auden, Eliot, Day Lewis, Hugh MacDiarmid, William Plomer, and, above all, of MacNeice, testifies to the importance of the jocular statement of the hardboiled truth. As MacNeice experiments richly with poetic drama for stage, screen, and radio, he advises his contemporaries that—just as light verse offers them a needed change from the intensity of the lyric—so drama offers them a change from the single voice to an expression of the many different people who inhabit any single poet. It is good for the poet to employ those forms which require collaboration with other craftsmen. He must always "collaborate" with his public; but in the film studio or the back rooms of a broadcasting station he may discover bits of himself that he would have missed entirely among the papers and books of his study.

In the most significant summary of the volume, found in its own Conclusion, MacNeice reiterates his initial contention that the poet is a blend of entertainer and critic. He is not photographic or scientific because he is always grinding an ax or "showing off" to his enemies or his friends. He records not merely the fact, but the fact plus, and modified by, his own emotional and cerebral reaction to it. As to the requirements for a modern poet, MacNeice offers a definition which has often been either admired or castigated: "I would have a poet able-bodied, fond of talking, a reader of newspapers, capable of pity and laughter, informed in economics, appreciative of women, involved in personal relationships, actively interested in politics, susceptible to physical impressions." [85] The perfectly obvious response is to point out that the description may be a better one of Louis MacNeice than of the poet per se. But there can be no question that it is basic to his whole philosophy of poetry and to his performance of that art.

MacNeice insists that the relationship between subject and form, not either alone or pre-eminently, makes a good poem. The matter of expression is dictated by the radical distinction between a disguise that deliberately hides or distorts and a form that amply reveals and gives independent life to the subject. MacNeice states once again his prime insistence that the younger poets are becoming more direct in their diction and style as they increasingly focus their attention on some idea or ideal from the same practical world which is inhabited by ordinary men.

MacNeice attempts to make a radical distinction between belief and propaganda. He observes that beliefs are increasing among the poets he knows, and he contends that this increase should encourage the production of a wider, more effective, and possibly a major poetry. Poets like Auden, Spender, and Day Lewis have adopted a system of beliefs into which they have not as yet completely grown. But that very adoption argues a sympathy for those forces which at that date—1938—and in that place—England—make for human progress. Poets should write honestly; poetry should arise out of their convictions and their lives; but the poet should neither hang back in an obsolete Romanticism, nor run ahead with wild enthusiasm for assurances that cannot be fulfilled. Only through such sympathy with the major movements of their time can modern artists become part of a major literature.

CHAPTER 3

Left of Center

TO MILITARY strategists, the Spanish Civil War proved the value of airplanes and tanks against civilian populations. To political idealists, it was the classic confrontation of Right and Left, Fascist and Communist. To socially conscious American writers of the era it was "Hemingway's war." For at least a generation of intellectuals, to have fought against Franco was the impeccable recommendation of liberalism—but a credential that later got some of them into trouble. In "Spain 1937," W. H. Auden describes the Iberian peninsula as merely an "arid square" of rock and sand "nipped off" from Africa. But, on its tableland, the central drama of Western man was being ignominiously staged; for in Spain "Our fever's menacing shapes are precise and alive."

MacNeice conveniently provides the data for the Proletarian involvement of his group of friends. Edward Upward, the early inspiration of Auden and Isherwood, asserted in a periodical essay that no contemporary writer (1940) could produce anything of value unless he were taking an active part in the "Worker's Movement." [1] Upward also wrote a novel about an introspective and neurotic youth who, after two hundred pages of fantasy, sees the light and goes out to find a worker—MacNeice remarks, "as if that would solve everything." Auden and Isherwood took their turn at manning the barricades by producing a "bad play, *On the Frontier.*" [2] Stephen Spender toured England with a lecture on "The Artist and Society," in which he attempted to make Picasso the evangel of Marxism.

MacNeice makes little reference to "the popular front" in his review "The Poet in England Today," but he wrote *Autumn Journal* in 1938 about Munich and the Spanish Civil War as his contribution to protest literature. He is frank to admit, both in the review and in the *Journal,* that he was convinced that the "*balance of right*" was with the pro-Communist government rather than with the pro-Fascist rebels. But he insists that the poet is not forced to choose between the Ivory Tower of I. A. Richards' complete severance of poetry from belief and the "Brazen Tower" of political propaganda. The Ivory Tower represents isolation from man in his togetherness, and the Brazen Tower represents isolation from men as individuals. To MacNeice, it is important to recognize that both are forms of imprisonment. The poet should sing about the whole life of total man but with his mouth, not with a megaphone.[3]

These comments of MacNeice, in his survey of 1940, make clear the ambivalence of his political position. He considers that the poet must include the political life of man in his poetry. In certain situations, the poet is convinced of the essential rightness of the Leftist position. But social significance is not the only significance required of poetry, and the old Romantic-Liberal emphasis upon man as a unique individual, even if essentially anarchic in concept, must also be permitted to function in the poet's life and in his art. Thus MacNeice defines for us the extent to which he went along with the dialectical enthusiasms of his friends, and the fashion in which he remained the separate, isolated critic.

I   Autumn Journal (1939)

In the Foreword to *Poems: 1925–1948*, MacNeice says that he considers *Autumn Journal* to be "in a sense, a failure; it fails in depth," and he adds, "we shall not be capable of depth—of tragedy or *great* poetry—until we have made sense of our world." It is quite understandable that the poet should feel that the verse diary of the public and private events from August, 1938, through January, 1939, would be so involved in the immediacy of event as to be all foreground and no depth, although, to be sure, with enough chiaroscuro. There is, also, good reason to enter the caveat that some very great poetry, including such different exhibits as Shakespeare's *Othello* and Eliot's *The Waste Land,* are great not because of the essential sense but because of the essential dilemma presented.

In this respect, *Autumn Journal* [4] joins their company; essentially, it explores a dilemma and climaxes in an insurmountable frustration. But MacNeice does not resolve the dilemma, nor does he lean the ladder of a philosophic system against the insurmountable wall. The weakness of Julian Symons' nickname for the

poem—"The Bourgeois's Progress" [5]—is precisely that in Bunyan's *Pilgrim's Progress*, Christian reached his goal and was illu-
minated by the heavenly vision. *Autumn Journal* records a shift of
attitude and a reluctant confrontation of political situations; but
the shift which begins with amazement and shock, ends only with
the restatement of the same personal "good-will" that the poet
recognized as ineffectual at the beginning. The poet, thoroughly
aware of the lack of a definitive philosophy in the *Journal*, defends
that deficiency by a reminder of the poem's genre: "In a journal or
a personal letter a man writes what he feels at the moment. . . .
I was writing it from August 1938 until the New Year and have
not altered any passages relating to public events in the light of
what happened after the time of writing." [6] He ascribes the philosophic limitations of the poem to his own desire to be honest and
to reveal only the things he was witnessing, thinking, and feeling
in the fall of 1938: "Nor am I attempting to offer what so many
people now demand from poets—a final verdict or a balanced
judgment. It is the nature of this poem to be neither final nor
balanced. . . . I refuse to be 'objective' or clean-cut at the cost of
honesty." [7]

The long poem of twenty-four cantos (approximately one hundred pages) is a major test of the technical skill which all the
critics seem to agree MacNeice pre-eminently has. The lines are
usually four to five feet in length, with varying numbers of un-
stressed syllables within the foot. Most often, the poem moves
rapidly with rhyme on the first–third or second–fourth lines—just
enough rhyme to keep the beat swinging along but not so much
that the recitation becomes singsong.

Canto I begins in Hampshire, amidst the domesticity of roses
on the breakfast table and bacon and eggs in a silver dish. Going
north to London on the train, the sight of a river reminds the poet
that he cannot get a corner on life's beauty. The essence of a river
is flow, and that of life, change. His meditation is interrupted as
he watches a woman get on at Surbiton, her face painted, hair
dyed, a run in her stockings, and a faded air of tired sexual attrac-
tion about her.

In London (Canto II), night is a spider web; lions from the zoo
roar beyond the hill, the meter clicks, and the cistern bubbles.
Lions must have reminded MacNeice of William Blake's "Tiger,
Tiger, Burning Bright"; but, oddly enough, he applies a parody of

the meter of that well-known poem to the spiders weaving webs, rather than to the lions roaring beyond the hill. The gods (perfect Being) are absent, and men (imperfect Becoming) are still. If he should die, he would then be pure non-being; but tomorrow is another day on which he can begin again the tasks he has begun so often before.

August is nearly over (Canto III); the good conformists are back from the beaches with enough tan to keep them going until the annual spree at Christmas. The poet muses that he, a conformist with a "slave-owner's mind," is also ready to accept the easy unearned profit and to occupy the undeserved niche at the top. But his worst temptation is not to affirm but to retreat—to murmur "Lord, I am not worthy"—and turn his face to the wall. He must look up and out; his feet may stumble at first, but they can learn to walk with others and, at last, to dance.

Canto IV (September) is a love poem to one who made many of his days intolerable and perplexed, but many more happy. London is littered with the memories of their kisses. If he must go on without her, he will always remember her shifting, transient moods and her candor and assurance. He has often suffered because of her unwillingness to flatter or respond, but he realizes now that this unwillingness expressed her own honesty and integrity. He resolves to develop just such a pattern of clear expression of clean-cut emotion.

Then on a beautiful day, Hitler speaks (Canto V). Everyone thinks "This must be wrong, it has happened before . . . we must be dreaming." The bloody frontier (Auden and Isherwood's *On the Frontier*) converges upon men's private lives. It is no use echoing the prayer of Jesus, "Take away this cup." We helped to fill it, and it is only logical that we should help to drink it. He looks at an eight-year-old eider-down wedding present, at linens bought in Ireland; and he wonders dully what the morning paper will say. His mind wanders back to his trip to Spain the preceding Easter (Canto VI), in which he was resolutely a tourist unresponsive to sullen faces and writings on walls. He came home and forgot Spain, but now he realizes that Spain is not to be forgotten.

The news is full of conferences, adjournments, ultimata, protest meetings in the park; and Hitler's voice keeps yelling over the wireless (Cantos VII, VIII). This international issue necessarily involves principle, but it will be settled in panic and self-deception. He returns to Birmingham where eight years ago he came with his wife to teach Classics. Now he is wifeless, and the national crisis has thrust him out of his ivory tower. Word comes that the crisis is postponed: Chamberlain has saved their skins and damned their consciences; and the Czechs go under without help or protest from their friends.

In October (Canto IX), the poet is back in London. The Greeks were set free by their belief in necessity, plotting their little lives with truth and humor between the "jealous heaven and the callous sea." But even in Greece, free speech ended on the pikes of Macedonia; and Athens became a mere university city. Philosophy narrowed its focus to putting the individual life in order and to keeping a quiet mind. The great talk still went on for a thousand years; but, instead of the epics of heroes, it became dapper little elegiac verses by professors about the transience of all affections and the golden mean between opposing ills. When the professor of Greek ought to remember the paragons of Hellas, he recalls instead the crooks, opportunists, fancy boys, the splitters of hairs, the demagogues and quacks, and especially all those slaves.

The return to his teaching duties reminds him of the beginnings of other school terms (Canto X). There was Marlborough College in England, where the boys took for granted that things would always get better and bigger, or, in parody of Matthew Arnold, when the boys had everything to expect and nothing to deplore. Then he passed four-foot-six and went to Merton College, Oxford. Life began to narrow; number two must mimic number one in everything. School was an initiation into life and all the more symbolic because initiates are always blindfolded; reflex action is all that is required to sleep in an office when things are normal; and, of course, things will always be normal in the British Isles.

In Canto XI the girl of Canto IV haunts his memory. Common sense says she will not return; that, if she did return, she would not stay. His pride tells him to cut his losses and consider her lost. He hates her and would like to murder her memory; he thinks of her with other men and jealousy consumes. He is forced to try to assess her paradoxes of spirit. Perhaps he may see her sometime during October.

It is Tuesday, October 25, 1938 (Canto XII), and the Roman weather suggests the Roman mob crying only for bread and circuses. On this foggy English night it is difficult to realize that the legions of barbarism are waiting at the gates. Plato's idealism was too bleak; Aristotle's linking of form and function is superior. All the poet wants is to be human, with the mind given its full due, but the body not distrusted. Humane studies led to cushy jobs, but tended to leave men spiritually bankrupt intellectual snobs. He is grateful for his comforts; better to have authentic mammon than worship a bogus god. After all, if he did not have a degree in Humane Letters, he might be a hod carrier. The Emperor takes his seat, and those who are about to die . . . come, draw the curtain.

Besides being good for the logical brain, Marlborough and Merton (Canto XIII) insured that a gentleman need never misplace his accents. The man with a Classical education and an honors degree (like the poet), considers that the man in the street has particular items of information but no general concepts. On the other hand, perhaps he is all general, with no particularities. One of the assets of Oxford is that the graduate can never really believe anything again. The next evening (Canto XIV) the poet drives to Oxford to vote and to drive voters to the polls. He goes mainly for fun, partly for the half-believed-in principle that the parliamentary system is the only weapon of the citizen against the legions' eagles of militarism and the lictors' axes of fascism. People who hate politics will lose their private values unless they work at the public gate for a better political system. The perfectionist waits forever in the fog; it is necessary to join the vulgar voters, to make a cross for Lindsay and leave a blank for Hogg. The nicest people in England have always been the least apt to solidarity, but now they must all align against the beast.

Canto XV describes the frenetic activity of a pleasure-loving people as they attempt to forget the war. But ghosts of dead soldiers from Gallipoli and Flanders of World War I, as well as those more recently dead, haunt their revels. The poet envies the men of action who are not too haunted to shoot to kill (Canto XVI). Yeats was too aware of the jumble of opposites for action, but his beloved Maude Gonne somehow made purpose out of them. The poet spits out his hatred of Ireland's grandiose airs, sob-stuff, laughter, and swagger. She is a bore and a bitch who gives her children neither sense nor money.

After breakfast, at nine o'clock in the morning, he sits looking at

the November sun (Canto XVII). But the ego cannot long remain
self-sufficient; others are always organic to the self. Even the sense
of taste provides communion with God in plant or beast; a fish
includes the sea, and all food is a sacramental feast. Aristotle considered man-in-action the essential and really existent man; one
may try to confine himself to himself if he can.

English poets should sing no more of the English countryside as
the Georgians did; Tennyson, in "Locksley Hall Sixty Years After,"
predicted correctly that the country dwindles and the factory
grows (Canto XVIII). Once men believed with bone and pulse,
not simply in the brain. Spiritual sloth grows in the nation. Who is
behind the church doors: Sleeping Beauty, the Holy Ghost, the
greatest happiness of the greatest number? As Nietzsche said,
maybe God is dead. If we pray, shall it be to the Unknown God of
decadent Athens, or to the pantheistic God Who is everywhere?
But, if we assume a God, then how can we explain empty stomachs, blindness, paralysis? God forbid a Hindu acquiescence, the
apotheosis of the status quo. December brings overdraft and defi-
cit, a "doped public" sucking a "dry dug," revival of the ghetto,
free speech gagged, concentration camps. There is no use to cry to
St. Paul to "Come over into Macedonia to help us"; we must now
help ourselves. Many renounce the responsibility of moral choice
and simply take orders from a square box containing a mad voice.

At last (Canto XIX), he can think of the lady of Cantos IV and
XI with no response of his pulse. When out of love the question is
how we could ever have been in it? Freedom is good but less
exciting than being drawn into the rush of the circling stars. His
thirst was worse at the end of the romance than at the beginning;
but he agrees ironically with Tennyson that it would have been
worse never to have drunk at all. On this busy morning he hopes
she is also busy; he wishes her luck and thanks her for the party.
Nelson still stands on a black pillar in the Square (Canto XX); in
the National Gallery the passions of artists are caught like frozen
flames. The unfounded confidence of the arrogant Old Masters
affronts modern and doubtful systems of values which only ask
that we be left alone to cultivate our Voltairean gardens. It is now
only a week to Christmas with its memories of childhood's thrill.
The Magi brought their luxury toys in homage of a child who was
born to capsize all their values. The herald angels sing on the
street corners, not about peace, but for the sake of copper coins.

The poet sits in his room in comfort before the fire (Canto XXI), for man cannot live by soul alone. Eternal spiritual life would be flat indeed compared to the collective creation of mind, body, and spirit. Like the spendthrift fire, let man spend himself recklessly but give a good return; may he burn the silent into sound, laugh at the dark, and jump to glory from a single spark to purge the world and warm it. He can understand a friend's wish to quit, to make the great refusal. But to have been born is in itself a triumph among all that waste of sperm. A fire should burn until it burns itself out.

It is December 19, and the first snow falls in London (Canto XXII). It is time to leave England for that land of Cockayne across the Channel. All the poet seeks are tourist values: eating and drinking are more important than thinking, looking more than doing, a casual friend better than a colleague, and work a dull convenience to provide eternal amusement. He needs the surface company of a sophisticated woman, whose soul would be quite out of the picture. He will not stay long in Paris; after a French Christmas, he will cross the Pyrenees into Spain "where there is pain and pride."

In Barcelona (Canto XXIII), a city of two and a half million people, there are no lights in the streets. War austerities are acceptable where human values remain. All the poet's heredity and upbringing have thrown him into the wrestling arms of the God who straddles the antinomies amongst which man lives. Jacob's thigh was withered in the struggle; the poet bears the marks of the drawn battle. He confesses that he has been a lover of defeat and sloth, an idle martyr. Having thrown away the roots of will and conscience, he now must search for both. He can no longer play the part of the Dying Gaul among the cushions. The planes from Majorca, "modern Valkyries," ride over the city to bomb, maim, and kill the stubborn fighters for freedom whose matter-of-fact faith and courage shame all niggling equivocations.

Canto XXIV begins with an invocation to sleep. In particular may the conflicting selves the poet has so long endured wake cured in Asclepius' temple. And may the wife with whom he shared an "idyll five years long" sleep serenely beyond the Atlantic. What shall we dream? Idle fancies or a real future we really plan to make? The poet dreams of a life of understanding, in which none is disbarred his natural music, where there is no hun-

ger, where thought is free, and where power and profit are fallen
together into disuse. But his coward doubts sleep lightly and mar
the dream. The New Year comes announced by bombs. It is too
late to dose the dead with honorable intentions. Tomorrow there
is water to be crossed: not the river of the dead nor the Lethe of
forgetfulness, but the Rubicon of decision. Later there will be
time to audit all accounts; later there will be sunlight, and the
equation will come out at last.

A year before, when Louis MacNeice wrote *Modern Poetry* in
1938, he shocked critics' row with his exceedingly matter-of-fact
definition of the poet as "able-bodied, fond of talking, a reader of
the newspapers, capable of pity and laughter, informed in economics, appreciative of women, involved in personal relationships, actively interested in politics, susceptible to physical
impressions." If Wordsworth aimed to write in the common language of men, MacNeice seems to enshrine the common man as
the ideal figure of the poet. In 1938 (the year covered by *Autumn Journal*) it is probably safe to say that the common man
was not a violently class-conscious member of the working class,
nor was he the upper-class product of Marlborough and Merton
College, tinged with Bloomsbury wit and London sophistication.
The real common man is probably a manual worker who aspires
to be a white-collar worker, who wants to become a small property owner, who, in turn, wants to become a big landlord.

In other words, the common man of England is the bourgeois
three-fourths of the nation. This class traditionally desires the
social changes which will make it possible to move up more read-
ily, but is terrified by violent changes which imperil the little advances it has already made.[8] In a sense, MacNeice has so identified himself with the common man as one who just happens to be
able to write poetry, that to a large extent this group's terrors and
inadequacies are his own. Because MacNeice is an honest man, as
well as a skillful poet, he recognizes that his gentle hedonism,
which is the bequest of nineteenth-century Liberalism, is too
gentle and too delicate to survive the coming clash of the classes.
He is revolted by the old excesses of fascism and cannot go all the
way to the Communist position, yet he is clearly dissatisfied with
the present condition of affairs.

Thus he is caught in an indecision which is lucidly mirrored in
Autumn Journal and which continues to haunt his later work.

Dragged out of his upper-class, cushioned existence by the Spanish Civil War, by the betrayal of Munich, and by the hysteria of Hitler, he is amazed and shocked that an alien scale of values should have the temerity to threaten his pleasant, indecisive life. He feels guilty of being part of the old world order that provided the forcing-frame for fascism and communism; but, most of all, he feels helpless to do anything about them and hopeless about a better future.

The basic question which underlies all the technical brilliance and badinage of the *Journal* might be stated baldly thus: What can my kind of man do, in this kind of a world, at this kind of moment? The manifest evasion of the poem makes the answer clear: Nothing. In his moving valediction on the past year, Mac-Neice blesses everybody: those who work for Christ, the humanist eager for a better life, the atheist, the devotee of a cause, the family man. But it is evident that the basic contradictions of such universal blessing tend to cancel each other: the Christian and the atheist, the bourgeois who would preserve the family and the Communist who would destroy it, the man who lives only for his little family circle and the man who owes a universal allegiance to the world. He dreams of a future which is admirable, but he recognizes both his tendency toward idle fancies rather than real plans and his coward doubts that a better world has any possibility of coming to pass. He is going to cross the water, not the Styx of the dead, nor the Lethe of forgetfulness, but the Rubicon of decision—When? Tomorrow. *Later* all accounts will be audited, *later* the sun will shine, the answer to the equation will come out at *last*.

Significantly, the final canto of the *Journal* is an "invocation." This is encouraging because an invocation ought to come at the beginning of divine worship to invite the presence and work of the Holy Ghost. But this invocation is different; it is an invitation to sleep and dream today and to act tomorrow. In 1934, Louis MacNeice could take consolation in "the perfection of a grilled steak." But he is David Daiches' "The Honest Man as Poet," [9] and he knows that steaks are irrelevant to any Hitlerian bill of fare. So he is bewildered, shocked, appalled. He is a man of good will at a time which clamors for deeds rather than intentions.

And so the poet plays, in the phrase of John Peale Bishop, "The Hamlet of L. MacNeice." [10] He is as irresolute as Shakespeare's

prince, but it is impossible to imagine him, even in the rashest
moment, stabbing Mr. Chamberlain, who plays the role of Polo-
nius at Munich (cf. the denouement of *Out of the Picture*). He
can go down to Oxford instead of Wittenberg to commit some
action which will redeem his will. His purpose is to help win an
election, which is promptly lost. He less dramatically rids himself
of his Ophelia, simply by the process of the erasure of time from
memory. He feels the bloody frontier converge on his bed, but he
does no more about it than does Hamlet in the face of Fortinbras'
troops. Both are haunted by father-ghosts, by soldier-ghosts, and
by the ghost of a kingdom's dead greatness.

Having rather thoroughly explored what MacNeice called the
"failure" of the *Journal*, perhaps it is not too late to mention some
of its successes. The thoughts and emotions of the poet, although
drawn out by a particular political crisis, are remarkably consistent with the mood and message of the earlier lyrics. The poet
repeats with new emphasis his belief in the necessity for an improved social and economic order, still using Ireland as his bad
example. He criticizes the kind of education he received because
it prepared boys for the old life which was already crumbling,
rather than making them fluid and effective for new and changing
conditions. He displays an increasing suspicion of abstractions in
favor of the sensations, experiences, and emotions of the present.
He recognizes that, in his basic desire to be human, his humane
studies may ironically have hindered rather than helped. He realizes now, as he had formerly sensed, that the professional men
who are led by their habits of thought to hate politics must fight
for a better political system if they are to retain any private
values.[11]

In addition, Cantos IV, XI, XIX, and XXIV, as a recent rework-
ing of the Meredithean "Modern Love" theme, are memorable
achievements. They manage to combine psychological honesty
with charming nostalgia. The jealousy, bitterness, and rejection
are not permitted to cancel the fascination, excitement, and
beauty of the relationship. Both poles of the tension are kept intact and powerful. The reader finds the image of the beloved as
fascinating as infuriating, and this kind of love-exacerbation
shares the Romantic insights of Dostoevsky and Freud.

A number of modern poets have presented the theme of a radical Christ domesticated by the complete inversion of His message.

Francis Thompson's "The Kingdom of God," A. E. Housman's "The Carpenter's Son" and "Easter Hymn," Edna St. Vincent Millay's "To Jesus on His Birthday," and T. S. Eliot's "Journey of the Magi" are all angry or ironical on this same central theme. In the second part of Canto XX, MacNeice has placed a lyric which belongs in this general tradition and one which may well be as good as any of these others.[12] Christmas is approaching, with the decoration of the shops and with the memory of childhood celebrations. The rustling of tissue paper opened up a "coral island" where we might land and eat our "lotus," but where we could never stay.

This gentle and circumstantial beginning moves directly to an angry and ironical passage which illustrates what Henry Adams called "the two thousand years' failure of Christianity." The Magi brought jewels, perfumes, and precious metals to the very person who would capsize their values and wreck their appropriateness. The smell of hay in the stable was peaceful, but Christ came not to bring peace but a sword. He cut the "Gordian knot of logical self-interest," and he moved beyond the philosophers to make stringent demands of the souls of men, to make the smooth lies of life rough, and to knock together the heads of church and state. Then, in honor of this spirit-affirming, flesh-denying Lord, modern Christians take over the pagan Saturnalia for their annual treat to the belly, and they studiously ignore the spirit while they gorge the flesh. So conscience still cries in the desert with sackcloth around his loins, and "Hark, the Herald Angels Sing" is the musical background for the begging of copper coins. This is light and angry verse; it is ironical verse in which the form and the substance show their diametrically opposed natures.

II Selected Poems (*1940*) *and* The Last Ditch (*1940*)

In March, 1940, Faber and Faber published a volume of twenty poems, selected by the poet from his earlier work.[13] From *Poems* (1935), he chose "An Eclogue for Christmas," "Eclogue by a Five-barred Gate," "Sunday Morning," "Birmingham," "Belfast," "An April Manifesto," "Museums," and "Ode." From *The Earth Compels* (1938), MacNeice selected "Carrickfergus," "June Thunder," "The Sunlight on the Garden," "Eclogue from Iceland" (originally in *Letters from Iceland*), "Leaving Barra" (originally in *I Crossed the Minch*), "Books, Do Not Look at Me," and "Bagpipe Music"

(originally in *I Crossed the Minch*). From *Autumn Journal*
(1939), he chose II. "Spider, spider, twisting tight"; IV, "September has come and I wake"; VII, "Conferences, adjournments, ulti-
matums"; IX, "Now we are back to normal"; XXIV, "Sleep, my
body, sleep, my ghost."

In the last week of March, Louis MacNeice finished a group of
poems which were published later that year by the Cuala Press in
Dublin, Ireland, under the general title *The Last Ditch*.[14] The un-
pretentious nature of this printing of four hundred and fifty copies
is suggested by the dedicatory quatrain, addressed to Eleanor
Clark:

> Without heroics, without belief
> I send you, as I am not rich,
> Nothing but odds and ends a thief
> Bundled up in the last ditch.

From many poets, such a modest disclaimer would be dis-
counted at less than face value; it would be assumed that this is
simply one of the many masks the poet may don or doff at will.
But the regular reader of MacNeice's poetry comes to believe precisely what the poet says about his verse. These poems will not be
"heroic," and they will be lacking in the power that comes from
coherent and passionately held "belief." The poet is "rich" technically and intellectually; but he is "not rich" in affirmation, confidence, or faith. These are slight poems, "odds or ends," the
"thief" of current history "bundled up in the last ditch"—the
Liberal with his back to the wall of his own limitations. In an
interview for the New York *Times*,[15] Louis MacNeice is reported
to have said that "The world is not very likely to see much war
poetry coming out of the present war between Germany, England
and France. . . . Prospects may improve if and when the war
speeds up a little, but right now there is too much boredom about
the whole thing to encourage either poets or poetry." That statement was made in February; this selection, finished the end of
March, in no way contradicts the general prediction.

The first poem, "Prognosis," provides an elegant and poignant
forecast of the possibilities of the spring of 1940. Using "slant
rhyme," MacNeice closes lines one, two, and four of his quatrains
with such combinations as "winter," "longer," and "stranger";

"burden," "garden," and "bargain." Clearly the poet has wiped his pen after *Autumn Journal*—and also sharpened it—to write these incisive, technically brilliant little quatrains. What is perhaps even more remarkable is the moving, evocative tone which comes to its climax in the simple-sad lines at the end:

> Will his name be Love
> And all his talk be crazy?
> Or will his name be Death
> And his message easy?

The poet bids winter farewell as he notes that the days are growing longer. A tea leaf in the cup heralds the arrival of a stranger. Will he bring business, gladness, or a cure for his own illness? Will he come to beg or bargain, to pester or to bluster, with the threat of a gun? Will he be John to herald a new Coming, or Jonah calling to repentance with the warning of inevitable catastrophe? Will he be Jason calling to adventure, or a mad crusader? Will his message be war, work, marriage? Will he answer questions, or be dark with evasion? Ultimately, will he be love or death?

Then follow sixteen poems which the author groups under the heading "The Coming of War." Four of these are Irish in setting as well as military in reference—"Dublin," "Cushendun," "Sligo and Mayo," and "Galway." Dublin never was the poet's town for birth, breeding, or schooling. Yet the Danish fort, garrison for the Saxon, the "Augustan capital / Of a Gaelic nation," by some juggler's trick poises "the toppling hour" and gives him time for thought. Dublin is "greyness run to flower"; gray stone, gray water, brick upon gray brick. The unrhymed trimeter lines suggest again MacNeice's new emphasis upon the brief, crisp statement. In "Cushendun," Georgian nature poetry, the poet celebrates fuchsia, ragweed, distant hills and a whitewashed house with a walled garden that is a place of easy forgetfulness—until from a little box in a dark green room, a well-bred voice talks about the war. In "Sligo" there are echoes of the same setting of flowers in soft country with browsing cattle. But in "Mayo" we have a place of tumbledown walls and brown water in desolate loughs, where turfstacks rise in the dark "Like the tombs of nameless kings." "Galway" describes the town in even shorter dimeter

lines with the trimeter refrain "The war came down on us here."
The first part of the poem draws the contrast between the idyllic
landscape and the coming of war. The second half, in longer, lyrical lines, asks why everything goes on as before when "doom" laps
at the door.

"Meeting Point" depicts the experience of the lover that "Time
was away and she was here." MacNeice is making interesting
metrical experiments in this collection. In "Meeting Point," the
five four-foot lines of each stanza rhyme *ababa*, with the first and
last lines duplicates. In "A Toast," the poet's refrain—"This is on
me and these are yours"—suggests that MacNeice is paying for
the drinks, but the qualities described in the toast belong to his
guest. The "London Rain" sets free the poet's fancy, and his
thought moves with the rain out across the countryside to the
warning beacons of the English Channel, where God and No-God
"Play at pitch and toss." Whichever wins makes no difference at
all. If God, He will give pardon when the sinner falls; if No-God,
"nothing will matter at all." The rain abates and logic rebukes
fancy. No metaphysics are necessary to establish the validity of
action, the meaning of right and wrong. The rain returns, and the
thinker falls asleep listening to its patter on the roof. The trimeter
six-line stanzas rhyme *abcbdb*, with the repetition of the same
word at the end of lines four and six.

"The British Museum Reading Room" seems to have been a
favorite of MacNeice or his editors because it is repeated in several anthologies and is frequently reprinted in journals. The poet
watches the various habitués of the place: some on commission;
others lovers of learning; those who have nothing better to do;
those who hope the books will deaden the "drumming of the
demon" in their ears. There are cranks, hacks, poverty-stricken
scholars; those who are too alive and those who are asleep; and
outside, in the Ionic portico or on the steps, refugees mumble in
guttural accents. In June, 1939, MacNeice wrote "Primrose Hill"
(cf. *Zoo*) about the area where he had a bachelor apartment not
far from the London Zoo. The trees have been cut away from the
crest of the hill for an antiaircraft emplacement, and the poet sees
the bare spot as a raft on the stormy seas of the surrounding trees.
But some day the raft will ride a stormier swell, the sirens will
howl, the searchlights quest, and the "impartial bombs will fall."

In July, 1938, MacNeice wrote a poem, "Departure Platform,"

inviting his beloved to get ready to take a trip. Wherever they go, the previously unseen land will be theirs because its stones are their bones, its rivers their blood. They seek in the distance for that "evasive universal" which can be known only "in dispersal." So they will take the hopes hoarded for a year and expend them in a fortnight. Ironically enough, as lovers, they really hope for nearness and dearness in—of all things—the distance. This philosophical love lyric is written in rather conventional quatrains rhyming *abca.*

The five "Novelettes" that follow the war poems in *The Last Ditch* are playful, pleasant, witty, and all give the impression of having been written long before in a more placid, less impersonal world. "The Old Story" retells the legend of fading charms; the woman was twenty and she is now thirty; and, to the poet (who was now thirty-three years of age himself), she seems so different that he cannot call her his love, or be at all sure to whom he is talking. In the second poem, the poet took his girl to see the ballet *Les Sylphides.* They seemed to be floating on a river in which there was neither separation nor ending. They were married in order to be together, but they found themselves divided by the morning tea, the evening paper, the children, and the tradesmen's bills. At night, as she watched his regular breathing, his wife wondered what had happened to the river and where the white, flower-like dancers had fled.

Another of these fragile, rather silly novelettes is about "The Gardener" who took such pride in his work because "*he was not quite all there*"; and, when he died, he went to "the land of the Ever Young." These slight vignettes, read in the right mood, might seem charming, but in most moods the pathos becomes bathos and the slight the silly. Perhaps silliest of all is "Christina," in which the "he" of the poem goes to bed with a lady. When he found out his companion's name, he suddenly saw a childhood doll named Christina, "dead on the nursery floor."

"Three Poems Apart," written in the summer of 1938, are only a bit more mature, perhaps adolescent instead of childish. The first poem reminds us that on summer evenings we take our loves for granted; but in the fall we are haunted by the limbs we only half remember. Now that he and his beloved are in bed, he wants the light switched off, her body fastened to his as "close as an eyelid," and for himself the rather Gargantuan metaphor of trains advancing, advancing farther and farther. The second poem is an *aubade* in which the poet looks down at the sleeping lover of a single night and wishes he could protract "this hour of quiet after passion." But the light steals into the room, illuminating the titles on books, and duty, and separate identity. The third relates more closely to the earlier poems of the collection as the poet treasures each sight and sound of a sunlit March, knowing that the world is on the brink of war, and hoping hopelessly for a permanence he knows cannot stay.

This pleasant collection ranges from the jog-trot rhythms of "Dublin" to the restrained lyricism of "Cushendun." There are many experiments in style, metrics, and rhyme pattern. The artist has clearly moved forward technically; but the question still remains of maturation of thought, for some of the poems are embarrassingly juvenile in tone, mood, and intention. The major dramatic device of the collection is the dialectic between the settled, safe past and the threats of war. But this dialectic never proceeds from the thesis-antithesis tension to a synthesis. The developing thought, a development still arrested at the shock level of *Autumn Journal*, seems to say three things very expertly, but loses all in the omission of formulating the necessary fourth. "When I was young" is poignantly and charmingly done; "This is the old England I love" is presented persuasively and nostalgically; "These are the pieces of the past after the bombs burst" is a much more muted and understated climax than in the previous diary-journal. But this climax is not a true one; it is a catastrophe after which the pieces need to be picked up and either restored to the old, settled relationships—which is manifestly impossible—or put together by a new logic to make a new and better pattern. The absence of the pattern gives the fast, light, eminently readable verse a tone of irrelevance and frivolity. And it is this same absence that darkens *The Last Ditch* with the shadow of defeatism.

This total lack of solution or hope led Conrad Aiken to liken the reading of Louis MacNeice's verse to a dip in the river. We dive into the bright, quick, deft current; we climb out and discover that we are hardly wet.[16] The poetry is all too topical, too transitory, too reportorial; it has the vividness of immediate confrontation with the object, and this confrontation produces a momentary magic. But we doubt that there is much residual magic, that quality of total union of thought and expression that leads us back to reread a poem because nothing else can express the idea quite so well. The sheer brilliance of "Meeting Point" and "A Toast" almost blinds us to the essential sadness that these relationships with a lover and a friend are in the past, unrecapturable, and unlikely to recur in tomorrow's world. *The Last Ditch* represents a very competent oiling of the artist's tools; but where does one go from "the last ditch"?

III Plant and Phantom (*1941*)

Plant and Phantom, a new collection of poems, published in April, 1941, by Faber and Faber, includes twenty-one selections from *The Last Ditch:* "Prognosis," "Departure Platform," "The British Museum Reading Room," "London Rain," "Trilogy for X" (called "Three Poems Apart" in *The Last Ditch*), "The Coming of War," [17] "Meeting Point," "A Toast," and five Novelettes: "The Old Story," "Suicide," "Les Sylphides," "The Gardener," and "Christina." It too, is dedicated to Eleanor Clark, with the motto from Nietzsche's *Thus Spoke Zarathustra: "ein Zwiespalt und Zwitter von Pflanze und von Gespenst."* [18]

The title poem is concerned, as all Liberals must be especially concerned in wartime, with the nature and destiny of man. The poet, in six eight-line, unrhymed stanzas, gives three answers. Man as creature of superstition is appropriately and primitively first. He consults leaves in the Sibyl's cave, he lurks in the shadows, he lives with hallucinations, ghosts, and mirages. He moves beyond the reach of the creatures of his own superstition, not by what he is, but by what he can build. The second definition of man is expressed by his oneness with the rest of Nature and by his mad revolt against it. The third definition, the exaltation of Promethean man, deals with man's nature in terms of "a riot of banners" and "organ-pipes in the sunset," and "orgy of brains" and "rampant" martyrdom. He feels in the void for the creative Word; he does not find it but feels its aura. Ever since, he peers within and behind everything, hoping at last to find the "Word Itself." From this trilogical poem, the poet turns to a series of dualisms.

"Stylite" depicts two pillars: one for the world-banning saint with closed eyes; the other, for a white Greek god with crisp-curled pubic hair and eyes fixed confidently on the world. The comparison of the two world views is not labored; it is simply indicated. On the surface, "Conversation" is about the vagrant eye

behind the façade word. Two ordinary people are talking, and the
eyes of one slip away "Into some black wood behind the skull."
But sometimes the eyes happen to meet, and the vagrancy is outward bound instead of inward turned. The eyes plumb the depths
of the other conversationalist as if searching for a lost purse or a
dropped stitch. When that happens, ordinary men return to normal, look the other straight in the eye as if to say "It will not
happen again," quickly put up a barrage of common sense to re-
pulse intimacy, but by mistake swear words slip in like "roses in
their talk." Presumably this well-wrought poem is about questing
man and the possibilities of human sharing which are blocked by
his sense of social decorum. "Entirely" presents man's search for
absolutes. If he could learn something entirely, if he could be entirely happy with someone, if decisions were entirely right or
wrong—but, of course, he can know only the conditional, the
"splash of words in passing," some "falling twigs of song."

"Picture Galleries" is, for MacNeice, a return to an old theme.
The pictures in the gallery at first are opiate, frozen still-lifes. But,
if we look at them a second time, we sometimes get a sense of
passion too great to bear. Or we are moved intellectually by the
ethical relativism of art: what Zurbaran found in serene, white-
robed Carthusian monks, Lautrec discovered for himself in
brothel and circus. The curator rings a bell; the viewers leave the
silent rooms which were crowded with dead voices. Outside, in
the open air, they still sense something "half-articulate and un-
safe."

"Order to View" is an Expressionistic fantasy with the most optimistic climax to date. The poet and a companion go to view a
house for rental—one they had known long before. Now, even
their memory is thwarted by the general air of decay and rotten-
ness: the bell rope does not pull; the whole place seems ill to
death; the world is closed. Then the wind stirs, clouds mass on the
horizon, a horse neighs, and "all the curtains flew out of / The
windows; the world was open." In a world where even the old,
familiar things look familiar no longer, the forces of elemental
Nature still survive; and the new world is there, open for the
entering.

Three new poems have been added to the Novelettes from *The
Last Ditch*. "Provence" is lovely with its juxtaposition of two generations: a couple planning marriage with a happy old man whose

wife and three children are dead. "The Preacher" is not a mono-
logue as it ought to have been to fit its subject, but it is dramatic
in the Browning fashion. The quatrains, rhyming *abcb,* describe a
cleric for whom every trip was on Charon's ferry; and, wherever
he went, he never really left the Catacombs. Unsmiling, he
showed men the Hell beneath their feet, and cried "Repent / For
the Kingdom of Death is at hand." At the age of sixty, he went
upstairs to die. Drawing in all his deeds, like a thread pulled in
beneath the door, he wrapped them around him until all that was
left was a ball of black with himself "at the centre of the ball."

The next ten poems all involve death or defeat. "Débâcle" contrasts the early years of empire building—a firm or a nation—with
the later years, when the heirs take the achievement of the past
for granted, and the bricks crumble, the old breaks up and dies
(cf. "The House That Jack Built"). "Exile," written in March,
1940, pictures the exiled patriot with one half hour of reprieve,
knowing that the blood which blackens the streets of Europe will
flow here, too. Florrie Forde is the heroine of "Death of an Actress." Old, huge, and painted, she collapsed at the age of sixty-
five after singing to wounded soldiers. Her voice was long gone;
but she could shimmy, wink, and evoke a warm, human, safe
world. Now that remnant of the older, brighter England is gone,
and we should gently cover the Babes in the Wood with leaves.
"Give us this day our daily news" is the invocation of the habitués
in the poem "Bar-Room Matins." With pretzels, chips, and beer,
they listen to the radio, grateful to be allowed to live in such a
catastrophic time when every failure has a perfect alibi for doing
nothing at all.

The human heart has forsaken its proper place in "Flight of the
Heart." It has built a copper tower with four exits but no entrance
for need to find its way in. And, if the tower falls, the heart will
retire to the cellar to get drunk in the dark. But, if the cellar roof
caves in, the heart will have no choice but to return to the "fore-
being of mankind" where it has always belonged. The form of the
poem is an illustration of Richard Crowder's contention that a
favorite pattern for both Edith Sitwell and Louis MacNeice was
the question-and-answer dialogue of the nursery rhyme. With
persuasive singsong and simple diction, the poem deals obliquely
with the alienation and displacement of modern man.[19]

"Refugees," in MacNeice's favorite *abcb* rhyme, shows the risen

Lazaruses as they go ashore for another chance. But chance is
dubious, fate is stingy, officialdom is blank; and the risen migrants
wait for "Something-or-Other" to turn up. In a superb transformation of images, "Jehu" moves from the quiet peace of New England to the ancient Hebrew usurper who shatters peace, kills his
lord, and orders that his lord's mother, magnificently evil Jezebel,
be flung down from the balcony to be trampled beneath horses'
hoofs. Now that the sand which seeped over Israel is blowing over
England, what role in the eternal drama will Britain play: mad
charioteer, the surgeon too late to heal, or the pampered queen
"who tittered in the face of death"?

In "O'Connell Bridge," it is October, 1939, and the poet
crosses the bridge which spans the river Liffey as it winds
through Dublin to the sea. He hears a burst of barrel-organ music,
a rain of riches; but the poet neither dances to the tune nor thanks
the organ grinder. Cold, lonely, and afraid, watching his past float
out to sea, he merely drops the silent coin in the waiting cap. "The
Death-Wish" argues that in this life people are forbidden to move
too lightly; therefore, they weigh themselves down with dead
habits, hopes, beliefs until this "ballast of unreality" sinks the
boat; and all their thinking, contriving, and planning drown in the
sea that never thinks. Since this is the fate of the majority of men,
it is strange that some should choose to meet death like madmen
or meteors, leaping in their impatience, mad to possess the sea as
a man in spring "desires to die in woman." "Autobiography" has
its origin in the poet's loss of his mother in his early boyhood. His
father was a preacher; his gentle mother wore a yellow dress; but,
when he was five, he heard the dark talking to the dead; and
when his terror called, nobody answered. From then on he
walked his chilly way alone. The childish rhymed couplets are
separated by the italicized refrain *Come back early or never
come.*

The eleven remaining poems in *Plant and Phantom* fall into no
pattern or unifying theme. "The Ear" complains that it has no
choice of callers; many visitors climb the "spiral staircase of the
ear." It would like to lie alone awhile in a deaf hollow wrapped in
a cocoon of self and silence. Instead, it is annoyed by will-o'-the-
wisps, the terrible monotony of the drone of the cock chafer, or
the bleak bad omen of a dog's bark. "Evening in Connecticut"
teaches the lesson that Nature is not to be trusted. Here is a

lovely, friendly lawn. But the leaves turn crimson; Nature grows red hair on the back of its hands and carries a heraldic ax which has the power to strike. The snow falls, covering lost travelers; it buries their graves deep; and the sun smiles in approval. Nature is not to be trusted; she is only herself, and the shadows grow longer.

Three octets follow. In "Business Men" the poet hears two men talking easily about their work. The windowpane reflects their faces, and the poet listens in a trance to two strangers talking his own familiar language after he has been sojourning in a strange land. In the "Night Club," the legshows and the brandies are over; and all await the next act. Salome comes in, bearing the "head of God knows whom." "Didymus" is a kind of brief preparatory study for the longer poem entitled "Didymus" in *Ten Burnt Offerings*. Didymus (or St. Thomas) loved the creature more than the Creator, but he could accept only what he could see. When he died, the swallow reflected in the river seemed to plunge into the wrong, the reflected sky.

"Plurality" is a major poem reflecting the poet's growing certainty of the incorrigible multiplicity of things (cf. "Snow"). This recognition by the philosopher-Classicist had been growing for some time, and the resulting poem is appropriately highly philosophic. All along the way the academician has gradually shifted his interest from Being to Becoming, from evasive Universals to concrete Particulars, from mankind to the individual man. The poem begins as an attack upon both Parmenides, the pre-Socratic Greek monist, and his modern disciples. The fallacy of the monist position lies in its terror of confusion, change, and diversity. So everything must become One Thing, all colors a dead ideal of the all-white Universal. When Eternity is now, "Now is therefore numb." If there is no distinction between essence and existence, there is no possibility of action or growth. Man is a "mere mirror of God."

Any philosophy that does not accept the central fact of change fails: the seasons are more important than the year; a thing, a beast, a man is essentially a becoming which is different from its beginning. Whenever we talk of Ultimate Value and Universal Form we are dealing with visions that ride upon storms; the value judgment must be made and the form sought, but they can never be maintained. Man might have been a beast, but he is not now;

and he feels himself increased. He is not yet a god, but he hankers after the pantheon, and so he constantly transcends the human span. He is conscious of things amiss, of guilt, inadequacy, the sick ego, the broken past, the speeding clock, waste, spite, and hate. But he is also conscious of love, joy, and power—never completely conscious but partly—"and that is much."

In many ways "Plurality" is the most important poem in the collection, and it most clearly wrestles with the task indicated at the book's beginning of defining the nature and destiny of man. It also represents that central shift in allegiances that marks the departure of the scholar from the academic ideal of classification, universality, and unity to a more lifelike devotion to process, change, and growth. This poem is, perhaps, the most hopeful one that the poet has written. If it is missed, it is very possible to miss a prime pivotal moment in the development of the poet.

"Plain Speaking" continues the emphasis upon discrete entities. The only way finally to define anything is by a tautology. If man attempts to define by comparison, he misses the thing in itself. If he attempts to reduce it to genus, basic similarity, and universal form, he kills the many to produce the one. A man is a man; a woman is a woman. A man may become tall as a tree, and a woman may become a whole world. But personal identity persists and event occurs. "Perdita" is the lost love who dwells in the attics of the mind. What became of all the plans we made? The time for their fulfillment is overdue, and in some metropolitan station the caterpillars of dreams await the butterfly flights of fancy.

In "The Dowser," the man seeking water feels an inkling, a whisper in the bones; the hazel rod bends, and he says "Dig." After two hours the spade clinks against not a well, but a tomb. The diggers back away from a sudden resurrection of the dead which sends flower colors into the sky. In "The Return" the poet raises, but leaves unanswered the question of whether the return is the birth of a child, the coming of spring, or a more generalized new Advent of joy to the world. At any rate, the central operation is clear. Out of all the lost things, the dead hopes, the broken relationships, the new birth will come, "jonquils out of hell," and with its coming bring imperative joy, sunlight dancing upon the water.

As *Autumn Journal* ended with an invocation to sleep, so *Plant and Phantom* closes on the lullaby cadence of "Cradle Song." The poet croons to his twenty-odd-year-old darling that, better than watching disaster fall and being racked by "the pity of it all," she should creep into the only heaven, the cave of sleep. The world will try to interrupt; the day will come too soon; the watchers on the wall will stay awake all night and they will know "the pity of it all." It is hard not to read this poem as more evasion than benediction, but it comes quietly and recessively at the end of a major collection that records major poetic and ideological developments in the life, mind, and art of the poet.

IV   The Poetry of W. B. Yeats (*1941*)

In a review of MacNeice's book on Yeats,[20] F. O. Matthiessen pointed out that MacNeice, as a young Irishman, is in a good position to tell about Yeats's background and to relate Yeats's political opinions, social prejudices, and cultural values to his national heritage. MacNeice, writing as a self-conscious member of a very different school of poetry, but as a young man who very much appreciates the poetry of the older man, sets himself to indicate what lessons his generation has learned from Yeats and what qualities of his poetry that younger generation has summarily rejected.[21]

If MacNeice were making a general anthology of shorter English poems, he would want to include about sixty by Yeats, more than from any other poet in the language. If he were called upon to defend such favoritism, he could only reply that the poets who interest him are the poets whom he likes to reread; and he finds himself turning more frequently to Yeats than to any other English poet: "I feel that in Yeats I have met a poet who is strange enough to excite my interest but is near enough to me myself to preclude my misrepresenting him too grossly."[22]

Before preparing a full-length study of the Irish poet, MacNeice wrote an epitaph for Yeats which was published in the *New Republic* (June 24, 1940). He pointed out that Yeats has had more critical compliments in the last ten years than any other poet of our time. While MacNeice considered it refreshing to see critics and younger poets committing themselves to such enthusiasm for an older contemporary, some of the grounds of adulation were critically suspect. MacNeice suggested that some of the critics were so wholehearted in their praise because they considered Yeats so "different," so "exotic," that they could laud him to the skies without committing themselves to a particular school of poetry or party of critical thought. In MacNeice's homely image: anyone can praise a bird-of-paradise, but he has to know something about chickens before he goes to buy Rhode Island Reds.

Naturally MacNeice disliked this accent upon exoticism—after all, had he not defined the poet as an ordinary man with specialized gifts? This dislike becomes a kind of thesis in the longer study in which he insists that Yeats was not so exotic as was popularly assumed and that the poet recognized his exoticism as a liability. MacNeice documents this last statement by pointing out that Yeats deliberately set out in his middle period to make his poetry less "poetic" and that in his later years he fought clear of the dead hand of Walter Pater. MacNeice makes a valid defense of his thesis, but it is quite clear that exoticism is not quite the same as poeticism or Romanticism, and the poet-critic proceeds as if, by freeing him of the latter charges, he has shielded him from the former description. He does succeed in showing a Yeats who emerges from an 1899 mood of "fin de siècle," but he says almost nothing of Yeats's later immersion in Theosophy, Rosicrucianism, and mysticism in general.

In the epitaph, MacNeice had pointed out that his enemies tend to regard Yeats as a knave or a fraud and, at best, as a "silly old thing"; but his admirers consider him God-intoxicated and therefore irreproachable. Surely it is irreproachable logic for MacNeice to point out that "silly old things" do not write fine poetry. The central issues of MacNeice's book on Yeats are rather uneven and slightly haphazard: Yeats's obsession with Art and Ireland, his extraordinary ability to write lyrics when he was very old, his high peak of creativity in *The Winding Stair*, but the undeniable virility of the gossipy, contumacious, magnificently eccentric poetry of his old age which is found in the collection *Last Poems*. He considers "The Circus Animals' Desertion" the most revealing poem in the last collection; for in it the old poet looks back with admirable ruthlessness on his various elaborate attempts to project himself on the world through Celtic legend, Maud Gonne, and symbolic drama. At this last moment, the self-centered old man rises far enough above his own personality to pin it down for what it was.[23]

The Poetry of W. B. Yeats is a strange critical study; but a book by one poet about another poet is likely to be. Instead of a critical self-forgetfulness by the author, the book tends to become a kind of dialogue of accusation, denial, comparison, and appreciation. This dialogue does not invalidate the study; in some curious ways the book is enriched as two poetic generations engage in discussion. At the same time, the study is at least as revealing of Mac-Neice as of Yeats; and about much of the author's critical judgments, the reader can only react with, "That's just what you would expect MacNeice to say. . . ."

The Preface is a philosophical-critical general statement about poetry itself. The author quotes and approves Samuel Johnson's requirement that "wit" in poetry should be both natural and new. MacNeice recognizes in Dr. Johnson's brief statement two continuing characteristics of a poem: that it correspond in some recognizable way to the world and the experiences of life—in this sense it is natural; and that it be somehow unique, special, and a brand-new thing in itself. The failure of criticism is that it finds itself powerless to assess the poem's "thingness," and therefore devotes its major attention to the simple issue of correspondence. This approach tends to substantiate Plato's criticism of all art as a poor imitation of an imitation, or what Aristotle called bastard reasoning. MacNeice confesses that he, too, fell into this critical trap in his book *Modern Poetry* (Chapter II) when he stressed the half-truth that poetry is about something, a form of communication. Poetry is this, he now says; but it is also a separate self, a physical organism in its own right.[24]

In the first chapter of *The Poetry of W. B. Yeats*, MacNeice accuses Yeats of being, all his life, the professed enemy of facts; and for this reason the poets of a younger generation were suspicious of him. In a reaction against Pure Form, against Art for Art's Sake, W. H. Auden and his friends asserted that a poem must be about something real, by which they often meant something contemporary. Thus they would point to a poem like Yeats's famous "Easter, 1916" and claim that it was a good poem precisely because it celebrated an important event in contemporary history.

MacNeice leans heavily on Freud in his description of the genesis of a poem. Man lives by egoism, by making logical distinctions; but he derives the driving force for his decisions from below his ego and his ideals from above it. Thus man has an animal sub-self and a mystical super-self. The poet is not necessarily either more animal or more mystical than other men; he may even be more

rational.[25] This business about an idealistic super-self brings up
the question of Yeats as mystic. MacNeice claims that Yeats believed in mysticism, but that he does not seem to have had, to any
unusual degree, direct mystical experience. Poetry was, for him, a
mystery cult, a ritual. But in this cult, which was non-moralistic in
character, he visualized himself as priest of the liturgy, not as the
saint of personal holiness.

MacNeice begins his critique of Yeats by indicating his two
main backgrounds—Ireland and the English Esthetic Movement.
He traces his poetic lineage through Keats, Tennyson, and Dante
Gabriel Rossetti. As T. S. Eliot pointed out in *After Strange Gods*,
Yeats felt the need of a religion. In his *Autobiography*, Yeats had
written: "I am very religious, and deprived by Huxley and Tyn-
dall, whom I detested, of the simple-minded religion of my childhood, I had made a new religion, almost an infallible church, of
poetic tradition. . . ." For this cult he found his sacred books in
Walter Pater's *Marius the Epicurean* and in Count Villiers de
l'Isle Adam's *Axel*.[26] In his introduction to the *Oxford Book of
Modern Verse*, Yeats wrote: "The revolt against Victorianism
meant to the young poet a revolt against irrelevant descriptions of
nature, the scientific and moral discursiveness of *In Memoriam*
. . . the political eloquence of Swinburne, the psychological curiosity of Browning, and the poetical diction of everybody." [27] The
old idols were replaced by Catullus, the Jacobean poets, Verlaine,
and Baudelaire. Just as Lionel Johnson proclaimed that life must
be ritual, so ritual became, for Yeats, the dominant poetic outlook
on life.

Throughout his life, Yeats harped upon the importance of passion in the Romantic, Pre-Raphaelite tradition. According to
Pater, it is great passion, especially the "poetic passion," which
gives us a quickened sense of the power and poignancy of life.
Along with this belief in the importance of passion, Pater supplied
Yeats with a conviction of the importance of style, a distrust of the
vulgar world, and an esthetic pantheism in which worship is paid
to material things because they are the representatives and
models of spiritual reality. Perhaps from the observation of the
role playing of Oscar Wilde, Yeats's mind "began drifting vaguely
towards that doctrine of 'the mask' which has convinced me that
every passionate man . . . is, as it were, linked with another age,

historical or imaginary, where alone he finds images that arouse his energy." [28]

De l'Isle Adam had called science "the oldest offspring of the chimeras" and had referred to "the monstrous paradox of progress." Yeats, who agreed with him in both respects, dispensed with the empirical method of arriving at truth by his doctrine of the Great Memory, a derivative of Plato's doctrine of recollection. Truth cannot be reached by induction; we are ourselves part of the Great Memory and the truth runs in our veins like blue blood. We shall recognize this truth, not in the laboratory, but when the critical faculty is stilled in the state of trance, or in the aristocratic and dreamlike ritual of social obligation. Of course, this concept meant that Yeats developed some strange prejudices; witness his inability to appreciate Ibsen—"the chosen author of very clever young journalists, who, condemned to their treadmill of abstraction, hated music and style"—and his violent opposition to the new Realism imported from the art schools of Paris.

As for his Irish background, in his early days Yeats tried to equate Ireland with a Celtic utopia, a land of beautiful dreams. But his experiences with public life and his admiration for Maud Gonne, along with his inability to commit himself to her political activism, disillusioned him in his middle years about Ireland. His early hero was, inevitably, Charles Stewart Parnell. The Easter Rising of 1916 shocked Yeats precisely because it was consummated by the vulgar kind of Fenian leader with whom Yeats could have very little personal sympathy or identification. It was only through friendship with John Millington Synge and a knowledge of his writing that Yeats came to appreciate the value of brute vitality—of, in his own words, "all that has edge, all that is salt in the mouth, all that is rough to the hand, all that heightens the emotions by contest, all that stings into life the sense of tragedy." [29] It was only after that recognition that Yeats began to develop his own elegant version of fascism, a political philosophy which was based upon the complementary worlds of the peasant and the aristocrat, and the brutal, violent men who were used in their seemingly willful careers by the eternal forces of cycle and renewal.

Yeats wrote in 1925 that, when he had been young, his Muse had been old; as he himself grew older, his Muse grew younger.

MacNeice, who entirely agrees with this self-analysis, considers
Yeats's development to be a study in rejuvenation.[30] His early
method had been to diffuse a poetic atmosphere through the close
concentration of poetic images. In later life, when he revised his
early poems, Yeats deliberately reduced the number of epithets by
about half. For example, he revised "The Sorrow of Love" by cutting the poetic epithets from seventeen to nine, stiffening the
verse, removing every hint of sloppiness, and adding words that
gave strength and glitter to the line. His lyrics of 1910, bound in
one volume with the satirical play *The Green Helmet*, reveal that
this development produced a manner which was deliberately flat,
austere, and bleak; but it had not yet produced his peculiar ability
to make something memorable and sensuous out of ordinary
words.[31]

    The Wild Swans at Coole, 1919, follows two very important
events: the Easter Rising in 1916 and his marriage in 1917. It is
difficult to imagine the impact of marriage upon a poet who, according to his friends, remained a virgin until he was forty. But,
while his poetry was becoming more physical and material in its
orientation, his wife brought her psychic gifts as a medium to the
marriage bed. It was she who introduced the poet to the extraordinary theosophical system which he outlined in *A Vision* and
which became, for a time, the major scaffolding of structure for
his poetry. And his cult of the body, so evident in the later books,
always had the qualification that the body rules by supernatural
right.[32]

    The Tower, published in 1928, and *The Winding Stair*, 1933,
MacNeice considers the highest achievements of Yeats's genius.
During this period Yeats was obsessed with the myth of Leda;
and MacNeice links this obsession with his desire to avoid the
split in Plato's thought between the worlds of Being and Becoming. The mythic union was also useful to vindicate those heroic,
passionate, and limited men who do not see beyond the narrow
scope of their own careers yet are nevertheless the instruments
used by dynamic eternal principles. MacNeice sums up Yeats's
logic in the following formula: "the eternal (Zeus) requires the
temporal (Leda), further (for the myth is complex) that the
human being (Leda) requires the animal (the swan), that God
and Nature in fact require each other and that the world will only
make sense in terms of an incarnation." [33]

MacNeice grouped Yeats's plays according to content and subject matter. This classification draws together the early tapestry-like fantasies. *The Countess Cathleen* (1892), *The Land of Heart's Desire* (1894), *Deirdre* (1907), *The Shadowy Waters* (verse version, 1906; acting version, 1911). Then there is the Cuchulain group which contains, in the order of the legend, *At the Hawk's Well* (1917); *The Green Helmet* (1910); *On Baile's Strand* (1904); *The Only Jealousy of Emer* (1919); and the very late short play, *The Death of Cuchulain*. Third, there are those plays which are near-fables or parable plays: *The King's Threshold* (1904), *The Hour-Glass* (1914), *The Cat and the Moon* (1926), *Calvary* (1920), and *The Resurrection* (1931). In this same category might be included *A Full Moon in March* and the play which it superseded, *The King of the Great Clock Tower*. Certain plays resist any attempt to classify them with the others; for instance, *Cathleen ni Houlihan* is nationalist propaganda; and *The Words upon the Windowpane* becomes a study of Swift, through the medium of spiritualism. If the plays were regrouped according to technique, a special group would emerge based on the technique of the Japanese *Noh* plays: *At the Hawk's Well, The Only Jealousy of Emer, The Dreaming of the Bones, Calvary, The Cat and the Moon,* and, only possibly, *The Resurrection*.

The most obvious characteristic of most of these dramas is their remoteness from life. The characters are taken either from legend or are modeled like the figures of nursery rhymes. In reaction against Ibsenism, these plays were to be unsullied by psychology, untroubled by contemporary problems, and uncompromised by the comic spirit. The theme and the language are all-important, as Yeats had insisted in an essay in *The Theatre* (1899): "The theatre began in ritual, and it cannot come to its greatness again without recalling words to their ancient sovereignty." [34]

Yeats kept writing until his death in January, 1939. If the poems of his early years tended to be languid, the work of his old age is full of zest in atonement. Many of them are "little mechanical songs," something between epigrams and nursery rhymes. On the surface light verse, even nonsense verse, the poems carry essentially the same ideas and the same passion as the more dignified utterances. Yeats's role in these poems is that of the singing fool in his dramas, and it can be traced back to Synge's belief in the primitive power of natural vigor, to Yeats's sensuality in old age, and to the dialectic of *A Vision* which recognized brutality as a necessary complement to beauty. Many years earlier, Yeats had written in *Stories of Red Hanrahan:* "a voice out of the Rose had told him how men would turn from the light of their own hearts, and bow down before outer order and outer fixity, and that then the light would cease, and none escape the curse except the foolish good man who could not think, and the passionate wicked man who would not." In his own old age, the light of a man's heart became the equivalent of sexual virility. And in "Prayer for Old Age," he begs that he may seem, even though he dies old, "a foolish, passionate man."

<h2 style="text-align:center">V   The Strings Are False:
An Unfinished Autobiography (1965)</h2>

In 1941, while London was under bombardment, Louis MacNeice came down from the city to visit Dr. E. R. Dodds, Regius Professor of Greek at Oxford. Perhaps the long thoughts occasioned by the involvement in global war prompted MacNeice to hand over a manuscript [35] which was to be put away, never referred to again, and only remembered when MacNeice died suddenly in September, 1963.

Upon examination it proved to contain three chapters of autobiographical writing in highly abbreviated script, followed by clear and easily legible longhand, except for a few typed paragraphs about the Oxford years which seem to be part of the text of a lecture given in 1939 or 1940 to an American audience. In good textual-critical form, Dr. Dodds calls this manuscript B. It bore no title, but was accompanied by a typed chapter with the superscription "A Visit to Spain: Easter 1936 (excerpted from a book, now in preparation, entitled *The Strings Are False*)."

Later, as literary executor, Dr. Dodds received another version of the same manuscript in two parts. The first part, A[1], is a folio notebook containing mutilated fragments of a first-draft introduction to the later B, and the first draft of a two-chapter portion of the revised B. From internal evidence it seems to have been written at Cornell in February or March, 1940. Manuscript A[2] is a continuation on loose sheets, unnumbered, with some pages obviously missing. Again it is the rough first draft of material reappearing in B. Comparison of manuscript B with the earlier drafts reveals retouching or complete rewriting of almost every paragraph, elimination of superfluities, sharpening of epigrams, and concretion of imagery. Thus Dr. Dodds reproduces B as it stands with the A¹ introduction as chapters I–XXXII. Chapters XXXIII–XXXVIII are derived from A². Appendix A gives "Landscapes of Childhood and Youth," and Appendix B contains a personal reminiscence and quotation from letters by John Hilton, a classmate of MacNeice's at both Marlborough and Oxford.

The Strings Are False is an honest, witty, sometimes tongue-in-cheek, and always dryly understated self-portrait. The chief topics are: childhood in an Ulster rectory; schooldays at Marlborough; Oxford in the 1920's; first marriage and a lectureship in Greek at Birmingham University; politics and poetry in the 1930's; the breakup of a marriage; and the coming of war. The subject of the topics, Louis MacNeice, tells only enough to be provocative. Always charming, often diffident, he remains the elusive cat that walks alone.

VI Christopher Columbus: *A Radio Play* (1944)

The first performance of the radio play *Christopher Columbus* was given by the British Broadcasting Corporation on October 12, 1942. Among the many British actors listed as performers in that broadcast, there appears the name of Hedli Anderson, who played the role of the Marquesa. This is the same Hedli to whom Louis MacNeice dedicated his next collection of poems, *Springboard,* and who later became the second Mrs. MacNeice. Among the more famous names to be found in the cast are Sir Laurence Olivier, who played the role of Columbus, and the English composer William Walton, who wrote the music for the presentation.

The Introduction takes the form of some comments on radio drama in general. How does the writer design a drama for the radio audience? MacNeice quite democratically insists that drama on the air does not require so much an education or intellectual hearing as a sensitive one.[36] But if the problems are raised that the radio audience is so easily bored, so attuned to bad art, and so unconscious that it is an audience, the author replies that the writer must forget about literature and concentrate upon sound. The scholar in MacNeice reminds us that to forget is not to deny literature; for literature begins as sound with the Homeric bard or Icelandic skald shouting over the clamor of a banquet, while tankards ring, babies squall, the fire is poked, and old men snore

and snuffle in their sleep. It is encouraging to remember that poetry is especially designed for this kind of an audience; it is the
most primitive form of literature and the one most likely to make
a rhythmic appeal to the ear alone. A printed page of poetry is
enough to frighten away the common man; but verse emerging
from the radio may not strike him as verse at all. He will listen to
the words and judge them on the basis of their emotional impact
and meaning.

By comparison with stage drama, the radio writer has a much
narrower time span; he has to move faster in building up his situation; he must be more careful not to confuse his hearers with side-
shows or involved references to past events; and the voices of his
actors must be somewhat less "stagy" than in the West End thea-
ters of London.

In *Christopher Columbus*, MacNeice employed the devices of
solo voices representing abstract qualities, and a Greek chorus to
express the cumulative social verdict; Doubt, Onlooker, Doubt
Chorus, Faith Chorus. Columbus is presented as a man obsessed
with certainty and exalted by a semi-religious faith in his calling.
Whether the monarchs wish to or not, they will have to hear him;
he is the Christopher, the bearer of Christ, the Dove that flies over
the waters, the Last Apostle, the remaker of the destinies of the
human race. In Act II, the protagonist claims that Isaiah, Esdras,
Job, and John the Divine all prophesied that he would come. And
he quotes from the Roman poet Seneca's prediction of a time
when a rolled map will be unfurled, and a new sail set forth to
uncover a new world. The radio drama ends with triumph as the
voice of the Onlooker surmises that the city of Seville will never
see a wilder celebration, with soldiers, coffers of gold, red savages
crowned with feathers, and the Discoverer himself

> With his pale face and his burning eyes, sitting his horse
> Like a Roman Emperor . . . or
> It might be fitter to say like the fifth
> Horseman of the Apocalypse.

In response to critics, and presumably because he felt that radio
drama needed some defense, MacNeice added an appendix to the
unpublished play. After the first transmission, a critic complained
that he should have ended the story with Columbus' later and

poignant record of decline and fall. But the author replies that this program was prepared to celebrate the 540th anniversary of the discovery of America; therefore, the occasion required an epic, rather than a biographical or psychological treatment.[37] In regard to the dialogue, he explains that he used an irregular blank verse based upon the rhythms of ordinary speech; but the lyrics were written in more regular form because they were designed to be sung or spoken with musical background.

Historically, MacNeice considered that Columbus was a legend first in his own mind and later to all the world. Therefore it was important that the emotional truth preserved in the legend be presented to the audience, rather than buried under a mass of historical detail. However, as the writer of a historical program, he remained well within the proper purview of history because everybody seems to agree that whether or not Columbus was a first-class sailor, he was a man of one idea and an almost mystical faith in his mission.

The figure of Beatriz Enriques gave offense to some listeners who may have assumed that MacNeice invented this long-suffering, always waiting mistress of the admiral. But she was in fact the mother of Columbus' son, Fernando Colon; and her role of neglected and unmarried mistress was introduced in order to emphasize just how far the discoverer's single-mindedness could go. As a fascinating little reminder of the scholarship of the playwright, the quotation from Seneca's *Medea,* with its forecast of the voyage of the Discoverer, was taken from Columbus' own translation found in his *Book of Prophecies,* which was written in 1501.[38]

VIII   Springboard (1945)

In 1947, Louis MacNeice was asked to prepare an article on the "English Literary Scene Today" for the New York *Times.* His first point provides a good basis for *Autumn Journal* and *Last Ditch;* his last point is a prophecy fulfilled by the later volume, *Springboard.* In the first place, he pointed out that before the war, far too many writers in England abrogated their rights and toadied to schools of thought which should have no control over the arts: "Leave it all to the Unconscious! or Leave it all to the Proletariat! Most of us have realized now that we cannot leave it all to anyone." [39] This conviction is not a new one with MacNeice; he held it at the very time he was writing the poetry of class-consciousness. However great were his personal doubts and reservations concerning the Messianic function of the working class, nevertheless he recognized it as the current movement.

His conclusion to "The English Literary Scene Today" suggests that he had been asked to prophesy concerning the evolution of English literature in the years ahead. He disowns the prophetic role, but he makes this valedictory response: "Since 1939 we seem to have become more humane; we have also become—in the widest sense of the word—more religious . . . many . . . have regained a sense of value, *i.e.*, of the value of people and things in themselves, of ends as distinct from means. We have escaped from nineteenth-century snobbery which disowned our Christian (and thereby our cultural) heritage. This should save us from totalitarian ways of thinking and also from the falser kinds of writing." [40]

Religious values in their wider sense is precisely the scope and concern of the new collection of poems published in 1945.[41] The title poem, "The Springboard," is built around the arresting image of a man, perched on a board high above London, who feels that he ought to dive like a bomber, both to wipe out his own original sin and, like the many who died in the war, to give his life for the people. The Christ image is clear, both in the oblique references to His temptation to throw Himself from the parapet of the Temple, and to original sin and redemptive sacrifice. The MacNeice image is also clear: the man is not paralyzed against the stars by fear; rather, his problem of unbelief holds him crucified in the sky. If he could be sure that his death would mend the world, or guarantee peace on earth, or build a utopia, or even ransom or reprieve his friends, he would be perfectly willing to pay the price. But, since he has long since ceased to believe in any of these possibilities, he hesitates endlessly, although he knows that at last he must dive if only to leave his friends "a grain of faith"—whatever that might be worth.

One of the most striking of MacNeice's religious poems, "Prayer in Mid-Passage," is included in this collection. In unorthodox but powerful fashion, God is named monster, guide, pattern of inhuman good, hard critic, fierce impersonality, silence and song, meaning and death. The central image is the Jacob vision of a "time-bound ladder" which may be climbed "out of time." Behind

the ladder lies the temptation of Lot's wife to turn back to the
"Cities of the Plain of Youth," the humanist tendency to have faith
in men alone and to be absorbed by memories of a past which
never really existed. Beyond the ladder, by the use of mere human
organs, men will manage to "transcend humanity" and move upward. The poet ends by dedicating this poem to the One Who is
both silence and song, the source of meaning, and the prospect of
death; but without Whom human breath would only be breath. A
choral version of this poem was appropriately sung at the memorial service after the poet's death.

The two themes of the title poem—war and man's function in
the modern world—are also the two major themes of the book.
The poet does not group the poems in this fashion, but the division seems to be demanded ideologically. "Brother Fire" is the
result of the incendiary bombing of London, when the feasting of
the flames was Lenten fare of fasting for the people of the city.
The fire forced them to ask if there might not be a great Will
which wills the natural world, but would prefer to eliminate man.
The people have to admit that the fire's elemental song of joy in
destruction is but the actualization of their own destructive
thoughts.

"The Trolls," written after an air raid in April, 1941, is clearly
indebted to Eliot's "Ash Wednesday" and "A Song for Simeon" for
its metrical structure, refrain, and the device of using a solemn
line from a continued theological argument for the beginning of
each stanza. The trolls are the "hulking, halfwit demons who rape
and slobber," the blind and ignorant forces of destruction that
assume death can destroy ideas. "Troll's Courtship" reveals that,
although these ignorant, destructive forces are in love only with
Death, they cannot seem to die.

The pattern of a "Convoy" (cf. "The Atlantic Tunnel") is rather
like the life of man. He sets a course to fulfill his soul's basic needs
of love and pride, but he often forgets that, like the protecting
destroyers and corvettes, his voyage home depends upon the im-
plementation of some very ruthless and pragmatic attitudes. In
"Sentries," men stand guard at the dangerous corners of the
world; and the poet hopes that these naïve champions may learn
to know what they believe, and to live what they know, before
chaos drags them under. In "Whit Monday," the bank holiday
crowds mill through the street, looking up to where an angel used

to be on a bombed church. Perhaps the Lord's Prayer is a stronger
rubric than the monolith of granite. But then again . . . *"I'll not
want"*—not when I'm dead; *"He makes me down to lie"*—in a
baptism of fire with death at my christening; *"The quiet waters
by"*—like the Thames, or the Salween, or the Don.

Two crazy songs, "Swing-Song" and "Nuts in May," have much
of the same gay, inconsequential lightness of social criticism as
"Bagpipe Music" from *I Crossed the Minch*. The girl of "Swing-
Song" is going deaf in a machine shop while her boyfriend flies for
the Royal Air Force. She walks alone and talks on the ground
while he talks to his friends in the sky: "K is for Kitty calling P for
Prue . . . / Bomb Doors Open . . . / Over to You." "Nuts in
May" represents a type of word experiment fairly unusual in Mac-
Neice, although he has always been addicted to the rhythm of
musical comedy, folk ballad, ragtime jazz. But in this poem his
special technical genius is shown by sound-alike phrases that
serve not merely for recitative swing, but are intellectually appropriate and imagistically precise: "bird-din," "sun-dint," "water-
wheels," "sun-peppered," "the guns unfold," "Pollen of death,"
"cowspit and bullspit and spirits of wine," "acid-drop," "angels are
frigid and shepherds are dumb," "die for your life." The poem is
essentially a cynical, modern version of the New Testament shepherds, who abide in the fields; they are now old, their flutes
broken, and their tales told. The angels now have become frigid;
their tail feathers shine in the high court of heaven; but, being
divine, they know no pity and give no quarter to their human
foes. Thus the annunciation to the shepherds becomes both "the
same again but different."

In "Neutrality," another bitter war song which skins the Irish
neutrality policy, every man has an area of neutrality in his own
heart, an area of withdrawal from life, of dream, gloom, and
doubt. But, if the Irish would look eastward they would see a dark
and dangerous continent, and, westward, the mackerel growing
fat on the flesh of their own kin. "Bottleneck," a very significant
poem, relates immediately to the title poem and "Neutrality." The
bottleneck is the high-minded Liberal who has been trained never
to fight "unless from a pure motive." Educated in progressive
schools, he will never make a soldier or a servant. He watches a
troopship depart with a "furtive footsore envy." He will always be
a noncombatant because his soul is too violent to kill anyone but

himself. In his mind a strange muddle of components press to be combined into that unified whole which will make action possible; but his compromises can never squeeze through the bottleneck of his idealism. It is highly possible that this is one of the most autobiographical poems in the collection, as well as a group portrait of the Liberal British intellectuals who were educated and reared as MacNeice was.

In "The Conscript," the soldier is rushed from camp to camp; he fulfills his citizenship by necessity, practices killing, and runs in a straight groove to disaster. But, because he is young, he has a central stalk which is vertical and points straight to the stars from its root in the spine. "The Mixer" is a portrait of a man who was deeply shocked by a night in Flanders in World War I. For twenty years he has suppressed his memory by keeping constantly in company; here he is alive and happy; but alone, he is colorless and self-accused. Now that he is caught in another war, he is reduced to a cipher. "Nostalgia" refers to those moments in the trenches when the old world of childhood and nature calls strongly, the trigger finger is slow, and the spirit lonely. The stars call; but earth and will are stronger and nearer, so the soldier stays at his duty.

The other chief division of the collection—and in many ways one more important than these random jottings on English life after five years of war—has to do with man's function in the modern world, or with what the poet describes in the Dedication "To Hedli," as turning his mind away from casual pleasure "towards a centre— / A zone which others too / And you / May choose to enter." This major theme might well be broken down into beginnings, problems of relationship, and the new world.

Certainly, not many collections of even modern poems have begun with an invocation by a foetus, but the first poem in this collection is "Prayer Before Birth." Some of the same wordplay used in "Nuts in May" is exhibited superlatively well in this initial poem. The unborn child prays that he might be protected from "the bloodsucking bat or the rat or the stoat or the / club-foot ghoul." He is afraid that the "human race may with tall walls wall me, / with strong drugs dope me, with wide lies lure me, / on black racks rack me, in blood-baths roll me." The intoxication of sound-alike words, while it successfully creates a mumbo jumbo of primitive incantation, is yet always intellectively secure and imagistically precise. The eight stanzas follow the poetic and intellectual pattern of initiation as they point out the dangers that lie in store for the unborn child; and the form of lines, diminishing in length but increasing in tempo, weaves a most effective spell against the disasters of faulty education and life's dehumanizing processes. The last line is brief and rhetorically powerful—"Otherwise kill me."

The second poem in this group on beginnings, although entitled "Precursors," might more appropriately have been called "Atavisms." With the new interest in sound-alikes, MacNeice describes the weather as "flat, matt, mute, unlivened, unexpectant." If only it would be broken by the battalions of rain, thunder, wind, or the transmutation of a harvest moon! In the midst of all this hushed flatness, only the insects dare to sing or dance. As a dancer, man is either an anachronism or has not yet really learned how to dance. But the poet has known one or two who had the gusto of a high wind or who could come shining through a storm.

"Explorations," a poetic version of a philosophic-evolutionary thought expressed by MacNeice in *Zoo*, as well as by Aristotle, Gerald Heard, Loren Eiseley, and many others, considers the possibility that man's great glory is not his superb adaptation to environment, but his fluidity and capacity to change to fit various environments and yet to fit none exactly. The precise adaptation of other mammals has proved a trap and a dead end, instead of an advantage. Thus, in "Explorations," the whale, the tapeworm, and the swallow are all considered as great successes in adaptation; but they are not models for men. We are unique; we are conscious and therefore we hope; we hope and therefore we despair. Our goal is not to be learned from whales or birds or worms; our goal is our own and must be won "by our own endeavour / And held on our own terms."

In "Mutations," the poet considers that, although there has been no definitive change in our species since Cro-Magnon Man, yet each man has known some remarkable mutations in his own mind. The scholar suddenly understands something he has thought about for years; the inveterate rake breaks through from lust into love—"the fuse is always laid to some annunciation." In "Thyestes," the son of Pelops and brother of Atreus seduced his brother's wife; and, in revenge, Atreus slew Thyestes' sons and served them to their father at a banquet. The tale reminds MacNeice that just as along the trail of time we have all been cannibals and incestuous, today we still "garnish to pollute and breed to kill." Then, with a sudden switch to religious imagery, we are all "messmates" in the "eucharist of crime" and heirs to two of the three black crosses that arose on Golgotha.

The final poem of beginnings, entitled "Postscript," deals in a remarkable transformation of image with the shift from prism to burning glass. When we were children, all language was a prism, spilling over with color and possibilities. As adults, the prism has turned to a burning glass suitable only for the practical purpose of heat or for the destructive purpose of burning. For an adult to know joy, it is necessary to shift the image backward and to remarry language with color and possibility. Presumably this is a versification of Jesus' requirement, "Except ye become as these little ones ye shall in no wise enter into the Kingdom of Heaven."

The second division of the poems on man's function in the modern world is the problem of human relationships. "Babel" raises the obvious complaint that the confusion of tongues is not just a biblical device to explain the existence of so many different languages, but the archetype of a problem of communication that exists between human beings in the same language group. The theme is expressed in the poignant refrain "Can't we ever, my love, speak in the same language?" In "Schizophrene," a dark and moving poem about the associations of a child with various common experiences, the water running in the bath suggests the biblical Flood and the will of a God Who chose that all His creatures should perish. The hiss of gas burning in the grate transports the child to a desert where her hand becomes alien and her brain turns to iron. The hum of telegraph wires carries ugly sexual overtones. Church bells ring with a threat of that moment when the world, which came out of chaos, will return to chaos again. A cock at dawn returns to biblical symbolism and a guilty denial for which the child would atone if she could; but, instead, she keeps on denying.

In "Alcohol" the Greek poet Bacchylides calls drink the great leveler of rich and poor. The Haves do not want to make choices, so they keep right on ordering the same-as-before; the Have-Nots have no choice, so they also order the same-as-before. After several of the same, the drinker is far back in the primitive history of the race. Men do not need to be fed on slogans; just give them beer or brandy or schnapps or gin and the self-betrayed will follow the old road which leads not out of the maze, but back in. "The Libertine" ran through women in his teens and twenties like a child looking for a lost toy; he never found the toy, and he has forgotten the faces. Now, in middle life—with his erotic program torn in two—if, by accident, he should meet a woman who would offer him the fulfillment of his manhood, his answer would be the same refrain as to all the other angels, goddesses, bitches— "O leave me easy, leave me alone."

The master of the pinprick in "The Satirist" can dissect anybody: hero, saint, or lover. He has no creativity at all; he bears no blossom even in season; his hobby is to give everyone else the lie. He becomes the lonely keeper of the log on a condemned ship. Oddly enough, it was high ideals which made him a satirist of everything which did not satisfy his large premises. In "This Way Out," the scholar always parted quickly and abruptly from his friends, although he loved friendship, saying, "I must; I have to work." His will moved and he returned to the lonely tasks of thought. His friends always asked regretfully, "You're not going yet?" and one day the answer was "I must; I have to die."

Although "The Casualty (in memoriam G. H. S.)" is a war poem, it should be classified under human relationships because the emphasis is not so much upon the accident of death, but the persisting relationship with friends. No matter how good an elegy the poet might write, if his friend were alive he would grin and say "Damn! . . . All clichés." He never expects to find another friend with whom he can be "silent knowledgeably." This is an interesting tribute from MacNeice, because T. S. Eliot remarked upon how disappointing MacNeice was to meet;[42] and the writer of a eulogy after MacNeice's death remarked that he was no talker, but a silent, companionable man—"a cat who walked by himself." [43] The poet's friend, who drowned in the mid-Atlantic, while he was still young, forces his way into the poet's dreams, smiling and swinging through the pearly sea as if he had something to report: How was it at the moment of death?—How is it now? As boys, they used to discuss death and to snicker at the solemn sureness of the preacher when he talked about immortality; but now his dead friend could talk as big as any—if he had breath. The poet attempts to correlate the memories of his friend that dart and trip through his mind: he had archaic gusto, and the lips of a Gothic imp; with inky hands, he made notes and fingered his piccolo; he belonged to that "high humble company" that lives outside of cliques, unbothered by fashion. As the poet glances over the snapshots of his dead friend, he marvels at his gift to be surprised at life, and therefore to be sympathetic and warm. He was awake to the "integrity of differences." Did he make one last integration and see the Form emerging from the formless when the Atlantic flowed over his head? Whether he did or not, his whole life was straining toward discovery; if he never made that discovery, then the loss is everybody's as well as his own because he is out of this life "and cannot start any more hares for ever."

Louis MacNeice arranged his volume with a dedication to Hedli Anderson, the epigraph "*Even poisons praise thee*" from George Herbert, most of the poems listed under Roman numeral I, and only three poems and a postscript following Roman numeral II. The second division of the collection has its own epigraph: "*Lascio lo fele e vo per dolci pomi,*" by Dante.[44] I have had the temerity to subdivide his divisions and to choose for concluding poems "Epitaph for Liberal Poets," "Prospect," and "The Kingdom." These seem to fit together because—instead of looking out at the current war, or back at man's beginnings, or around at man's relationships—they look forward to ask important questions about tomorrow's world.

"Epitaph for Liberal Poets" is a highly personal poem in which the poet considers the plight of those who have been trained in individualism and the humane tradition, and who will now be superseded by the "tight-lipped technocratic Conquistadores." This is not the first time individualism has died; for, when Catullus passed from the scene, he gave place to men who were born old, who were adaptable to any circumstances, and who did not care enough even to be jealous of his wild, warm lyrics. So today there is no need to whine, because there is no way out. The Liberal will vanish; but perhaps he will leave behind certain frozen words which some day may melt and "accentuate a thirst" for tomorrow's men. "Prospect" continues the thought that today's world, empty of song, spelling out a Machiavellian creed, has no place for individualistic, therefore anarchic men. Even though every sand-castle dream crumbles, men know that rooted in the future there will grow "a plant of tenderness."

As a continuation of this same idea, but in a more comprehensive and hopeful form, "The Kingdom" is the most important poem in the collection, and perhaps expresses an ultimate wisdom of Louis MacNeice's thought and genius. A longer poem, two hundred and eighty-six lines in eight cantos, the Kingdom of the poem seems to be composed of those rugged individuals who, daring to be themselves in a recalcitrant world, give hope and courage to others to do likewise. This humanistic Kingdom exalts the anarchic qualities of the unique individual and claims that its highest aim is the fullest realization of them. Perhaps because the message is affirmative rather than negative, earnest rather than casual, the tone of the diction is decidedly quiet and flat, almost with the diffidence of a young man making his maiden avowal of faith. Under the crust of bureaucracy, says the poet, there is a Kingdom of individuals, each equal in difference and separately sovereign. Among them may be found the candid scholar, the unselfish priest, the uncomplaining mother, active men who are kind, contemplatives who are generous, happy-go-lucky saints, and peace-loving buccaneers. These people vindicate the human species, and they can be found everywhere.

Then the poet proceeds to point out some prime specimens. In Canto II there is an old man who dresses in tweeds but has none of the squire's presumption. He is gentle with flowers, and his memory and life are full of wisps of nature. There is a mother (Canto III) who has a stroke; her family full of the immediate emergency, fails to recognize its own tragedy. It was she who made the home, who gave the family cohesion, who carved out the little, self-respecting, sane island amidst chaos; without her, chaos will take back its own. There is a ship's officer (Canto IV), a heavy drinker and a man quick to anger, but full of earthy manliness and independence. He loves the vigorous life of a "brave unforced solidarity" and finds his own meaning in this elemental fellowship. This vignette is perhaps the most suspect since we cannot help wondering in what sense the organization of a ship can be called a "brave unforced solidarity." MacNeice's experience as perpetual passenger is perhaps romanticizing his insight into the life of the crew.

Canto V depicts a large, classic-looking girl who finds herself an antique goddess among the little people of earth. A Doric rivergoddess, she pours out of her pitcher water which is wild, anarchic, pure, and healing—but it seems ice-cold to modern men.

She has vitality of her own, but the reaction of others fills her with self-doubt and fear. She must simply go on being the individual she was meant to be, whether she fits or not, because her true citizenship is in the Kingdom.

There is also a dapper little man (Canto VI) who works obscurely in scientific research. He makes a religion out of his work and a church out of his laboratory. His friends complain that his mind is painfully one-track. But this concentration on the task immediately at hand is his glory and his honor—the certificate of his membership in the Kingdom. The old preacher (Canto VII), who is conducting the funeral service for a friend of forty years, seems to make a dreadful error as he assures the congregation that all is well with the child. But his friend had always retained the high seriousness and integrity of childhood, and the minister himself lived the life of a generous puritan—lyrical, strong, kind, and truthful. Perhaps this canto may be somewhat indebted to the clergyman-bishop father whom Louis MacNeice continued to admire personally long after he had lost his faith in traditional religion.

These, then, are individuals of a Kingdom in which each subject is a king. They are not cranks, self-deceiving realists, self-seeking altruists, self-indulgent penitents. They have been chosen and called to enter the Kingdom because, even if they are grotesque, they are also beautiful; and, though willful, they are also wise and "hard as meteorites." These are the "archetype and the vindication of history."

It is easy to see why F. W. Dupee spoke of the language of "The Kingdom" as "strangely without nerve or color" and of the individuals of the cantos as "characters . . more quaint than fine." [45] The quiet understatement of MacNeice's verse may be conscious or unconscious. If the latter, it represents the diffidence of a writer more apt to diagnose than prescribe, to criticize than eulogize. If the former, the writer knows that a starry-eyed enthusiasm will not be persuasive to his generation. Instead, the basic belief must emerge almost in spite of the form of statement. The choice of character does verge on the quaint because of the frequent mixture of humor and seriousness characteristic not only of the poetry of MacNeice but of many of his contemporaries as well —the inescapable truth told in a breezy, droll manner. If Cantos I and VIII are given their full weight, it is apparent that the poet is very earnest about an unaccustomed role—that of *vates,* seer, and hope-giver. That MacNeice is constitutionally unlikely to assume this role makes this exception (also *Autumn Sequel*) all the more impressive and persuasive. It is as if he were to say: All right, I am one of the Liberals who have gone to the wall. I have been unable to become a wholehearted adherent of Freudianism or collectivism. Fascism is my born enemy.

What is left is only this reaffirmed, basic belief in the importance of the individual and a confidence that, wherever a man dares to live his own life, he fulfills the human ideal and encourages others to dare their own self-realization. This may be a painfully meager answer, but it goes a long way to rescue the poet from the charge of defeatism and despair. Lest the reader should miss this theme, MacNeice pointed out the individualism of the collection in a specific note: "Many of my titles in this book have the definite article, e.g. 'The Satirist,' 'The Conscript.' The reader must not think that I am offering him a set of Theophrastean characters, I am not generalising; 'The Conscript' does not stand for all conscripts but for an imagined individual; any such individual seems to me to have an absolute quality which the definite article recognises. . . ." [46]

VIII   The Dark Tower and Other Radio Scripts (*1947*)

Louis MacNeice decided to publish his radio scripts[47] both because of the interest shown in the publication of the script of *The Rescue,* written by his friend, Edward Sackville-West, and in order that the publication of other scripts might throw more light on what at the time was a new and challenging art medium. Because his Introduction to *Christopher Columbus* had essayed a general exposition of radio dramatic writing, MacNeice does not labor again the main points outlined there; but he does make some corrections in emphasis. In the earlier introduction he had said that the radio writer "must move on a more or less primitive plane." Now he restates that requirement by saying that the radio scriptwriter must remember that he is primarily an entertainer.

In the Conclusion to *Modern Poetry* he had earlier indicated that one prime function of the modern poet is to be an entertainer. In the *Columbus* Introduction he wrote: "As compared with most contemporary literature, the objective elements will preponderate over the subjective, statement over allusion, synthesis over analysis." This idea is not such a new one either because, in the Conclusion to *Modern Poetry*, he had stated that the modern poet must offer not only entertainment plus criticism, but also fact plus emotional reaction. In his later qualification of this position he simply underlines the word "fact." The psychological novel, concerned chiefly with subjective experience, deals largely in *oratio obliqua.* A radio play must be much more predominantly *oratio recta.*[48] The subjective may be dealt with, but it becomes objectified by the very fact of its spokenness.

In this age of "irreconcilable idioms," [49] MacNeice has often heard writers expressing their longing for some sort of group life. He considers that, for the modern poet, such a desire is doomed to disappointment; he is *ipso facto* a spiritual isolationist who would lose far more than he would gain were he to immerse his individuality in a poetic pool. For example, of all the poets MacNeice knows, there are only a very few with whom he has any desire to discuss poetry and only one from whom he can accept frequent criticism. While this isolation is probably both healthy and necessary, the poet envies the playwright and the musician who can work in groups. But he has the opportunity in radio drama to become part of a producing team. He must learn to cooperate effectively with all the other persons whose work will go through the same process—into a microphone at their end, and out the other end through a radio. MacNeice testifies that this fellowship can be enjoyable as well as effective. The department in the B.B.C. of which he was a member at the date of writing compares very well for intelligence with almost any contemporary salon of literati. Actually, he claims that, on the whole, his radio colleagues are "quicker-witted, more versatile, less egocentric, less conventional, more humane" than his fellow poets.[50]

The Dark Tower is a radio parable play dedicated to Benjamin Britten, the composer of special music for the production, and the drama was first broadcast in the B.B.C. Home Service on January 21, 1946. As a parable play, it belongs to that class of writing which includes *Everyman,* Spenser's *The Faerie Queene,* and Bunyan's *The Pilgrim's Progress*—although it certainly cannot bear comparison with any of these. MacNeice's impression was that pure Realism was almost played out in his day, although most works of fiction would remain nominally realistic on the surface. But the single-track mind and the single-plane novel or play were almost bound to falsify the contemporary world. Freud had clearly proved that there may be method in madness and both fact in fantasy and fantasy in fact. If this is the case, mere surface "reportage"could no longer masquerade as art.

The title of the play was suggested by Robert Browning's poem "Childe Roland to the Dark Tower Came." The theme is the age-old questing instinct of man, dissatisfied with what he has, insistent that there is something better to be found, and dedicated to the pilgrimage which leads from one to the other. Both Browning and MacNeice leave the poem-parable indeterminate as to whether or not Roland finds his heart's desire once he reaches the Tower. Both suggest by dialogue and setting that the Tower is a miserable rather than a glorious place, and that the end of the quest may be death instead of fulfillment.

In the MacNeice drama, the Parrot (an image MacNeice had used earlier and was to use later) represents the jeering, belittling voices that keep men from any great achievement. The Raven which encourages heroic exertion may also be the symbol of heroic death. At the close of the brief play, Roland says he will blow his horn of challenge although he is a family black sheep and an unbeliever in the magic of the Tower. He has never done anything in his life of his own free will, and perhaps by this challenge to his death he "will bequeath free will to others." [51] The Tower grows in size, and its shadow lies cold upon the pilgrim. Although Roland is aware of his great danger, nevertheless he challenges the Dragon, "who makes men beasts," to come out; here is a man, let the enemy do his worst. The secondary plane of symbolic meaning is one that MacNeice has often constructed in his poems: the world too large for a man to challenge, the loss of the old confidence of belief that his fathers knew, and the certainty of defeat; yet the only recourse is to challenge the overwhelming powers anyway, in order to show the measure of a man.

Sunbeams in His Hat, a study of Chekhov as a man, was first broadcast on the B.B.C. Home Service, July 16, 1944. MacNeice had made an initial feature-biography treatment in 1941, but he rewrote and enlarged it for the anniversary of Chekhov's death in 1944. His special intention was to correct the popular misconception which considers Chekhov as a synonym for melancholy and which so often makes the performance of his plays dull and dead. The major challenge of such a program is how to select those few significant "shots" which, put together, will make a coherent whole. Using the hackneyed device of the flashback, MacNeice begins with Chekhov on the morning of his death and ends with that evening.

As the *Dark Tower* was presented in dream form, this biographically factual drama on Chekhov uses a dream as the omen which prepares the audience for the playwright's death. Thus the River dream becomes not only foreboding but a symbol of transition and continuity. In the flashback to a conversation with Maxim Gorki and Leo Tolstoy, Chekhov describes his literary motive as "trying to catch a sunbeam" and put it in his hat.[52] The others drown him in laughter, their argument forgotten. Tolstoy, still half-choking with laughter, calls Chekhov incorrigible. Chekhov muses, as the flashback fades, "They can both have been right in contrast to me. The artist must grind an axe: Tolstoy thinks so, Gorki thinks so—of course they are different axes. But poor Anton Pavlovitch [Chekhov]—he just hasn't got an axe to grind. Even Souvorin used to rebuke me for it. He said I was indifferent to good and evil."

The Nosebag, the direct and simple dramatization of a traditional Russian folk story usually entitled "The Soldier and Death," was first broadcast in the B.B.C. Home Service on March 13, 1944. Although MacNeice prefers *The Dark Tower*, this radio drama is far better in regard to comic and dramatic elements, as well as having a comforting completeness of plot. The theme is the intrepid but simple soldier, who, with the aid of a magic feedbag, manages to trap death, and even to graduate from Hell to Heaven.

The "March Hare Saga" is composed of *The March Hare Resigns* and *Salute to All Fools*. The March Hare role was written especially to be played by Esmé Percy. The playwright describes the technique as "a little-bit-of-mud-for-everyone," [53] and he considers it successful because both programs managed to outrage a large number of listeners. The listener reaction was probably partly due to the suspicion that satire must always be partisan and partly to the desire to classify everything—pure fun, pure satire— no mixtures of serious meaning expressed in frivolous tones. Since this very mixture of the serious and the frivolous is a favorite technique of MacNeice and his friends, this audience reaction might have warned them that their favorite technique had the tendency to limit both their readers and their listeners to the cosmopolitan sophisticate.

In line with the principles enunciated in the Introduction to the plays, the playwright's first object was entertainment. Nonsense verse ought to be entertaining and on a "primitive" enough level to reach the radio audience. But, just as the nonsense verses of Lewis Carroll bore a criticism of contemporary life, these scripts were designed to do the same. *The March Hare Resigns* is the more lyrical of the two dramas because its basic theme is the clash between the sympathetic poetic madness of the Hare and the repellent pedestrian madness of all the people who consider themselves sane.

Salute to All Fools has saltier dialogue and more bite in its social criticism. Appropriately broadcast on April 1, 1946, the drama portrays the March Hare on the quest for truth. He interviews Journalists' Truth, Poetic Truth, Scientific Truth, Tory Truth, the Freudian Analyst, the Marxist, a Yogi, a Gael, and a Photographer; and he decides that all these truths are not only partial but suspect even in their own departments. They toast: Up the rebels! Up the Oedipus Complex! Up the Upper Ten! Up the Inevitability of History! Up the Circulation of the Late Night Final! Up the Immanent and Transcendent Rope! Up the New Era of Atomic Energy! Up the Beautiful Ineffectual Angel who is older than the rocks on which she sits!—but the March Hare can only murmur: Up the Garden Path. April Fools—all of them.

In the 1930's, Louis MacNeice was challenged by the enthusiastic involvement of his closest friends in the Proletarian movement of the British Left. *Autumn Journal* (1938) makes it clear that he admits that the "balance of right" belonged to the pro-Communist Spanish government rather than to the pro-Fascist rebels. Characteristically, after MacNeice has carefully weighed the merits of "ivory tower" poetic isolationism against "brazen tower" poetic propagandism, he chooses neither. Instead, he reverts to the old Liberal-Romantic doctrine of the unique and ultimate value of the individual. While, as a poet of the whole life of man he must sing about social concerns, he retains his central allegiance to an older-fashioned, humanistic individualism.

MacNeice proceeds along this *via media* with increasing difficulty and final frustration. After he had visited Spain, he tried to forget the angry faces and the apocalyptic writing on the walls.

Discovering that they could neither be forgotten nor dismissed, he explores in *Autumn Journal* the crisis for the Liberal mind of a totalitarian world and confronts the historical dilemma, but he offers no resolutions either personal or public.

In *The Last Ditch*, he reluctantly portrays the embattled Liberal with his back against the wall of his own limitations. He considers, in the classical tradition of Meredith's *The Ordeal of Richard Feverel*, that those limitations are partly self-imposed and partly the result of a faulty education ("Bottleneck"). A poet who had always been obsessed with a sense of eschatological doom, MacNeice writes with increasing frequency and implacability of the coming *dies irae*.

The heroes of his radio dramas are men like Columbus with an almost divine sense of mission, who thus are able to view history in the uncomplicated terms of personal destiny. But the British Liberal, with a full stock of tepid good will, is empty of passionately held convictions. MacNeice describes this frustrated figure in many guises, but always with the same stance—the diver paralyzed on his springboard, not by fear of war's violence, but by doubt of life's meaning. He is the Onlooker in *Christopher Columbus*, a Joseph Conrad hero who joins neither Doubt Chorus nor Faith Chorus but stands unhappily uninvolved. He is the perennially confused youth who can sing about the older "Merrie England" that he knew and loved; he can recognize uneasily its need for social, economic, and political reform; he can show us the pieces of the old harmony left scattered by falling bombs—but he cannot either reassemble the pieces in their old shape or create a new and better pattern than the old.

In the face of these agonizing difficulties, the poet is tempted by three possible recessions: that old interest in comatose sleep that snored through his *juvenilia;* the shallow laughter of the March Hare who relegates everything to humor and has only one reply—"April fool"; or the recessiveness, already mentioned, of retreat from public to private concerns, from mankind to the intrinsic merit of the individual. As the poet stands before the Dark Tower, an unheroic hero about to go doubtfully to certain death, he chooses the last recession—individualism, to take with him into battle. Like an agnostic rosary, he strings together the beads of individuals he has known, and from whom his praying fingers can take comfort and solace.

Quaint and irrelevant as many of his individuals may be, the recession has gain as well as loss. The agony of his frustration often seems to push the poet into a marvelous fertility of technical expression and experiment. And more important ideologically, the new "pluralism" ("Plurality") of the poet links his poetry closer to the haphazard life of common men than the well-ordered universe of an Oxford don. When the attempt of *Plant and Phantom* to reduce pluralism to monism has failed, MacNeice is left with the path traveled by the French Existentialists: from the one to the many, from being to becoming, from the universal to the individual, from essence to existence, and from classification in terms of value to development in terms of organic growth. Thus in "Plain Speaking" he makes the same affirmation—the only definition is a tautology—that Albert Camus does in *The Myth of Sisyphus*.

CHAPTER 4

The Disillusioned Liberal

WITH characteristic lightness of touch, Louis MacNeice iron-ically summed up the critical consensus on his work in an article in the *New Statesman and Nation,* entitled "Poetry, the Public and the Critic": "I am a writer they can place quite simply: I am a surprisingly feminine, essentially masculine poet, whose gift is primarily lyrical and basically satirical, swayed by and im-mune to politics, with and without a religious sense, and I am technically slapdash and technically meticulous, with a predilec-tion for flat and halting and lilting and Swinburnian rhythms, and I have a personal and impersonal approach, with a remarkably wide and consistently narrow range, and I have developed a good deal and I have not developed at all." [1]

There is no hint of bitterness in this witty summary of the critics' dicta on his work. There is, however, surprising agreement by the critics that *Holes in the Sky: Poems 1944-1947* [2] represents some kind of crisis in the poet's craft; but their analysis of just what kind of crisis amusingly illustrates the poet's estimate of their general lack of agreement. William Van O'Connor, who says there is nothing wrong with the poet or his poetry, calls his critical review of *Holes in the Sky,* "Master of His Idiom." [3] Denis Bot-terill states flatly "that Louis MacNeice is facing some . . . con-flict seems to me to be implicit in *Holes in the Sky.* . . . The old technical mastery of loose rhythm is still apparent," but the whole collection has a "nagging touch of despair." Is the problem that he now rates himself as one of those minor poets who are discussed in his poem "Elegy for Minor Poets"? Or is the clue to be found in the date of the book's genesis, indicated by the subtitle *Poems, 1944-1947* just because those were war years in which no one could expect anything much from any poet? Or, as with Arthur Rimbaud and George Gascoyne, was the divine game of poetry beginning to pall, and was the poet wondering if philosophy might not be nearer the truth? [4]

Horace Gregory, who insists that something has gone "terribly astray," asks three questions: Was the influence of the group bad for MacNeice? Mr. Gregory feels that only young people can take shelter under the protection of group writing and group publicity. Now in middle life, MacNeice must stand on his own despite the close resemblances between his language and that of W. H. Auden. Second, could MacNeice have done better writing adaptations from the Classics, since this is his major professional orientation? Third, was he flitting back and forth between the older Auden group in England and the younger Irish poets, and finding himself at home in neither camp? [5]

Out of the plethora of diagnosis and prescription, three possible explanations emerge. First, *Holes in the Sky* does seem to represent some kind of a crisis in the poet's craft. Second, the dates of the poems need to be compared with the poet's birth in September of 1907, as a mathematical reminder that he was now entering middle age. In the motto poem of *Holes in the Sky*, the poet wrote: "Double your stakes, says the clock / To the aging dancer." Perhaps to the aging poetic dancer the old tunes and the old routines no longer seemed so bright when tapped out by feet that were fortying. As Mr. O'Connor claims, he is still "master of his idiom"; but perhaps that idiom has begun to show the strain, to become inadequate for the new things the poet wants to say. Or worse, perhaps it is beginning to act as a technical strait jacket confining him to the old jingles and the old themes.

The third possible explanation is the very clear evidence adduced in Chapter 3 of this study that the young man who faced the war as a Liberal came out of the war with a thoroughly battered Liberalism—and even with the conviction that the old Liberalism had no place in the new world. "What is truth? says Pilate" at the beginning of the motto poem. Perhaps the poet, like Pilate, is seeking for a new set of beliefs to meet the new, challenging situation. In the last two lines of the poem, the child answers Pilate's question by scanning the stars and replying: "Holes in the sky." As we turn to a consideration of the volume, we will find a few such holes but many more repetitions of the old techniques and much more nostalgia for a past no longer relevant. In one of the poems of the collection, MacNeice states "And what happens next on the programme we do not know." *Holes in the Sky* represents "we do not know"; *Ten Burnt Offerings* of four years later represents "what happens next on the programme."

I   Holes in the Sky: Poems 1944–1947

The first poem in *Holes in the Sky*, "The Streets of Laredo," raises the problem, along with five other poems in the collection, of the poet's craft. Based on an American cowboy song of the same name, the original tune was specially arranged by William Alwyn so that the poem could be sung by Louis MacNeice's second wife, the actress and singer Hedli Anderson. Perhaps one of the best poems in the entire volume, its virtues point to the technical achievements of the past. In speed and rhythm, it ranks with "Bagpipe Music." It swings along on a ballad line and incongruously tells about the incendiary bombing of London and the final fires of the Last Judgment. This is MacNeice's old trick of sounding casual about momentous themes, and it is handled extraordinarily well. Perhaps the most remarkable poetic tour de force is the elegant subtlety of the shift from Laredo to bombed London, from the London of World War II to the London of Sir Christopher Wren and the fire of 1666, from the architect Wren to the evangelist Bunyan, from Bunyan the preacher with his call to repentance to Blake of the apocalyptic vision.

Having traveled by these infinitely subtle gradations from a cowboy town to the final judgment of men, the Angel of Death whispers:

> O late, very late, have I come to Laredo
> A whimsical bride in my new scarlet dress
> But at last I took pity on those who were waiting
> To see my regalia and feel my caress.
>
> Now ring the bells gaily and play the hose daily,
> Put splints on your legs, put a gag on your breath;
> O you streets of Laredo, you streets of Laredo,
> Lay down the red carpet—My dowry is death.

It is indeed impressive to begin with a ragbag full of unassorted materials and come out with a terrifying, unified picture of the Final Judgment. But the very splendor of technique points to a mastery which is mature and to a style which has been used be-

fore. Perhaps this is the high water mark that MacNeice can reach
by use of wit, ballad refrain, current reportage, war imagery, the
subtle transformations of history, and the eschatological sense that
everything is going to end—soon.

The "Elegy for Minor Poets" raises a question which the text
does not answer: was Louis MacNeice thus classifying himself?
Perhaps the force of the last stanza should lead to a revision of the
critics' question. The poet says that we later suitors of the muse
(who does not grow old) do the right thing in hanging a trophy
on the grave of each bygone poet. These "debtors preclude our
scorn"; did we not "underwrite them when we were born?" Whatever that last line may mean, it might suggest that all poets of our
day are minor simply because of the time into which they were
born. It does not seem a definitive labeling by the poet of his own
rank as minor. These dead poets were minor because some were
too happy or sad, too soon or late; some thought too much, some
too little; some were not better poets because they were the
world's best talkers. They knew all the words but failed "to
achieve the Word." All in all, the poem is a persuasive, moving
elegy with just the hint of self-reference to add the spice of question to the flavor.

"Autolycus," a poem named for a character in Shakespeare's
The Winter's Tale, refers to the last period of Shakespeare's
dramaturgy when he turned from taut plots and complex characters to romances with happy endings. The dramatic mainsprings
were the old gags of babies exposed, identities confused, and
queens restored. How could Shakespeare have remained so innocent? But "the master pedlar with your confidence tricks" balanced the innocence with pickpockets and rogues from East-
cheap. MacNeice's question seems to be: Why does Shakespeare
pluck "heartstrings in the name of mirth" and hawk such entertainment as leaves the client brooding? His answer is, that although Shakespeare was more self-reliant than latter-day poetic
dramatists, he too, was "born and grew up in a fix." Whatever
bearing this poem may have on Shakespeare criticism, it shows
the modern poet's continuing concern with an honest relationship
between writer and reader. MacNeice finds no solutions or final
answers to contemporary problems: (a) Shall he talk large about
areas in which he has thought small? (b) Shall he simply admit

that he has no answers? (c) Shall he continue writing at all? The answer of Autolycus may be MacNeice's answer: writers are not required to solve all problems; they are in the same "fix" with the reader, and they serve him best by their heightened sensitivity to the problem and by their extraordinary gift for stating the alternatives.

"Slow Movement" traces the quietly terrifying experience of a man who awakens in a train, with no reminder of the preceding day except yesterday's newspaper wadded under the seat. It is very early in the morning, and the girl across the aisle has not yet opened her eyes. The train stops in the middle of fields—there is absolute cessation of motion and sound; ". . . what happens next on the programme we do not know"; perhaps the train will begin again; or the girl will open her eyes; and, in so doing, she will "open ours." The title comes from the image of a viola player's hand sawing rhythmically in the slow movement of a musical composition.

The poet transforms that undulating hand into a fish in a glass tank, first darting away, then nibbling invisible weeds, at last lying on the aquarium floor with not a bubble rising. As the exploration of that sudden startled moment of coming out of sleep, the poem is complete in itself and entirely valid. We include it in the discussion of the poet's craft because of the bare possibility that this experience may relate to the poet's creative predicament of 1944–47. Perhaps for him, too, the slow movement has elaborated all its motifs, and only a lingering repetition is left before the movement sinks to silence. In which case, the crucial question is, indeed, "what happens next on the programme"?

At least ten of the poems in this collection arise out of the post-war situation or mood. A recurrent shelving of the war years as unimportant, as somehow not counting, is found in "Hiatus." Civilians in the towns of England felt that they had remained exactly the same age they were in 1939, as if they had stood in a timeless food queue all through the war. When they spoke of "last year," they meant the last year of peace. But eyes pucker, mouths crease; and, when the soldiers return who were schoolboys in the 1930's, they have reached their manhood in the hiatus. War has made some dark things clear, and some clear things dark. Another poem, "Aftermath," shows the end of the war as loosening the social bond that held people together through the emergency. Now they play with a pack of cards, each one separate; no suit is wild, and the joker of death has been withdrawn.

"Bluebells" is full of the delicate nuances of a love that began during the war and must now adjust to the postwar years. During the war, the lovers kept hoping for peace; now that it is peacetime, for what do they hope? They actually miss the menace of planes in the sky; the sun is too bright, and Nature is out of gear. They turn into a wood where bluebells grow, and there the woman discovers the image of "blue snow" to describe her feelings. She can only hope that somehow her "cold gentleness" will "irradiate him."

Tam Cari Capitis [6] begins with the cliché that the world is never quite the same after the death of a friend, but the poem moves quickly to the less usual idea that he is missed most, not in the full "floodlit moments," but as a help to kill time drop-by-drop at games like darts or chess. Even those games had exciting moments when the tap, as it were, was turned on full. Although "Week-End" is very much like "Bluebells," it can be included in this postwar grouping largely because of its mood. A pair of lovers go off for a weekend to "blend their persons," but something is wrong. The poet likens the process to joint authorship, white pages, ink that was supposed to flow "like a virgin river," but instead the click of an unexpected comma sends authors and lovers back to the beginning of the sentence.

"Street Scene" is a camera flash in the old MacNeice manner: a wartime spring, a swaggering Canadian sergeant, a street singer with a fantastically lovely voice, sentimental tunes that actualize each man's private dream; singer departs, sergeant dives for a pub, silence follows song. "The Drunkard" is not necessarily a war or postwar vignette; but by its tone of weary, disillusioning descent from the ideal to the actual, it seems to fit the postwar mood. The drunkard on his way home is undergoing Purgatory in reverse. When he was drunk, the "barmaid was a Madonna"; there was adoration in the gaze of a drunken comrade that made even "pissing under the stars an act of creation." But now, on his homeward way, he slips back into time and down toward Hell; and the questing tongue cannot even taste the departed sacrament of drunkenness. "Hands and Eyes" repeats the same theme of human and animal, young and old, doing their futile best and always failing just a bit. The hands are those of an old shepherd, an infant, and a chimpanzee. The eyes belong to a prostitute, a cat, and an alpine climber. Each soul burns in a cold church the best it may, whether the air be foul or blustering. If there were a God to see all hands and eyes, to hear all prayers, would He have mercy on all?

In *Holes in the Sky*, a child utters the words in the motto poem which become the title of the collection. So in addition to concern for the poet's craft, and the delineation of the postwar feeling, there are a number of poems which are concerned with childhood in general and with the poet's childhood in particular. "Twelfth Night" does not seem so much to celebrate the Epiphany—the shining forth of Christ's glory to the Gentile world represented by the Magi—as the end of the Christmas season. It laments boys who grow up; snows that melt, and, now that Christmas trees must be removed, an undecorated world in which to live. "Aubade for Infants" is an attempt, in the tradition of William Blake's *Songs of Innocence,* to express in verse the feelings and vision of a very small child. Indeed, the MacNeice lines "Something bright / Ignites the dumps of sodden clouds, / Loud and laughing, a fiery face . . ." may well owe some structure of imagery to Blake's line from "Mad Song": "Like a fiend in a cloud." The child is young; the child is also immeasurably old and wise, having flung the dawn song to mother earth before he was born.

The two longest poems in the volume, "The Stygian Banks" and "Letter from India," raise two questions: Why have children, and what happens to the individual in a society when the birth rate is completely out of control? "The Stygian Banks" begins with Troilus' speech from Act III, Scene ii, of Shakespeare's *Troilus and Cressida:* "Like a strange soul upon the Stygian banks / Staying for waftage." In seven cantos, MacNeice addresses himself to the reason people have children. Is it in order to keep themselves young, by following their children's growth to move backward from experience to innocence, to live England's history over again as it appears in the experience and growth of a child? Canto II warns that lives are together, yet separate, like notes in music. Son does not repeat father, nor can a man be his own neighbor. In a brilliantly sharp passage, the poet proclaims:

I am alone
And you are alone and he and she are alone
But in that we carry our grounds we can superimpose them,
No more fusing them than a pack of cards is fused
Yet the Jack comes next to the Queen. Though when they are dealt
You will often fail of the sequence; only you know
That there were such cards in the pack, there are other people
And moss-roses and beanfields and in yourself
Monk and lover and a battered hoop
With you for once behind it—and a coffin
With you for once inside it.

Canto III is based upon the archetype of the nursery rhyme
"Rockabye Baby." It is spring, and the birthright of the child is
never to be grown up, never completed or final. In the same sense,
this is the victory of the baby "when the bough breaks." It may all
end in a topple, a clink, a shutter released; but the dead baby still
has its exposure to experience, the transient becomes the permanent by having been seen, and the roses sealed within the dead
eyes are always red.

In Canto IV this world is shown as a walled garden within
which each generation follows the age-old patterns with different
individuals. To look beyond the wall is like gazing from Being
into Non-Being. But the lover's eyes slip beyond the beloved, beyond generation, to look over the wall. The tired man in the wartime queue, with senses dulled by fatigue, looks beyond the wall
and wonders if, instead of Non-Being, beyond the wall is the reality that makes the walled garden possible. Chaucer's Alison walks
through a spring garden with her arms full of flowers (Canto V),
and we have children in order to be childlike, to taste again
through their palates the green of salad, the red of radish. But we
err if we think the walled garden is our home; instead, we are
ineradicably a pilgrim people, and home is only an inn with a sign
clanking in the night.

Canto VI makes oblique reference to the Shakespeare lines at
the beginning of the poem. The lisping child reaches out to fly
with the bird and to embrace the sea. But some prescient ones
hear the drums of Judgment, so they slacken their pace and im-
plore everything else to take them away. But everything else is
finite and the Judgment is eternal, so no shelter is offered to the
reluctant travelers. During the war years, there were moments

when men stopped haggling for profit long enough to cooperate in the air raids. If they could stop now to look about them and call a tree a tree, this would be the beginning of worldly wisdom.

The final canto brings us back to Troilus, patrolling the Stygian banks, eager to cross. But the value is not on the farther side of the river but within his own eagerness. To the question raised by the poem, there is no answer. But man's glory is to raise the question, and even a false coin "presumes a true mint somewhere." A child's hoop is far from a perfect circle, yet it holds the road. The road is far from straight, but it leads from town to town. The imperfect circle implies perfection *where?* What is man's glory? The answer—no answers here—is the question! And now it is spring.

The other long poem, "Letter from India (for Hedli)," is Mac-Neice's version of William Butler Yeats's theme in "Sailing to Byzantium." Just as Yeats lamented a land so fecund that it could be described only in terms of "salmon-falls" and "mackerel-crowded seas," so MacNeice sees India as a place "where men as fungi burgeon" and the population "breed and broil, breed and brawl." He and Hedli have been writing to each other; their letters cross in the mail; and these letters become the thin connection for the poet with a land where individuals count. The humanist in Mac-Neice is deeply wounded at the sight of a refugee camp in the Sheikhupura High School, where no one has a place of his own, or the slightest privacy, or permanence. Unlike Yeats's evaluation of the artifice of beauty, the hoarded beauties of Buddhist stupa and Mogul tomb cannot atone to MacNeice for this maelstrom of people "where no person counts." The three central themes which the poet juggles and attempts to draw together into some kind of unity at the close are the burgeoning population of India, her life wish which verges on death wish, and the individualism Europeans take for granted. The poet unifies the disparate visions by calling their correspondence the wedding of East and West, and by forecasting their personal reunion—Hedli who is "proud and finite" and yet on whose breast he finds a serene and undistressed East which includes both directions of the compass and yet is neither.

The general theme of childhood is continued by the poet but is narrowed to his nostalgia for his own childhood and to the persons and places he then knew. In "Carrick Revisited," the poet returns to the Carrickfergus of his childhood, the Particular where he landed out of the sea of the Universal. He was torn before birth from the land of his fathers and schooled from the age of ten in a land with accent foreign to his ears. This place was his "bridgehead into reality," but it was equally the "concealment" of reality. "Slum Song" is the Irish equivalent of "Song from India." In the slums of Dublin, "fermenting with children," the growing years are confined in cruel poverty. The youths play cards by broken fanlights; the grown men play the horses; the old man smokes his pipe and laments his lost manhood—all to the refrain "wander near and far," which, in the final quatrain becomes the evening star, both near and far.

In "The Strand," there is a stretch of wet sand where, sixteen years before, his father at age sixty made paddling footsteps. Although his life was "responsibly compiled / Account books of a devout, precise routine," something in the square, black figure stayed solitary and wild. It was sixteen years ago that the father and son walked together on the sand; the father had twelve more years to live; now the poet walks on the same strand and finds there no sign of the visitor who has gone home. "Last Before America" depicts a scene the Irish youth might well have seen: the last rakings of the hay harvest before the family group breaks up, part to stay in Ireland, part to travel to the new world. Pennsylvania or Boston made no difference; it was to a better land because a land of impossible promise. They traveled away from death; yet they, too, died. The emigrants' last view would be certain low islands pointing toward the west, looking like cubs that have lost their mother.

"Godfather," which begins with the word "Elusive," is indeed an elusive poem. Perhaps actually the boy's godfather, he is speedily transformed in the poem to a being who whisks out through revolving doors as the youth enters a café; who is carefree in air raids; and, since godfather may also be death, leaves stone tablets like visiting cards in the graveyard. "Woods" records the poet's father's conviction that English landscape is tame. He never became native to woods; bogs always seemed to him the place to walk. But the boy entered the English woods with Malory's knights, Keats's nymphs, and Shakespeare's *Midsummer Night's Dream,* so the woods to him were an enchanted world. Yet, as he thought about it, he could understand his father's verdict. They were woods, but not forest; one entered them and left them; they were always connected with a manor, village, or farm. The real world of escape would be the neolithic wilds of County Mayo.

"Relics" evidently arises from a return to Oxford, as the poet's mind ranges back along a rosary of relics: leather-bound books, stone buildings, Oxford arches, crocketed pinnacles on the towers, and spires looking down upon an area in which the prehistoric Beaker people of England raised their religious edifices. In "Carol," MacNeice and a lady friend decide to end carol singing by exposing all the grafted growth of ages of blind faith to the searching power of thought. "So why sing carols, darling?" The Christmas angel replies that, although today is today and the Son of God may have vanished from the earth, man is still a spirit who lives on symbols. Money chimes feebly and matter cannot sing; so man should begin again to sing carols.

Holes in the Sky includes a number of Nature poems in which the "pathetic" or "Romantic fallacy" is run backwards and Nature reveals qualities of human nature. "Littoral" shows the sea in many colors and rhythms; it is so "burgeoning with minutiae" that it is like a philosopher who makes cat's cradles of string with his hands while his brain is hard at work elsewhere, or like a widow knitting for her sons but thinking about a tomb in a foreign land. Whether the sea is brain (philosopher) or heart (mother) to whom men are nothings, easily ignored, men recognize they are so afraid of the Unknowable that, like children, they each fill a pail with a little spade and have their own domesticated seashore.

"Western Landscape" is one of the longer poems with more complex philosophical meanings. It, "The Stygian Banks," and "Letter from India" are all representative of a new MacNeice style in which the old diction and the equal number of accents (although not of syllables) in each line is linked to a more elaborate, complex structure of thought than to the old quick-image and instant-symbol. The poet seeks to honor the landscape of Western Ireland in "doggerel." For him, it is Lethe and lotus, although he calls himself the bastard of Western urbanization and claims that he is disfranchised in this country which was once his own. In the middle stanza of the three-stanza poem, the poet considers St. Brandan, a "spindrift hermit" who stood upon this very sea wall and knotted the horizon around his waist. Because he had God, a feeling for the ocean, a moving body, and an unmoved soul, he became part of a fused whole. He chose loneliness as the only life for him; it was also the best because the beyond was there. On this same shore the poet meditates that the special quality of this land is quartz and bog, brute and ghost, land reluctant to be solid, wishing always to be sea. He is no St. Brandan, free of all roots; nor is he rooted peasant and thus united with the land. But he adds one stone to an indifferent cairn and utters the incantation: "With a stone on the cairn, with a word on the wind, with a prayer in the flesh let me honour this country."

Looking down from above, in "Under the Mountain," the sea is a feather, the field a flap buttoned down by the haycocks, and the house an obsolete gadget. But, when the observer comes down from the mountain, the water is scummy; the seaweed stinks; the field is a back-aching crop; and the house, a "maelstrom of loves and hates." But, since the observer came down, this is obviously where he belongs. MacNeice takes the phrase from the Revelation of John the Divine for the poem "No More Sea" and conjectures about a far-future scholar who, finding a fossil shell in that dry world, would try to imagine what it would be like to be an islander, individualistic, and embroiled with ocean.

Three of the Nature poems seem to repeat the theme of Keats's "Grecian Urn"—art, having captured life, has made love immortal. The paintings have been brought out from their wartime hiding in the Welsh caves and are rehung in the poem, "The National Gallery." Theirs is a world in which saints may be gorgeous and hedonists ascetic, in which the senses may know unending joy. The still life lives, and the portrayed flesh and features die. If the gallery windows are opened to let in the air that blows from unconfined and fuller times, it would "rekindle a pentecost in Trafalgar Square." In "The Cromlech," a circle of upright stones has been placed in that arrangement by some group related to the Druids of ancient Britain. The poet places Tom and Tessy, young and supple, against a cromlech, obtuse and old. Both groups are real, he insists, because there is no Life without lives, or values without facts. Thus Tom is here, Tessy is here, the Cromlech is here, and appearance has become reality. "The Cyclist" has precisely the same pattern as "The Cromlech." In the background is the great horse chiseled by prehistoric people out of a chalky hill.

In the foreground ride innumerable boys on their bicycles. When they are on the level or climbing up a hill, they must strain "left, right-left," but when they coast down the long slopes without pedaling, they become as timeless and unending as the great, chalk horse.

II Collected Poems: 1925–1948

This collection of one hundred and eighty-five poems represents the bulk of Louis MacNeice's published verse up to its date of publication in 1949.[7] The volume has nine overlapping divisions: I, 1933–37; II, 1925–29; III, 1931–35; IV, 1936–38; V, *Autumn Journal:* 1939; VI, 1939–40; VII, 1941–44; VIII, 1944–47; IX, 1940–48. The books in which these poems previously appeared include: *Oxford Poetry, 1929* (Section II), edited by Louis MacNeice and Stephen Spender; *Blind Fireworks,* 1929 (II); *Poems,* 1935 (I); *Out of the Picture,* 1937 (IV); *Letters from Iceland,* 1937 (I, IV); *The Earth Compels,* 1938 (IV); *Autumn Journal,* 1939 (V); *Plant and Phantom,* 1941 (VII); *Springboard,* 1944 (VIII); and *Holes in the Sky,* 1948 (IX).

The order of poems within each section is not necessarily chronological, although the earliest poem in the collection is "Genesis" (summer, 1925), and the latest, excepting the dedicatory sestina, is "The Window" (October, 1948). The volume does not include any of MacNeice's translations. Although another collection, *Eighty-Five Poems,* appeared in 1959, *Collected Poems: 1925–1948* remained the most complete one-volume exhibit of MacNeice's poetic work until the appearance of *Collected Poems,* edited by E. R. Dodds in 1967. In the Preface of the 1949 collection, the author states that he feels that, after the lapse of three or four years, an author does well to leave not-so-well alone; and he has resisted the temptation to make many revisions, but within that time he has revised to some minor extent.

There are a few poems included which had not appeared in previous volumes, and one of the most interesting is the dedicatory sestina "To Hedli." The form is especially challenging and involved—six six-line stanzas of irregular pentameter. If the closing words of each line of the first stanza were numbered 1–6, the rhyme scheme of the second stanza would use those same words in the pattern 6–1–5–2–4–3, and each succeeding stanza would

bear the same rhyme relation to its previous stanza. This sets up
the challenge for the poet to develop a page-and-a-half poem with
only six terminal words for all the lines.

The sheer virtuosity of the achievement resides in the fact that
the poem is highly significant in meaning and progress of thought,
as well as devious and complex in prosody. The poet may act
younger than his chronological age, but his thoughts are older. He
has lived too much in the present, looking askance at the coming
gods, and alienated from the gods who had created his fathers in
their image. He stands dumbfounded by the angry questions that
his time pours on the authorities of the past. He lays his ear to the
ground to discover where the Word, like a bulb, is waiting to
make the world gush green (cf. Dylan Thomas' phrase "the green
fuse") through the work of younger poets rather than the present
poets who are growing older.

Once the poet was content with the quick, dazzling image, with
answers which were quick and smooth, with archetypes from
some long-gone writer. But now he is not content. The leaves are
turning, gilt is flaking off all the private images, and all the poets
he knows are condemned to silence unless they can guess some of
the answers which the grim past has cached in the present—answers which are only groped after in this volume. The poet hopes
Hedli will turn the pages and give kind greeting to his waifs and
wraiths of imagery. Then the poet murmurs to himself, "Older
and Older. Which was the right turning?" He speaks of his poetry
as half-blind questions which still lack answers, and the lack
grows no less as he grows older. He has rhythm, image, and half-
answers at half volume. Such as it is, he hopes Hedli will accept it
in November, 1948, as an early Christmas present.

There are few poets who have been so disarmingly frank about
their lacks and limitations. Seemingly, this dedicatory sestina is
the perfect evidence for the trauma of self-examination suggested
by the mood of *Holes in the Sky*. Now, less than a year later, the
mood still holds sway over the poet's mind, and has become far
more explicit in his verse. In this one poem, we find the poet's
sense of growing older, his alienation from the older gods
matched by his horror of the coming ones, his loss of satisfaction
in past technical achievements and the frustration of not yet having reached a new style of writing, his troubling recognition of all
the questions for which he has only half-answers, and his honest

admission that vigor and volume are now at only half-strength.

"The North Sea," "Mahabalipuram," and "The Window" are longer poems which had been published previously in periodicals. The first is complex, but perhaps less realized in idea and image than "To Hedli." The central framework is the story of Sir Patrick Spens and the ballad based on his exploits. The primary image is the porthole of a Scandinavian steamer that sails the same route as the poet had traveled the year before. The traveler assumes that the sea is simply an interval of nothing between ports. But perhaps it is actually the reverse, and the sea journey is all and timeless. The strong secondary image is a Viking ship with "round bright shields on a long gunwale," itching to give the lie to steam and progress. The third image is a hypothetical battleship, swinging its gun turret to take full aim and annihilate the cargo vessel. All that any sailor can do on such a sea is sail on his previous understanding; he is fortunate to have embarked at all, even if his ship never finds a home or a landing. Probably the poet loaded the poem with too heavy a freight of image and meaning. The reading is rough seas, and the cargo decidedly heterogeneous.

"Mahabalipuram," like "Letter from India," arises from a visit to that Asiatic subcontinent. An ancient Hindu temple, dedicated to the worship of a god in the form of a *lingam* (phallus), fronts on the sea. Worshipers come here no more, but the cowherds and Krishna continue to dance on the rock. In "Letter from India," the Western poet was appalled at the fecundity of the Hindu people and at the resultant loss of individualism. But in "Mahabalipuram," worship of the male symbol of generation does not horrify him; he views the carvings on the rock as an Indian variant of Keats's "Grecian Urn." There is the pastoral eternality of Krishna's herds and milkmaids, as well as the dark horror of Vishnu and Shiva. There was a great moment of creative innocence when, thirteen centuries before, an artist looked at this great undifferentiated heap of granite and saw in it the manifold forms of elephant, serpent, antelope, and god.

This sculpture, both austere and orgiastic, confuses us intellectually, but it is the stuff of our dreams and the movements of our bodies if only we had not forgotten how to dance in the Western world. Thus the idyll of the simple and beautiful rustics is trapped forever in the rock. Tourists file by the figure of a creator who is also destroyer, a featureless phallus of granite, "as abstract / As the North Pole." The visitors move on; the waves launched in Australia assault the temple; but the travelers have known for a moment the impact of an avatar, a god taking form and moving their limbs in rhythm with those ageless limbs carved in rock.

"The window," written in October, 1948, is an important variation on the theme of the preceding poem. Canto I describes a bouquet of flowers on a window sill, framed by curtains, and painted by the artist from inside the room, with the light in back of the bouquet. Canto II introduces the central problem of how it is possible, in a "world of flux and bonfires," to achieve something of the coherence, permanence, and order that the artist creates in his painting. The artist's hourglass lies on its side, and no sand slips from credit to debit. Our human hourglass is vertical and nothing can stop its sandy flow.

But there is another flow we know: the impulses that draw us outside ourselves, traitors to self-interest and losers of our own life; these forces are contrasted with those that turn inward upon the waiting self. Is it possible to pronounce a betrothal between the outrush and the backwash? Canto III attempts to give at least a "half-way answer" to the urgent question. We stand on the "edge of senselessness" to mate, breed, and build. We force the primal mud to dance a ballet. Without knowing the how of the process, we can affirm that what art sets in antithesis to life is the very thing we lay claim to in living. Neither "miracle" nor "catalysis" is an adequate explanation of the how of the process; but the poet, like a parent, must take on trust that we can find form and that our lives can transcend the light and shade of living. Then let the poet "jettison his doubt" and see that there is profit where there was loss, that even the face of doom can be gentle. The window in the artist's picture opens, the air blows in, and a sweet scent pervades the room.

It is quite probable that, at this moment in his career, this poem chronicles as much of a victory of faith as MacNeice is capable of. He must jettison his doubt—very good; but when he has jettisoned doubt, what will he see? That even the face of doom can be gentle. This is measured victory. To see it as either full victory or defeat is to ignore one of the poles of tension. But, even as a limited victory, it augurs well for the poetry which will follow the moment of vision and hope.

III   Goethe's Faust (*Parts I and II*), *1951*

In the spring of 1949, when the British Broadcasting Corporation invited Louis MacNeice to prepare a special radio version of *Faust* in honor of Goethe's centenary, he at first declined for the very good reasons that he knew "next to no German" and had always rather disliked Goethe. But when his friend, the eminent German scholar, E. L. Stahl, expressed his willingness to go over the work with him line by line, MacNeice embarked on the "foolhardy" adventure.

MacNeice's version translates about eight thousand of the twelve thousand lines of the original. Although this abridgement was meant primarily for broadcasting, it seemed to the poet that the work might be improved by abridgement, and he recalled that Goethe himself had admitted that the drama needed cutting. MacNeice aimed at a line-for-line translation with a prosody equivalent to or identical with Goethe's own poetic form. The Oxford University paperback reprint edition of 1960 [8] quotes a London *Times* Literary Supplement endorsement of the translation as "an accurate animated version of *Faust*. . . . Mr. MacNeice has taken very few liberties with Goethe's verse; and there can be no doubt of his exceptional artistry, tact, and agility of mind. A new translation of *Faust* has long been called for; the present one, by a distinguished contemporary poet, should make Goethe's great drama accessible to many potential readers who have been put off by the older translations."

The reprint goes on to mention Barker Fairley's enthusiastic review in the *Partisan Review:* "This is what lovers of *Faust* have been waiting for ever since Shelley gave up the task too soon—a poet-translator, not a pedant, one who brought with him something of the creative force that shaped the German poem. Naturally we come to this volume with high expectations and the reward is there. There is scarcely a page without the felicities and surprises that only a poet can spring."

My colleague in the Language-Literature Division of the University of South Florida, Dr. Rainulf A. Stelzmann, assures me that, on the whole, MacNeice's translation is quite adequate. He finds occasions on which the author deviates from the German to turn a pleasing phrase and some on which, even with the help of Dr. Stahl, MacNeice seems to have misunderstood the text.

For example, Professor Stelzmann points out within the narrow confines of pages 168–94 a number of such faults. On page 168, MacNeice uses "yeomanry" and "landlords" where "mercenary soldiers" and "innkeepers" would be more accurate. The next page translates "his fairest" whereas the German suggests "anybody's fairest," or a lady of easy virtue. The rather clumsy phrase (p. 174) "what that technique you use meant," might more accurately be translated "what your art was leading us to." The phrase "feel appalled" (p. 177) rather secularizes the German "fear and trembling" or "awe." The "commander-in-chief" (p. 180) is a rather blown-up version of "butler" or "chamberlain." Some misunderstanding is indicated (p. 194) in the translation of "It is easier to discover a louse in a fur coat than 'a knave in the bosom' " as "The knave in the bosom/Lies low like a fraud/But the lice in the sheepskin/Come gladly abroad."

Dr. Stelzmann points out, however, in extenuation of the translation, that some awkwardness or lack of accuracy may well have been enforced by the ambitious attempt to retain the metrical pattern of the original. One of Dr. Stelzmann's advanced students, Mrs. Robert L. Zetler, pointed out the rather abrupt and heavy-footed translation of the much-admired invocation of Gretchen before the statue of the Mater Dolorosa (p. 120) as "Mary, bow down,/Beneath thy woeful crown,/Thy gracious face on me undone!" Again, in partial defense, it might be pointed out that MacNeice's style quite consistently leans toward the simple rather than the elaborate, the flippant rather than the reverent. Certainly the translation is a technical tour de force for a poet who is at home in the ancient tongues, but to whom German was relatively new ground, even with expert help.

IV   Ten Burnt Offerings (1952)

These poems[9] are a product of a year spent in Greece with the British Council, March, 1950, through April, 1951; and they are printed in the order of composition. Some had appeared previously in *The New Statesman and Nation, World Review,* and *Botteghe Oscure;* some had been used in broadcasts of the B.B.C. The dedicatory poem is dated May Day, 1951, a date significant of both the first day of spring and the time for a Communist parade and demonstration. But significantly, the poem has nothing to do with either; it deals instead with the great hope of all poets.

The lines are a series of paradoxes leading up to the final phoenix transmutation. Every voyage is a death, each action a loss, a poem sings its own death song, and its meaning is borne like a cross. But the poet loves to feed the flames of creativity with whatever pittances he is able to give. The words die by burning, in order that the Word may live. It is a commonplace to say that the words of Scripture are not the Word of God in and of themselves but that they become the Living Word when they are communicated to believing hearers. It is something like this that the poet is writing and hoping—that the dry words of his text may become for the reader the Living Word of transforming experience.

The collection is made up of ten long poems; each is composed of four contrasting movements, perhaps indebted to T. S. Eliot's *Four Quartets*. The political huckstering and the barroom clichés of the past are absent. The only descriptions of the Greek landscape are those which are integral to the meaning of the poems. The poet's interests are often religious: the Mars Hill of Paul's Sermon in Athens (II, "Areopagus"); Doubting Thomas, Apostle to India (IV, "Didymus"); a little Easter Hymn for Christ's Resurrection (III, "Cock o' the North"); a Canticle of Francis of Assisi (V, "Our Sister Water"); Jacob's Ladder (VIII, "Day of Returning").

The lecturer in Classical languages reveals his historical interests in: I, "Suite for Recorders" (the Elizabethans); III, "Cock o' the North" (Lord Byron and Meleager); IV, "The Island" (flight of Icarus); VIII, "Day of Returning" (Homecoming of Odysseus). The poet also contributes in "The Death of a Cat" (IX) to the Eliot cat-cult a brilliant and moving poem which somehow manages to be consequential. The collection ends with an unabashed love lyric "Flowers in the Interval" (X).

The extraordinary capability of the poet for technical dexterity is seen in the wide range of style and the very difficult metrical challenges he sets and meets: rhyme according to many diverse prosodies, some unryhmed passages, short lines and long, some with dense diction and slow movement, others swift as popular ballads, parodies by the dozen, blank verse, quatrains, tercets, sestets, octets, *terza rima* pure and bastardized, and some rhythms and rhymes which are quite original to the poet. *Ten Burnt Offerings* represents the mature, reflective MacNeice whom both the poet and the critics had been awaiting.

In "Suite for Recorders" (I), the poet takes a rather insignificant passage from Shakespeare's *As You Like It*—"it strikes a man more dead than a great reckoning in a little room"—and gives it a Tudor momentousness that makes the pages ring with the authentic tone of Elizabethan rhetoric. Canto I has ten quatrains of tetrameter, rhyming *abcc*, with some of the rhymes ghost or slant, and some of the rhythms sprung. The lines give the effect of great condensation, and the often elliptical thought is rather difficult to follow. In this collection, MacNeice has clearly abandoned the simplicity of style which had hitherto been his trademark, although the long poems in *Holes in the Sky* had given warning of this growing complexity of structure, dialectic, and reference.

The first four quatrains of "Suite for Recorders" gather up some of the ingredients of the English Renaissance: the shepherds and nymphs of pastoral poetry, Sir Walter Raleigh's adventures both on the sea and in the Queen's court, Marlowe and the flowering of the drama, the romantic Tudor admiration of Leander's watery rendezvous with Hero, and the dream of Eldorado. It is notable that all these ingredients involve death; death on beds of flowers, on the headsman's block, in a tavern, on the sea, in a vain quest. These many changes played on the central theme of death probably take their keynote from the Shakespearean passage "strikes a man more dead. . . ." The modern poet sees Black Jenny spinning a coarse pall both for Persepolis in ancient Persia and the Communist May Day of the Proletarian revolution. Now the great reckonings of history come, in which neither the cheat nor the schemer outlives or outdies his youthful beauty. Death is even nascent in fertility—"black fingers . . . bear fruit"; and spring pays off every reckoning.

Canto II, a brilliant evocation of the golden precariousness of the Elizabethan Age, is in six-line stanzas, rhyming *abcded*, with the rhyming lines trimeter and the unrhyming lines running from seven to nine feet. As Shakespeare suggested, great reckonings take place in "little rooms," little plots, little lifetimes, while the shrill recorders play after meat. The Elizabethan courtiers, nobles, and adventures are depicted as "Mayflies [variant of May Day] in a silver web which dangled over chaos." The lovely arabesques of Elizabethan music spray up against the silence of the headsman coming with his ax. The courtier hides a knife behind his smile; the ecclesiastic has "faggots in his eyes"; the cautious scholar

treasures forbidden books in his private library. All three are conscious of the web deep in their bowels, and they know that, in the
contest between old faith and new learning (cf. Donne's "An
Anatomie of the World"), no one dares to explore the question
of causality.

All the rich costuming is only stage props for men and women
who have been inadequately briefed to make one first, last appearance, which, even if it is not word-perfect, they will never
have a chance to repeat. Was it a golden age, an age of discovery?
It was also an age of "madrigals and liars," an age when men died
young. They revolted on tightropes; they tasted the blithe despair
of youth; caught in the dubious web, they tested their white lies
against the black truth. They were violent and bloody men, with
starved and sweaty servants whom Spenser, Sidney, Marlowe,
and Shakespeare liked to disguise as mimic shepherds. If their life
was a game, an art, an orgy, it was also a mortification leading to
premature death. And they left behind flowers, second best experiences, a starting point—or was it a blind end, the spring of a
trap?

The eleven quatrains of Canto III, rhyming *aabb* in iambic
tetrameter, begin with pride in history, in ancestry, in posterity,
and a naïve acceptance of the "gag" that we are "members one of
another." We do not produce the higher consciousness; neither
Tamberlaine with his crown nor Corydon with his flowery wreath
was satisfied; our alter egos chose us, not we them. So the dark
nothings of negatives is the setting in which these brief candles
magnificently blaze. These "angry ghosts . . . threw their voices
. . . Greatly in a little room."

Canto IV is a pastoral in four unrhymed stanzas of alternate six-
and three-foot lines. It is quite possible that the "Her" of the canto
is a personification of the bucolic peace of the countryside. If so,
then this is a pastoral elegy. She passed this way and will never
return until Judgment Day, which is also May Day when Maypole
ribbons are wound around the Cross. Battles were once fought on
this spot, so the shepherd urges his flock to beware the rusty wire
and the tank-traps. He plays on a borrowed pipe; he is only a
hireling shepherd (Gospel of John 10:12); but, although his hire
is due, it goes unpaid and his songs go unheard. But the flocks
shall hear in the twilight the song he sings of Her.

The second poem, "Areopagus," is distinguished technically

only in the third canto, where, in each six-line stanza, the last word of line one ends line six; the last word of line two, line four; and the last word of line three, line five. The first five lines of each stanza are in tetrameter, with a final pentametric line. Canto I shows the Hebrew-Christian Saul-Paul preaching in Greece the land of olives, an appetizer with a stone in it for the tired mind, a snub to the ancient gods, a titillation to the philosophers of Athens, and a threat to a historic cult and culture: ". . . he whetted the blade/Of the wit of his faith to slice their pagan/Prides to the quick."

It is the condition of man (Canto II), both in the Classical and the Christian worlds, to have inherited some curses and to breed others of their own. It was late in time for the Classical deities, but early for Paul and Christ. Mary and Jesus had not yet been scaled down to fit an ikon or a niche. Christ on the Cross was fresh reality, a moment in time, before the bishops and the organization builders gilded the nails and boxed the Cross into a square from which it could not escape. In a "flash on a lonely dust-white road," Paul was converted on his way to Damascus. The scales fell from his eyes in the city, but was the experience on the road a new opening or an old trap?

Canto III picks up Paul's reference (Acts of the Apostles 17:23) to the Athenian altar dedicated "to an Unknown God." The poet decides that such a designation would be proper for the god of modern men. If possible, because their tradition is Christian, it would be good for the unknown god to be Christ; but if necessary, it could be the Furies, for all must pay for their sins. What is unknown is dreaded, but yet it could turn out to be kind. Even of the Furies, he writes, "The fiery pack bays no more; their note is new." The poet asks Paul to postpone the day of doom. After all, even in Classical antiquity Orestes was finally acquitted. The body may seem to Paul a tomb; but to others it has seemed bread, wine, and flowers in bloom. Can modern man find a way to transform his Furies (avenging demons) into Eumenides (ministering angels)? The poem ends on the note of reconciliation of Christianity and Greek mythology, Furies and Eumenides: "Nurses of fear and hope, come taste our honey, taste our wine."

Lord Byron's *Don Juan* had a marked effect on Auden and Mac-Neice's *Letters from Iceland*. D. Burnham, in a *Commonweal* article, points out the obvious attractiveness of Byron's manner to

Auden and his group: "The witty use of the colloquial even for serious purpose, the easy mixture of present-day and past, the scholarly background supplying an additional background but never obtrusively: this is simply the way the mind of an educated, sophisticated, well-informed man naturally works. . . ."[10] With its title and motto from *Don Juan*, "Cock o' the North" is not only about Byron at Missolonghi, but sections of it are parodies of his style. The first fourteen lines of Canto I have the metrical form of the nursery rhyme "Little Jack Horner." The next four lines are based on Byron's famous anapaests, "The Destruction of Sennacherib." The next eight lines seem to echo the stately cadences of Lord Edward Elgar's "Pomp and Circumstance," and the last four lines are a little Easter Hymn celebrating the resurrection of Christ. With its metrical brilliance and speed of movement, the canto describes Byron's aristocratic background, the influence of Miltiades, the pose of his character Don Juan, and "the glory that was Greece"; but they all end in the swamps and fevers of Missolonghi.

Canto II likens Byron to Meleager the Argonaut, slayer of the Calydonian boar, of whom it was prophesied to his mother that he would live as long as a certain brand remained unburned. After he killed his uncles in an argument over the boar, his mother Althea threw the brand into the fire and thus killed her own son. Canto III mingles the images of Easter candles, cannon, boar, and flame. The physician delivers the verdict that the vein might just as well be closed; Lord Byron is dying of excessive leeching without ever having used his sword in battle.

Canto IV is constructed on the basic rhythms of Robert Burns's "Scots, wha hae wi' Wallace bled," but it would be a mistake to imagine that the parodic verse style makes the meaning of the poem artificial or cheap. There can be no mistaking the sincerity with which this last canto weaves in and out from Burns through "Lord Randal, My Son," to Meleager's boar and the Turkish curved sword which becomes the boar's tusk in the night. The dying Byron cries:

> Mither! Mither! *Crede Biron!*
> Was it my fault you bore me lame
>   To a warld o' sharks and dandies?
> To thae bricht lichts where licht is nane?
>   Christ gies licht but nae to pagans!

And, at the close, Byron calls to his mother in Aberdeen to throw his brand in the fire; "I will hae the courage o' my fear/And blaze a path to silence." The most astonishing thing about this whirling farrago of styles and speeds is its emotional impact as it shows the Scottish peer wasting all his beauty, genius, and youth in a dubious battle with fevers and factions in a Greek swamp.

Poem IV, "Didymus," considered by some critics to be the finest poem of the collection, is based on the legend that the Doubting Thomas of the Scriptures ("Except I shall see in his hands the print of the nails, and put my finger into the print of the nails, and put my hand into his side, I will not believe" John, 20:25) became the great Christian missionary to India, and finally India's patron saint. Canto I, in free verse, begins with the India against which Thomas is pitted: a land in which a child is "Born every second and reborn regardless," which worships a phallus of blind, indifferent, incredibly fertile procreation (cf. "Mahabalipuram"), a phallus which appears like a column of mute black stone hung around with grace notes. Thomas is no prince nor sage nor god. His only weapons are troubled eyes, a questioning mind, and two plain crossed sticks. In the crypt (Canto II) of a simple Portuguese "Church of the Little Mount" lies the body of the patron saint of India. Peter would have won India by talking big; John would have performed a miracle; Paul would have laid abstract to abstract. All Thomas has is two clumsy fisherman hands, but they have been plunged into the wounds of Christ. The history of India is full of the stories of kings who never raised a single hand to help their people although their religion describes gods who could at will sprout hands. Thomas has only two hands, but they are strong, and they can meet in prayer.

In the third canto, Thomas soliloquizes on the blessedness of those who believe spontaneously and who ask no difficult questions, to whom all water is wine, and who have the faith to wait. He doubts that he has any right to preach or write in the name of Christ. He knows that the oppressed Indian masses can find and keep the Great Friend, Jesus Christ—but is Christ also Thomas' friend? The soliloquy continues in Canto IV. Is it possible for Thomas, in his blindness, to preach light to India? The millions of India gobble crumbs from Shiva's table until his dancing foot comes down to crush them indifferently. Thomas' gospel grants to each ant its worth, but it is a gospel by proxy because Thomas preaches a faith he dares not claim as his own. His hands failed once because they needed a test. Those same hands that taught him once that spirit can also be man now grope through the dark to prove that all men are spirit. The proof of his groping is found in a bare church on a bare plaque which yet is somehow adequate: "To one who had thrust his fingers into the wounds of God."

The first canto of Poem V, "Our Sister Water," is a variation of Francis of Assisi's famous Canticle: the world's best and the heart's best is water. MacNeice would add to Francis' description: water is not only humble, precious, and chaste; she is also sometimes spendthrift and harlot. Pindar praised the virtues of water to the oligarchs, but Keats lamented the transitoriness of fame by describing himself as one "whose name was writ in water." Wine is related to luxury; milk, to babies; water, to dying men. Thales was right in saying that man's origin was neither in fire nor air nor earth, but in water.

On a hot day in a dry country the poet orders a cup of Turkish coffee. It is placed on the table—at a price; and beside it—quite free—stands a glass of water, a tower of liquid light. In such dry lands, men tell tall tales about the demons of the dust; but they can be matched any day by those *jongleurs de Dieu,* the dancing waters.

Canto II is composed of eight-line stanzas rhyming *aabbccdd,* generally seven feet in length, and predominantly iambic in stress. With his special flair for contemporaneity and the relevance of the poet's work to the modern industrial world, MacNeice shifts gears abruptly but quite logically from *Sor Acqua* to John Watt and the steam engine. In the 1770's Watt came to Birmingham, and there he murdered Sister Water, boiling her into steam, because he wanted to use not her but her ghost. He and Matthew Boulton built the Soho Foundry to manufacture English locomotives. The founders would be deeply shocked to know that today the Soho factory makes only weighing machines because they had a soft spot for things that puff and bray. The grave of John Watt is the grave of the whole steam age. Although steam comes from water, the two things Watt, with his dry Northern mouth, really loved, were steam and cash—both of them dry.

Canto III takes its starting point from Canto I, with Canto II as a kind of modern application of the theme. The poet, who is still

drinking his cup of Turkish coffee, considers the water in his
homeland in the West, squelching around the ankles of peasant
girls, or lifted up, a "bucket of windblown gold." He thinks of
water in the East: borne by humpbacked oxen of India down a
ramp to fill the pitchers of girls in saris; or in rice paddies, or in
pools of Moghul gardens. In this Middle Eastern land, the "red
mouths of water melons gape and slobber" while women with
dark handkerchiefs, dark glasses, and dark eyes fidget past. There
on the table stands the tumbler of water, a perfect example of
great in little: a leaf from the rod with which Moses smote the
rock to bring the gushing water; the "still waters" of David's
psalm. Water is the miracle out of a rock, a royal flush in the
hand, a river nymph on the table, a tumbler, a chameleon, a
clown, the conjurer of God.

Canto IV, in rhymed couplets of irregular length, reminds us
that water is the beginning, the birthright we sold for a "mess of
lungs and limbs." Like the water from which we came, we are
constant only in our variability. When Keats withdrew to Rome
and illness, he left water a new name for her archives—Adonais,
maiden knight of the sensual world. We and water are both alive.
We roll up on the solid black earth, or spray into the thin air, yet
at last we must fall back to the bed in which we were conceived
and born, the bed of the ocean, the bed of our own death.

Poem VI, "The Island," probably the least significant of the
poems, is certainly the most difficult to pin down to geographical
locations. In all four of its cantos the poet seems to refer to the
island of Ogygia, the place the nymph Calypso held Odysseus
captive until Hermes came with the ultimatum of the Olympian
gods that he must be released. The first canto (seven six-line
stanzas rhyming *abcded,* with five four-foot lines and a final three-
foot line) describes the island dawn amid a symphony of donkeys,
with the light flowing down the mountains like water. In the past,
as now, the Sun proved to be a deceiver, promising no more than
he could give, but more than men could receive: wealth, glory,
freedom, life. When Icarus flew too high, that freedom lopped off
his wings like a knife, and he fell by this island. It is now a place
where laboring wisdom leaves things until tomorrow. It asks for
no freedoms, only a time of reprieve.

The second canto describes a Greek mountain village where
there is no horizon across the sea but where letters arrive from

emigrants in Cleveland and Detroit. According to tradition, on this spot Hermes gave the message of the gods to Calypso. The Western world was the land of the dead for ancients; now the skyscrapers of New York support the little cottages of Greece. The third canto (eleven triplets rhyming *aba* with lines alternately long and short) depicts an August siesta, with the traveler at peace, grateful that the world is not a shambles after all. The cicadas make a noise like a sawmill, and the sheep he tries to count in order to sleep look at him with the outraged, sullen stare of refugees. The sleeper dreams that he is running with dogs at his heels; the dogs turn into wolves, the wolves into men, and he is driven before a judge, seated in his glory on vast gray rocks, wearing a dirty wig, himself frightened, with a tic beating in his cheek. When the sleeper awakes, he reflects that the inhabitants of these islands are prisoners, men who do not believe in freedom, or who have forgotten what it means, or who have never known it at all. The fourth canto (nine six-line stanzas rhyming *abcaad* in four-foot lines) is quiet with the approach of evening and the smooth sound of water running down the irrigation canals. The sun sets swaggeringly, and its place is taken by a new moon. Many who were reared on this island now live in foreign lands where their lot is improved. But they have had to learn how to get along without their island wine and oil and the slow island concord of life.

Poem VII, "Day of Renewal," is the most autobiographical of the ten poems; and, in regard to the practice of poetry, it is the most significant. The first canto (six eight-line stanzas of pentameter, rhyming *abcbdefd*, with the final line in each stanza in tetrameter) states the immediate problem quite boldly: "Do I prefer to forget it?" with the antecedent of "it" an unwritten but understood "middle age." If this poem were written in the first half of 1951, the poet was forty-three years of age and obviously concerned about it:

> This middle stretch
> Of life is bad for poets; a sombre view
> Where neither works nor days look innocent
> And both seem now too many, now too few.

With the Hesiodic echo in the third line, the poet turns from his works to his days. As a boy of ten, he was told that presents must

now be useful; but he kept turning back to the beginning of each
fairy tale. His birthday candles increased in number, until they
vanished altogether. He found it hard to accept a prosaic place of
birth and liked to imagine a different, wilder, mountainous birthplace. His deepest desire was just to be, not to have to become;
but only Death, traveling westward, is; life becomes. Even places
become dated and dead. So he began, with the heredity of physi-
ology, and with his mind shaped by taboos and values. What he is
remains just what he is; it may be predetermined to the insignifi-
cance of a comma; nevertheless, it somehow manages to keep its
time, place, and glory.

The second canto reflects the boyish note of the preceding canto
both by the choice of Dick Whittington and his cat as the main
characters and by the deliberate and delightful echoes of the
rhythm and cadence of "Humpty-Dumpty," "Ding-Dong Bell,"
and "Ride a Cock Horse." Like the story of Whittington, life is all
bits and pieces: a banquet and a barefoot mile, toasts and prices,
gifts and leases which expire. The events are like the clothes in a
man's closet, each eloquent of a single event, a rainstorm, a funeral, a voyage to India. Perhaps in that same closet are all the
unanswered questions of childhood: Why? When? Who put us
here? Who'll pull us out? And what about my next birthday?

The third canto, in blank verse, names over some of the poet's
own milestones, the "private code-words" of his time and place;
age twenty-one was the time of the economic slump; thirty, the
fear of war; forty, and his arm sore from shots. Now he is forty-
three, at sea in the very early morning, heading into the port of
Athens.

In the fourth canto (eleven quatrains of tetrameter, rhyming
abcb) the child is still within him; and that inner boy still lights
candle beacons both for victory and defeat. Fall is a special time
for him:

> For all my years are based on autumn,
> Blurred with blue smoke, charred by flame,
> Thrusting burnt offerings on a god
> Who cannot answer to his name.

With that one reference to the title phrase, the poet shifts to the
mythological figure of Cadmus, who founded a city and sowed

dragon teeth of his fears. Each dark furrow sprouts with eyes; from each eye glitters a spear. And the prayer for helpers ends in mutual clashes of personality and temperament. However, it must not be forgotten that some still survive to lay stones, light fires, and build cities. We all want to eat our cake and have it too. Perhaps we can, by seeing to it that no flame shines less than all the flames, and that through the smoke there drifts a god—not the god of the beginning of the canto, who cannot answer to his name —but "a god who needs no name."

Weighted down by the dubiety of the poem and the agonized honesty of the poet, it is easy to count the doubts and miss the affirmations. But it is important to remember that the poet called this poem "Day of Renewal." The notes of renewal include the survivors of life's clashes who build houses and cities and who light the fires of homes. It is possible for a man to eat his own cake, without eating the cakes of other men, or losing the cake of the world. The builders and the sharers worship a god who needs no name precisely because he is self-identifying; he bears his own credentials in their lives.

Poem VIII, "Day of Returning," has a Miltonic quality that arises out of its cheerful juxtaposition of Classical mythology and biblical character. The two who return are Odysseus and Jacob, and they bear more similarities than we would expect. The first canto has quite experimental prosodic form and represents Mac-Neice's interest in formal complexity. There are seven quatrains in the canto; each quatrain has the first line of seven metrical feet, the second of six, the third of five and the fourth of three; quatrains one, three, five, and seven end with "Ithaca"; quatrains one, two, four, and six end the second line with "wept." We are back on the Island of Ogygia; Odysseus kneels on the beach, with his back to the terraces of Calypso's island, to the sound of that sweet, enchanting voice, and to the sight of that weeping face. He looks out toward the terraced sea that hides Ithaca and yearns for the crisp commands of his wife Penelope as she works in kitchen and laundry. Here the bed is too soft, the wine is never rough, and the scent of flowers is always too heavy. We are all sometimes homeless (Canto II), homesick; godless, and godfearing. The poet paints a prim picture of Methodist piety: hard work in hope of an afterlife, the prim repose on Sunday of working hands, the harmonium in the parlor. The immortal life Calypso offers is only

an islanded escape from time and home. Penelope never escaped;
her husband did and "found that bliss a prison" where he wept
every day for his wife, for his dog, and for real people who live
ordinary lives. Odysseus longs for his "day of returning" (Canto
III); for who can bear the love of a goddess—unreal, immortal,
ageless, too smooth, with no problems. This island can never be
home.

The fourth canto introduces the story of Jacob in seven seven-
line stanzas of tetrameter, rhyming *abcdedf*. Like Odysseus, Jacob
has been called crafty. He robbed his brother, hoaxed his father,
and was altogether a practical man. But he also had his hours of
vision—that ladder with angels, like bees, searching for honey in
the hearts of men and making them feel suddenly happy when
they found it. There was that night he wrestled with God and was
left with a limp in the thigh and a job to do—to father a chosen
people. Laban exacted seven years of toil and then tried to cheat
him; his wives and children were jealous of one another. There
was the year that Joseph was lost, and that other year when he
was found, with corn, in Egypt. He continues to be troubled by a
recurring nightmare about a dark, stony place and an adversary
against whom he has no chance. He wakes in a sweat in the dark;
but, being a practical man, he reaches out his hand and finds that
it is his own domestic darkness. The ache in his thigh convinces
him that he is at home, no more a chooser, but chosen to father
the chosen. He has little to ask of God except that day should
return "each day of returning."

To lovers of the feline, Poem IX, "The Death of a Cat," will be
deeply moving; to many others, trivial and disgusting. The first
canto is composed of four six-line stanzas of blank verse. Something is gone from the apartment in Athens, an absence that re-
proves the master's negligence. The poet was absent when the cat
was missing for six nights, during two of which he was dead. The
cat returned to a closed apartment door in Athens, "his life in
tatters." Now the poet looks about the room with vague dislike,
because it is a room with too many exits, with frosted glass where
the cat "lurked and fizzed, the family puck."

But what difference does it make that a cat is dead? To begin
an answer to that question (Canto II), he was beautiful: with
blue crisp fur, a white collar and white paws, and eyes with the
light which is held in a rock crystal. A dancer, incurably male, he

was a clown, a fencer, an odalisque. His was a self-contained life, and he was more than an object. In his eyes glowed the "light that was locked in the stone" long before the poet's time or his own. To a cat, Athens was canyons of angry sounds, of catastrophe and cataclysm, all its smells and sounds in cataracts. The wheels of the city "ravelled out his being" until he ended in "one high horrible twang of breaking catgut." He dragged himself back home by obstinate instinct, by following a dark thread spun out of the labyrinth of his "catsoul"—and the thread snapped a few yards from his closed door. His purpose gone, only pain remained. Is all this grief out of proportion (Canto IV)? Certainly. Is it simply sentimentality? Possibly. After all, even the *Greek Anthology* laments its pets in the late, non-Classical period. So this poem is to be considered an epitaph: to a person in a small way, who touched human lives with a "whisk of delight."

Poem X, "Flowers in the Interval," is a rich, joyful love poem by a poet who wrote several notable poems about love, but always with seeming difficulty. MacNeice generally was hampered by his own astringent masculinity, robbed of imagery by his honesty, and frustrated by his preference to express weighty things in light verse. This poem is perhaps the greatest fullness of love poetry that he ever managed in its union of image, emotion, and melody. In the first canto (three seven-line stanzas, in unequal lines, rhyming *abacded*), the poet offers these poems in the Yeatsian phrase "of heartfelt artifice" to the woman who is "ivoried warmth," whose hair curled over her forehead, and who gazed at him with "ambivalent/Tigercat eyes." He came across her when she was still a dreaming princess beneath a spell. When her waking power spread out, thorns blossomed; and she made the commonplace rare. She is all the places (Canto II) he has been with her, but also all the places she has been without him. She is the Alps of her early years, the Berlin of the prewar years; but still she stands unique in her own right and light; and he is grateful.

In the third canto (thirteen triplets of pentameter, rhyming *aba cac dcd*, etc., and a single last line), the beloved intoxicates like all the drinks that they have had together. Each ray of her influence "distills/A benediction" and puts an end to doubt. She is the corn-and-fire dance, a caryatid, the moods of the sun and the water; she is a view into the wideness of space, but brought near. The fourth canto (ten six-line stanzas of tetrameter rhyming *abcbcd*) celebrates the singing voice of his actress wife. In a voice like "still grey dawn," she sings the works of Villon, Sidney, Campion, and Purcell. They are restored to life by her interpretation, both on the stage and here with him "on the edge of the world." The dreaming princess and her sleeping castle are both his. When she awakes, she sprinkles "all his days with daylight." When the wind and the night begin to trouble, he crosses his fingers, grits his teeth, and waits for her face to appear. It is incredible to him that her presence never fails to give a "timeless perfume to each moment."

V   Autumn Sequel: A Rhetorical Poem in XXVI Cantos (*1954*)

In the autumn of 1938, Louis MacNeice had written a long occasional poem, *Autumn Journal,* dealing with the personal and political events of that fall leading up to Christmas. Since that year was the period of Chamberlain's appeasement of Hitler at Munich, the betrayal of the Czechs, and the bombing of Barcelona, political events and the poet's personal reaction dominate the book. Fifteen years later, the poet produced a sequel, also occasional, but with some significant shifts in attention.[11] One of the most notable is the preponderance in the sequel of the personal over the political. The disquieting factor about this shift is that the personal references deal so often with the tired, the dead, or the dying.

Excerpts from this poem had already appeared in the *London Magazine* and *Encounter,* and major portions of it had been broadcast by the B.B.C. in the summer of 1954. The motto from Walt Whitman—"Do I contradict myself?/Very well then I contradict myself . . ."—raises some interesting questions: Is the contradiction the relation of *Autumn Journal* to *Autumn Sequel,* or is there an integral contradiction with the *Sequel* itself? Certainly after an interval of fifteen years, a sequel raises the additional questions of both motivation and continuity. Why was it written, and is it a continuation of the same or is it different from the original work?

Perhaps the proper place to start would be to point out similarities between the *Journal* and the *Sequel.* A reviewer in the London *Times,* November 20, 1954, was convinced that the *Sequel* was made of pretty familiar stuff: "Here once again are the brightly-coloured pub-talk, the Epicurean devotion to individual

friendships, the nostalgic pictures of childhood or Oxford days." [12]
The invidious reference to the diction of the poem is a substantial
one, for *Holes in the Sky* concluded with several long poems
which presented a pattern of philosophical complexity, imagistic
density, and more abstract language than would be expected from
the rapid-fire, read-as-you-run poet. This new form then dominated the next volume, *Ten Burnt Offerings*, the chief work of the
mature poet.

Now, in *Autumn Sequel*, many passages slip back into the old
manner—so many, in fact, that the whole volume has a retrospective ring. *Terza rima* suggests Lord Byron and the ottava rima
form used in *Don Juan* and imitated by Auden in *Letters from
Iceland*. Clearly this kind of rhythm—a favorite of Eliot, Auden,
and MacLeish—goes back to the early youth and the first literary
associations of Louis MacNeice. The volume also strikes a retrospective note by the examples of the poet's virtuosity as a parodist
of Yeats, William Empson, and Dylan Thomas. As for MacNeice's
capacity to say deeper things than can be contained in folk-ballad
rhythms, the *Sequel* is not only retrospective but retrogressive.
There is a possible explanation in the title, which clearly points to
a connection with something in the past. Perhaps as the poet reread *Autumn Journal* and planned a sequel, he both consciously
and unconsciously imitated his own earlier style of utterance.

However, he did not necessarily imitate all his earlier subject
matter. For example, the *Times* reviewer points out his devotion
to individual friends. It is quite true that there are so many references to friends of the poet, particularly deceased friends, that
long sections of the poem read like the obituary column of a metropolitan London daily. However, it is important to note two special circumstances related to these Epicurean friendships: first,
the obvious postwar toll of middle age which makes many of the
references necessarily obituary in nature; second, in *Springboard*,
MacNeice included the important poem "The Kingdom" which is
his own special and private answer to a totalitarian world. The
citizens of the kingdom were all individualists, and their portraits
were based on real persons.

In the *Sequel* the friends mentioned are what another reviewer
called "anarchs and artists whose unruly creativity is the life-
giving antidote to the monotonous rhythms of an age whose pulse
beat is that of the machines we mind and which do not mind

us." [13] Here is an old and a new reason for the mention of friends in the *Sequel*. It is entirely appropriate for MacNeice, after the personal friendships extolled in "The Kingdom," to document his thesis with the men and women he knows and trusts the most, in and out of this world. Thus, in this chapter, the long lists of friends are treated not only as similarities with the old, but also as characteristics of the new MacNeice.

The nostalgic pictures of childhood and Oxford days are certainly present in *Autumn Sequel*, but far fewer in number depict childhood than in earlier collections. In fact, the only substantial reference to the poet's childhood is a passage that arises from the coincidence that he was visiting Norwich on Halloween—and what person does not remember his childhood on All Hallows' Eve? In Canto XVII, he recalls tiptoed visits with the cook on Halloween. She was a Catholic farmer's daughter who entertained the rather serious rectory children with laughter, jokes, riddles, and divination of the tea leaves left in a cup. Then the boy would turn unwillingly to creep back into a cold bed in a cold room.

On the other hand, there are a number of references to Oxford. The poet visits his old college in October (Canto XII), when both buildings and fellows seem "all dead stone." He leaves the station and heads for a book contract and a steak. On the way he passes a shop where Esther (all the names of friends are fictitious) once bought whiteheart cherries in June and the canal where Gavin and he had a cosmic conversation one long afternoon when they were becalmed in a hired canoe. And he thinks of the clique he had belonged to when he came up to Oxford in 1926. Now he and Boyce return in middle age to Oxford to dine "In Wolsey's arrogant hall" and to bow their heads to a Latin grace.

In Canto XIV he cherishes some rather frank recollections of the Oxford boys who regularly crossed the "Bridge of Booze" which led to the "Castle Crapulous," or who became habitués of "Queer Street with Baroque doorways," where from the shadows shrill voices fluted "My dear! My dear!" Others went to call on "Potiphar's wife" or the "Moabite Madames." Still others turned to political clubs, where the lust was for power and where everyone toasted the Status Quo. Still others became worshipers in the temple of "Aesthetic Bliss," where they prayed for the time when science and god would be replaced by good taste and beauty. He makes brief reference to one other visit to Oxford (Canto XXI) on November 30, when he delivers a lecture and spends a dreamless night.

Autumn Sequel maintains its retrospective air by occasional familiar echoes from previous works. In Canto I the poet refers to the Regent's Park Zoo. Fifteen years before, when he wrote his journal within hearing of the animals in the zoo on Primrose Hill, some of the trees had been cut down for gun emplacements. That same year, in *Zoo*, he included some references to the proximity of his apartment to it.

MacNeice often referred in his poetry and prose to the insidious role of propaganda in the modern world. In *Autumn Sequel* he uses the striking image—for the voice of propaganda and the resulting consensus of popular opinion—of a parrot, raucous-voiced, full of cackle and meaninglessness, an image he had used effectively before in two radio plays, *Out of the Picture* and *The Dark Tower* (cf. "Barcelona in Wartime" and *The Strings are False*, p. 186). With some slight bow to Matthew Arnold's characterization of Shelley, the Parrot is introduced in Canto I "Clapping his trap with gay but meaningless wings." In Canto VII, the Parrot, along with the clock, is one of the main enemies of the life of freedom and creativity as it is lived by the poet's friends. In Canto XI, the Parrot cackles that this age is not a fit one for lovelorn melancholy; it is the time for brass tacks and cold analysis. Canto XVIII, a lament for Gwilym, refers to that poet as one who would always throw the Parrot's lie back in its beak.

Previously, we have noted the poet's frequent use of religious archetypes, in the Jungian sense of the word. In Canto III, he returns to one of the earliest of all archetypes by the transformation of a tree inscribed with the initials of young lovers into the tree in the Eden garden with its atavistic memories of original and lasting sin. Then later, in the same canto, when the loudspeaker at the Zoo announces that it is closing time for Regent's Park, he develops the announcement into an incantation: "All out!"—of Regent's Park, of Mount Everest, of the Garden of Eden.

His closely related interest in childhood memories and religious themes is evidenced by the frequent references to Christmas. At the close of Canto XX of *Autumn Journal,* he wrote a sensitive and bitter ode to Christmas and the visit of the Magi. In Canto VII of the *Sequel,* he asks how long it will be until Christmas. Then he meditates upon the star that "sprouts in each man's heart." At the center of the maze of life each man must fight the antagonists of greed, spite, doubt, and malice; but, standing beside the battle, there is the eternal bride like a "half opened rose." On a visit to Bath (Canto XXI) he sees holly trees loaded with berries and ponders the irony of red blood at Bath, of shepherds who chase a star; and he thinks of the nonsense Lord Chesterfield would have made of the Three Kings.

Canto XXIII celebrates a mild December with an outburst against yuletide good will toward men whose guts he hates, or perhaps he is damning their lack of guts, corrupted by some political theory. The Three Kings are three foolish old men making tracks in the sand, following a star, a wild light that refuses to let the soul relax, and which, at the end, will lead them only to a child. Standing in the department of the Ancient East in the British Museum, the poet conjectures about the origin of the Magi. Did one come from Egypt with its reminder of the constant renewal of life by the flooding of the Nile; or from Babylon like Gilgamesh to find the cure for the death of his best friend; or from India where the god Shiv destroys while he creates? MacNeice strikes a note already old in English poetry by asking whether they were bound to Bethlehem or to Birmingham—both towns being essentially the same. The birth of Christ must stand in conjunction not only with the great gods of history, and the fall of Rome, but also with a Russian firing squad preparing to make or remake history.

As of old, the poet is a great visitor of picture galleries. On Friday, September 25, 1953 (Canto VIII), he stands before the paintings of a master, who, though old, with a brush strapped to his wrist, still celebrates the beauty of velvet, of ostrich feathers, of breast and of thigh. Science, ethics, and politics stand somehow aloof from life; the artists eat meat, paddle around in dung, tear off women's clothing. The Muse prefers for its favorites the halt and the blind, the fanatics and the simple-minded. Unresponsive to the merely able, she favors dying kings, setting suns, hatching eggs, and kissing lips. We go to art galleries, decides the poet, to escape mankind by rediscovering it. Devlin looks at a self-portrait of Rembrandt and muses how many thousand pots of beer and tots of schnapps it took to produce that face. But then, Devlin is most at home in low, rowdy places.

Some of the same concern about MacNeice's craft as a poet that he had expressed in *Holes in the Sky* is also a gnawing concern in the *Sequel.* During the war, MacNeice served in the European Service of the British Broadcasting Corporation. After the war he stayed on to work with it (Canto IV), but the old scripts that cheered the Greek, Polish, or Czech resistance had now become ancient history (Canto V). The old actors had to play new roles with the same old voices. He is challenged by the thought that perhaps he too is just an actor whose Muse has defaulted, and that now he can only lament the Maker he might have been. But he pushes this thought, along with the nagging of two black telephones on the desk, out of his mind; and he gets ready for a nine-day trip to Wales for a rendezvous with a girl, or perhaps with a goddess, "to consort with whom is death." Somehow, two cantos later, he seems to have been reassured; for, when he gives a fanfare for the Makers of books and of deeds, he includes himself in the creative company: "Let us make. And set the weather fair" (Canto VII).

If it is true that *Autumn Sequel* echoes too faithfully and too familiarly the old MacNeice technique; it is also to be noted that there are some significant differences. The most noticeable quantitative change—and the most important in regard to direction—is the treatment of friendships of the past. The number mentioned (all under pseudonyms) makes a list that becomes a modern epic catalogue: Gavin (Graham Shepard), Gwilym (Dylan Thomas), Aidan, Isabel, Calum, Aloys (Ernst Stahl), Devlin, Hilary, Jenny, Blundell, McQuitty, Maguire, Stretton, Reilly, Price, Harrap, Owen (L. C. Powys), Boyce (E. R. Dodds), Egdon (W. H. Auden), Evans, Costa, Wimbush, Gorman. Of some, the poet is content with references to their baldness or their taste in food; but others become full-scale portraits.

Gavin (Canto II), for example, had no patience with the forlornness of John Keats. He was interested in the "Gates of Horn," women's calves, thighs, buttocks, and breasts, in all the innocence and ardor of his lust. He was wild, witty, and boisterously loyal to his five senses. But ten years ago this autumn, he drowned as a war casualty in the Atlantic; now he sleeps quite alone. He had been at Oxford with MacNeice and had enjoyed "cosmic conversation" with him there. In his student rooms, he flamboyantly conjured up fictitious abbeys where the nuns wore crimson hose and farthingales of flame.

Harrap (Canto IV) is the friend who invites MacNeice to enter the European Service of the B.B.C., there to learn how to set "traps for . . . neutral listeners, Yank or Turk." He accepts the job and goes to work with Devlin as his colleague and with Herriot as his boss. At the time of writing the *Sequel*, Harrap is dead; nine years before the poet had visited him for the last time in Wiltshire.

Boyce (Canto VI) was a friend whom he could call a "Yeasayer" and an opener of doors. He liked to visit him in his potting shed, where he watered the plants with twinkling bits of Greek wisdom. The great "No-God" has made this age his own by making nothing in it appear worthwhile. Boyce could plant a *Yea* against the most obstinate *No*. Amending a corrupt and glossed text of Plotinus, he knew that, although this was not a battle which could be completely won, nevertheless it was one which must be fought. On the poet's October visit to Oxford, he travels by bus to the village where Boyce lives and faithfully cultivates his garden; nevertheless, the gardener can spot the flaw in each political scheme and schemer. He knows how often fetters are forged in the name of freedom. MacNeice finds him among his books, shining "like a straight candle in a crooked world."

When MacNeice wrote *Autumn Journal*, he claimed he had known several Yea-sayers and openers of doors; in *Autumn Sequel* he considered Owen, with his white hair and his love of birds and butterflies, to be one of that elect company. He goes to see Owen (Canto XXII), once tall, sun-crowned, healthy; now half-lame, deaf, and blind, but still repeating his old motto, "Rejoice, rejoice!" while leaning on two sticks. More than thirty years before this old teacher had taught MacNeice the names of butterflies and the tricks of Latin elegies.

The most extended comments are about Gwilym (Canto XVIII), who can be identified quite firmly as Dylan Thomas. Gwilym comes to visit London the first of September. The friends swap tall stories and memories amid much laughter and beer. The visitor is a poet, a jester, and a bard. He is alert to those who would like to censor his freedom and confine his art. He will not be bought. They have only one riotous night together, and then Gwilym is bound "Carmarthenwards." On Saturday, November 7, while reading what the sports writers say about coming events, MacNeice reads that Gwilym lies in a coma in New York City.

The following Monday, Gwilym is dead; and their meeting three weeks before was their last.

It seems difficult to accept the death of one seen so lately with a card up his sleeve; jester, quester, and bard. He was one who always threw the Parrot's lie back in its beak. He knew some mountains must be climbed simply because they were there and also because they were high. He rhymed slowly and meticulously, interested in all that was ancient, primitive, mythological, "a bulbous Taliessin, and bow-tied Silenus." Gwilym burned instead of rotting; he earned his death instead of merely dying. Aristotle asked of the poet what he had to contribute to civic virtue, but it was difficult to see Gwilym in terms of civic virtues; he was all fire, and Demos is huge and lukewarm. The crowd may rule the streets of the city; Gwilym owned the sky.

Five years before MacNeice had bought a pair of shoes in Gwilym's company to travel to Drumcliff to attend the funeral of William Butler Yeats. Now he would travel to Wales in the same shoes for Gwilym's funeral (Canto XX). Just before the funeral he stopped at random at a Welsh thatched inn for a morning drink and found a crowd of Gwilym's friends already there. At the graveside service, he thought that whatever Gwilym took "From this small corner of Wales survives in what he gave." Leaving the churchyard, he had three illusions: first, that they had left Gwilym behind; second, that Gwilym had slipped off somewhere "into the grace of some afterlife"; third, that he would soon come walking over, full of flesh and wit and heart. On November 25, MacNeice was back again in London. Will Gwilym keep his friends waiting just as he used to? Indeed he will.

MacNeice often celebrated his personal friendships in verse. But ever since writing his poem "The Kingdom," these friendships moved out of personal privacy into social and philosophical significance. They are not simply friends; they are yea-sayers, openers of doors, the best pledges to the future, the real citizens of the kingdom of individualism.

As a lecturer in Classics, Louis MacNeice always had a strong sense of the intersections of history with modern life, but *Autumn Sequel* seems to be even fuller of such depth-reference in time than most of his work. Canto I refers to the black bureau of history where pale clerks correct the minutes of all the previous meetings, where lies are proved to be lies, but in which a man learns that

"Justice lies betwixt and between,/'A cool head but no cynic.'" It always seems that the pimps stand on the right hand of God, but "there is another hand." Ancient history keeps running into modern war. A dive-bombed jeep is just as broken and useless as a bronze wheel from Agamemnon's chariot (Canto II).

Through several passages in the poem, MacNeice carries on a dialogue with Thucydides, who pricked both the war lords and the demagogues, but still loved Athens (Canto I). Athens was crowded with the people's faith and hope, yet Plataea and Melos through their servitude paid for Athen's freedom (Canto VIII).

MacNeice continues his perennial argument with Aristotle about the arts (Canto XIX). The philosopher smiles and reminds that there are two schools of thought: one reviles the notion that any artist should consciously fulfill a social role; the other, along with Aristotle, files art in the civil service department. In Athens, Pheidias had free ivory and gold to finish the great statue of Athena. But MacNeice replies that other statues on the Acropolis were used as rubble to plug gaps in the walls. Aristotle replies that these were primitive works; masonry was short; and they were all practical men. MacNeice replies that the same practical Athenians with the same practical ends in view were beginning to bawl that injustice pays; it is necessary to knock your neighbor down so that you may stand; imperialism exists in order to raise the standard of living at home. MacNeice then proceeds to read from the daily paper about the experimental bombing in Kenya to shock the terrorists. He tosses the paper in the basket and replaces Aristotle and Thucydides on their shelves. Contemporary history makes bleak reading.

Closely related to MacNeice's strong sense of time is his equally strong sense of place. Not only are Oxford, London, Wiltshire, and Wales extolled, but there are fascinating historical descriptions of Bath, Norwich, and Glastonbury. In these the poet draws sharp the contrast between the genius of the Augustan Age of the eighteenth century and the Gothic age of vision and romance (Cantos XXI, XXII).

Perhaps it is permissible to mention the frequent and central references of the poet to his wife as one of the chief of those who inhabit the Kingdom. In Canto VI, when he lists some of his friends for special mention, he refers to one whom he had not yet met fifteen years before, the one for whom all his years were warned to wait, and "without whom Spring would be empty, the Fall merely a fall." In Canto XXIV, he leaves the British Museum on December 23 and returns to his home, a cheerful, gay place— made that way by his wife. The poet admits that his education and experience have made him readier to "scoff rather than bless"; and, unless the facts require a verdict of neutrality, he is more likely to say no. But "for this once [he will] say Yes." Very early on Christmas morning (Canto XXV), he goes to the broadcasting studio while it is still dark. Then he takes an empty train back on Christmas Day, moving by slow degrees toward his home and that one central person who takes the view that life is holy. The train brings the poet closer to his home, closer to his wife, and closer to that central view.

A major difference in *Sequel* from MacNeice's earlier poetry is to be found in Cantos XIV–XV. The poet has often cast his poems in the form of dreams, usually those related to his child-hood, or of a semi-mythological character. But in these two cantos, he describes an allegorical nightmare far more detailed and horri-ble than anything he has ever written. He stands with the esthetes before an official portrait behind which there lurks an "ape scratching his arse and his ear." He asks a question of the portrait, and the ape points to an area of thin paint, whereupon the ob-server tumbles in, and finds himself among men in damp tunnels, wearing helmets, masks, and mud-stained overalls.

It is a black labyrinth full of meaningless activity—highly or-ganized, yet blind. A faceless warder unlocks a door marked in red "By Order: Private: No Exit: Danger." But the door leads to a blind wall. The workmen hoist their battering ram and break through to a window, then to a door, and finally to the light. As they all watch the door, a queen bee flies out, followed by a male drone. The observer who watches them make love in the air, is saddened by the realization that the queen will now shed her wings and have no more flight, light, love, or freedom.

While he is still meditating on this melancholy thought, a circus barker persuades him to go on a ride. Immersed in a rubbery duct, the poet slithers wormlike through its coils. The duct moves as he moves, and whispers "Follow me! Give up everything." In the fat, intestinal darkness, the worm clings close and confides that within him there are darker and obscurer cells. Since life means to rise toward the sky but always falls, "Who would choose life?" The observer cries that he chooses life: to grow and decay, to weep and rejoice, "to be what I was and shall be." When we live, we pay a debt that no one can prove that we really owe; but the more we pay the debt, the more the capital comes back to us. We must live, give, make, and act, insists the observer. Man is never free from the blatant beast; but he can also never be severed from the castle of the Grail.

The observer's stirring dissent at the close of the nightmare makes the allegory clear. Primarily a foetal dream of a womblike existence, it also, like William Blake's "The Book of Thel," attempts to prepare the unborn child for life, but more successfully than in Blake's poem of birth-rejection. There are the officially conventional explanations of life, with apes hiding within. To insist upon further or clearer explanations is to fall through the thin paint of the social veneer into a meaningless place of blind labor and startling signs. But the will to life and freedom are strong, so the observer breaks out (or is born). The flight of bee and drone represent not only the domestication and settling down of love, but also the disillusionment subsequent to any flight of faith or creative energy.

Now the observer turns to the other alternative, an alternative presented in *Zoo* and *Holes in the Sky:* he may live a subterranean life without flight, love, creativity, or faith. He can become so adapted to his visceral environment that he will enjoy the damp security of his obscure coil and never be tempted to emerge. This life of conformity is what most men choose: they never ask piercing questions of the official ethic; they never struggle hard enough to break through to the window and the door that let in the light; they watch love in amazement but have no share in it; they adapt to their own little task in their own little place and choose security rather than risk. But the poetic observer demands life, risk, love, and light. Thus he takes his stand with all his friends of the Kingdom who are the anarchs and makers of the world.

CHAPTER 5

The Classical Humanist

THE writers of obituaries are always challenged by the need to sum up, and therefore, to attempt to reassess early tendencies in the light of final destinations. After all the years in which critics saw Louis MacNeice as standing in the shadow of W. H. Auden, or casually dismissed him as the most technically gifted of the "Thirties Poets," the final obituaries of 1963 tend to do penance for these easy critical judgments. The obituary in the London *Times* admits that he always had less in common with this poetic group than had appeared at the time. It recognizes that although his best friends became at least mildly Marxist, he was never politically or philosophically committed to communism. It points out that he was essentially from the start what he certainly was at the end—a "broadly liberal humanist." [1] Thus his poetry was "seldom intensely emotional or rhetorical and never flamboyant; but highly individual feeling and imagination are married in it to verse of amazing variety and fluency, and to technical skill of a dazzling order." [2]

Stephen Spender, who perhaps had opportunity to know Mac-Neice better than most, entitled an article on his friend "Songs of an Unsung Classicist." [3] In the article, Spender claims that Louis MacNeice was one of the best poets of the century, and he laments that he was also one of the most neglected. He classifies him as "a classically trained, Renaissance-admiring rationalist" and as an "individualistic humanist." He points out the richness of his poetry in its reference to Latin, Greek, and other literatures, as well as to painting. He distinguishes the special quality of his poetic diction as "a tone of eloquent, elegant, witty, and erudite discourse." He considers it important to recognize that he is essentially a "worldly poet." Although by reason of his mind, education, and special talents, he is superior to the world, he never ceases to belong to it. The idea of happiness imagined in his best poetry is "of a society in which sensual, esthetic-minded, amusing, scholarly people are able to communicate with one another, without mystification and with perfect tolerance and understanding." This kind of communication explains, for Spender, MacNeice's strengths, his limitations, and the curious judgment that, with great poetic gifts and with a genuinely poetic personality, he used these to express "ideas and situations that are essentially those of prose." [4] This last, of course, is a judgment which MacNeice would gladly have risen from his grave to dispute.

But both the objective analysis of the *Times* obituary and the highly personal essay of a close friend agree on the common ground that Louis MacNeice was essentially a Classical humanist, and on this note the final chapter of this book, as of the poet's life, rests.

I Visitations (*1958*)

We cannot be grateful enough to Louis MacNeice for his revelatory dedications, which often strike the dominant mood of a whole collection of poems, or of an era in the poet's life. In his dedication "To Hedli," he uses the key phrases: the "running of days," the "march . . . of events," "public fears," and "the timeless vagrant." A close examination of the poems[5] dictates their consideration under the headings: the poet and his public ("public fears"), the movement of life (the "running of days"), and the immediate experience of timeless mystery ("timeless vagrant").

Just as the dedication suggests that the poet writes on a deeper and more significant level than the public catchwords of either stooges or pundits, the first three poems are all concerned with the relationship of the poet to his time and to his public. "To the Public" begins with an exposé of poets as a thick-skinned, grasping, eavesdropping, lawless lot; but it ends with the insistence that they are also characterized by the possession of more common sense than the "Common Man." "To Posterity" refers to the time hailed by scientists when words and books will be outdated and other media of communication will be discovered. The poet wonders if colors and tastes will be the same then as they are now for us when they are "framed in words." Will grass be quite as green, or sky quite as blue, or will all their birds be wingless? "April Fool" is highly reminiscent of the two plays of the "March Hare Saga": *The March Hare Resigns* and *Salute to All Fools*. A madcap series of jolly snatches that seem to "Keep the sound but ditch the sense," it soon becomes apparent that the poet does just the opposite. He may keep the sounds right, but his mad way of looking at things makes his point of view, April Fool, and the March Hare more rational and realistic than the sober but bumbling world.

The last seven poems in the collection are the title poems, "Visitations." Janet Fiscalini has suggested that these, and some other poems, might be called poetic essays in the "immediate experience of mystery." [6] The first visitation is by the innocent and bucolic spirits of pastoral lovers who haunt our less innocent lives and perhaps call us when dying to lands unknown. The second visitation is by that special moment of vision which takes away loneliness and makes things dearer and somehow redeemable. The third depicts a merman and a mermaid, each on lonely rocks, who while away their time killing ships. But at last both throw themselves into the sea and swim unerringly to meet.

The fourth visitation is the revelation of that special quality which makes some persons unique and individual. Man, woman, and child; king, queen, and clown; the living and the dead—the unique few will find a way to communicate to us their richer story. The fifth is literally the visitation of an angel of the night who makes his dinner hosts feel both comfort and danger. The sixth celebrates the elusive visits of the Muse. Inspiration may leap from the very large or the very small—here, there, or anywhere. The artist who has the burden and birthright of poetry must watch and listen everywhere. Thus the moment of inspiration is defined as the time when the "unimmediately apparent" becomes the Immediate.

The last of the seven visitations begins with the archetype of Elijah, who, looking for God in the whirlwind, hears Him in the still, small voice. The poet sits in the cave of his own mind. Amid ill winds and stray atoms, the entrance of the cave is darkened by "Suddenly Something, or Someone." And out of this presence blossoms the pure understanding of the past and a surer affirmation of the future.

The striking thing about the structure of these poems is that they are neither the glib music-hall rhythms of the early poems nor the complex, long-lined difficult poems of *Ten Burnt Offerings;* they are both. In "Visitations" the poet has found the way to use the doggerel casual to express the philosophical complex. This is both an unlikely and a remarkable poetic achievement.

There are three more poems in *Visitations* which can be classed as the apprehension of mystery. MacNeice dates his "Visit to Rouen" as the fifth centenary of the Rehabilitation of Joan of Arc. In these lines which Dudley Fitts called "pious banalities" [7] the poet is simply exploring the two levels of Rouen; that of shop-keepers' exploitation of a commercial opportunity and that of the "voices" that called to Joan in the dusk. Evidently it was an unforgivable offense to Fitts that the poem should imply that both levels are true and valid. In "Easter Returns," very similar in intellective pattern, the man recalls the majesty of Easter to the believing child; and then he makes a pun on the Anglican classification of a "movable feast" (religious celebrations that occur on differing dates each year) by calling Easter a "removed feast" for adults who have lost their faith. But whether men have relinquished their childhood faith or not, the poet points out that, whenever a man finds a green shoot growing out of a wounded mind, the myth becomes actual again.

"The Other Wing," which had been published earlier as an "Ariel Poem for Christmas" (1954), is an outstanding poem in two regards: the brilliance of the intellectual conception and the vivid sharpness of the diction. Zeus is the first of three nativities, as the Curetes clash their shields together in the Cretan cave on Mount Ida, to drown the cries of the infant god, lest his father Cronos should find and devour him. Then, enthroned in his "talk-happy heaven," Zeus in turn gives birth to Athena, who bursts full-grown from his brow. All the artists strive to make her likeness, and her temple at Athens becomes one of the greatest wonders of the ancient world. But the "other wing" of the British Museum ("first on the left beyond these black-figure vases") contains the antiquities of another even more significant birth: that of Jesus in the manger of Bethlehem. Curiously, the Jesus birth is shown in conjunction with the birth of a grave-wrapped mummy (probably suggested by the figure of Lazarus whom Jesus raised from the dead). The "long thin pupa" of the mummy must always wait for and be warmed by the voice of the small round birth. And Jesus, referred to as "poor Tom o'Bethlehem," has scarcely enough fire to warm himself.

Besides the dazzling series of images and the startling surprises

of the thought, the language brilliantly evokes the metallic clatter
of the armored nursemaids of Mount Ida:

> Rat-tat-tat-tash of shields upon Ida
> Among pellmell rocks and harum-scarum
> Ibex and tettix; willy-nilly
> The infant cried while the tenterhook heaven
> Cranes through the cracks of its blue enamel
> To spot the usurper but metal on metal
> Drowns him and saves him, drowns and saves.

The third major theme of the collection must be stated somewhat ponderously as the movement of life, including both the
personal life of youth, middle age, and death, and the cyclical,
spiral, or repetitious life of all men in history. Two characteristics
of general interest are that, first, the reader cannot avoid the sense
that altogether too many of these poems are about revisits, or returns to familiar places and to the memories of events that happened long ago. This gives a curious sense of looking back over
one's shoulder upon any action taking place in the poems. Second,
and closely related to the first, it is important to note how many of
these poems, like the dramatic monologues of Robert Browning,
revolve about a closed setting, one person or mind, one mood or
one action, and what Miss Fiscalini calls "a significant doubling of
time," [8] that sense of the revisited past which has changed in sad
and disappointing ways.

"Sailing Orders" is a poem about the dreams of youth and first
love, dreams bound to be disappointed, but which still require
belief in order to exist at all. In "Time for a Smoke," the poet,
smoking a cigarette, sits outside that familiar British Museum and
tries to remember on which floor of the hotel across the street he
stayed as a boy. As he looks at the primitive Easter Island idols
guarding the entrance, at the hand holding his cigarette, he meditates on a "hand's view of London," a hand still bearing the feel of
everything it has touched. He remembers himself as a boy dash-
ing into the museum at the moment of opening, and racing up the
stairs to see if he could beat the elevator. Out of the meditation
there emerges a glorification of the childhood vision: hands, boy,
and a bird. They have no ideals, no history, only wings. This
poem, like the series of "Visitations," achieves the union of his

early manner—"time for a smoke"—and his later, more portentous subject matter.

Although a number of poems may be dominated by a middle-aged point of view, only one, "Dreams in Middle Age," refers to the experience directly. The poet recalls the vivid and melodramatic nightmares of his youth. His dreams now burst at the seams with petty details, all the debris of the day before, faces and figures in ledgers. If these are the dreams of middle age, then let the nightmares of youth return. He would rather be engulfed by the lurid dark, be trampled by black horses, and let fierce hands feed all the petty details of his workaday world as "dying values to the undying furnace." Soon enough the watch will cry at the door "Bring out your dead!" They must be themselves, or more than themselves, and thus alive.

Three poems are especially concerned with death. In "Beni Hasan" the poet is on a Nile steamer passing the rock-cut tombs. The holes in the cliffs look like eyes so long dead that they are equally indifferent to their own death and to the poet's. Here Mac-Neice is overwhelmed, as was frequently the case, with the sense of the long drift of human history and the indifference of a thousand years to human and personal values. The witty title "Figure of Eight" suggests the shape of two similar and opposed experiences. The youth rides the bus with supreme impatience because it is taking him to a rendezvous with a girl; the older man rides the train with extreme reluctance because he will meet death at the station. "Death of an Old Lady" is one of the brief personal vignettes MacNeice etches incisively. Years ago the lady saw the steamship "Titanic" set out on its maiden voyage to collide with an iceberg. Now, at the age of eighty, she sets out toward her own iceberg.

The remainder of the poems have to do with the movement of life. The "Donegal Triptych" is a miniature masterpiece. The first poem claims that the idea of history as cyclical is as false as that which claims history is the record of straightforward progress. The second offers rebuttal by claiming that age means change and change means renewal; therefore man's history is a cycle, but one that goes up! The third poem takes the median position: earth is a halfway house between sky and sea. We come from the sea; we live where the two spirals intersect; the wind blows us away to return to the whole lost race of men.

The five poems of "A Hand of Snapshots" follow a similar pattern. The structure of the first is based on the childish ritual of asking questions in the form of a riddle. In "The Left-Behind," the things left are poverty—the fire that gives no warmth; youth—the ship that chose to run on a rock; the unborn—more than enough fish to fill the ocean; and death—the clock that strikes when it has stopped. In "The Back-Again," a farm boy has been to the city and now has returned for a visit home. Wearing his city tie, he feels very superior until he recognizes that, if his farmer brother is an oaf, he is one with dignity and sense. Oddly, the subject of "The Gone-Tomorrow" is a two-year-old child. "The Once-in-Passing" concerns the visitor for one month who can imagine himself only as part of the permanent.

"The Here-and-Never" is a tongue-twister like "Peter Picked a Peck of Pickled Peppers," and thus reveals the weakness of this spare and clean-cut series of quatrains. Too often the poet plays the game of meaning-opposites and sound-alikes just for the virtuosity of being absolutely the best at "metrical parlor games." [9] Thus the poet informs us that it is *here* and *now*, but it has never been *there* and *now* or *here* and *then*; it is *coming* and *going*, but never *coming* the same or the same *gone*; here it is *living* and *dying*, but never *lifelong dying* or *dead-alive*. The moral is impeccable: "here means now to the opened eye" and "both mean ever, though never again." But the language smacks of bright boys playing brittle games.

"Wessex Guidebook" might be described as the county from the point of view of Thomas Hardy. The seasons and the hills may have fostered man, but "they never loved him." "The Rest House" was situated near Nimule, where the Nile flows north from Uganda into the Southern Sudan. The poet notes the flow from the primitive heartland of the continent to the sophisticated delta land of one of the great cultures of the ancient world. He is moved to muse that man's life is also an inescapable drift from too little history to too much. "Return to Lahore" (another of the "return motifs") came from a visit to the Indian city in 1955, which he had last seen during the communal troubles of 1947. Then it was shaken by the excitement of riots; now he sees it in the dullness of peace; but Lahore itself remains indifferent and itself.

"Jigsaws" is a series of five poems demonstrating only the poet's technical dexterity in the first selection, but uniting prosodic skill to meaning in the other four. The first seems to be about "cuckoo-spit and dew" and the Berkeleyan position that, if the viewer is gone, the view also departs. The second point expresses every man's occasional disgust with property when he wishes a poltergeist would tear everything to pieces so that the ingrown souls might have an outing. The third assures humanity that the gulf between human and brute is "deep but not wide," for men are nine-tenths submerged beast, and only one-tenth added intellect. In the fourth poem, the quality of George Herbert, a poet Mac-Neice very much admired, is somehow suggested by the naïve question-and-answer form, as well as by the beautifully spare symmetry. The situation is the postoperative illusion that it all happened to someone else—but where is he? The fifth points out both the absolute necessity of God to men who swear, and the recognition by every man that there is an Unknown which nevertheless "is There."

Other poems which relate to the movement of life include "The Burnt Bridge," the epitome of the youthful romantic dream of dragons and fair ladies on burning bridges. But the chivalric vision is set side by side with the middle-aged caustic comment that there are no dragons, and the whole quest ends beside a shoreless and therefore entirely unapproachable sea. "The Tree of Guilt" weds both the archetypes of the Tree in the Garden and the Cross on the hill. We sense the tree first as an omen; but, when we look for it, we see leaves sprout out of the bare gibbet-arms; and we note that the trunk is covered with hearts, darts, and lovers' initials. So we carve our initials, imbibe our anodyne, fall asleep, and wake to discover that the branches have once again become gibbet-arms with a noose dangling there.

The "House on a Cliff" equates domestic security with the emptiness of nature. Indoors, there is a tiny oil lamp, the sound of the wind, and a locked heart; outdoors, there is a lighthouse signal on a waste of sea, the wind, and the lost key. So the poem continues, showing the sheltered life as the microcosm of the empty macrocosm of the universe, a life which finally betrays the purposeful man who sleeps inside, talking to himself at cross-purposes.

II Eighty-Five Poems: Selected by the Author (*1959*)
and Solstices (*1961*)

Eighty-Five Poems[10] repeats as its dedication the poem "to Hedli" which was originally the dedicatory poem of *Collected Poems, 1925–1948*. In the Foreword, MacNeice assures the reader that these eighty-five poems are not necessarily his best poems, nor even the ones which he happens to like best. His main object in selection was to illustrate different phases and types of his own work. The poems are arranged in eight groupings which defy the reader to find any principle of organization. The third division is composed largely of Irish poems, but the other seven divisions are non-chronological, non-thematic, and non-prosodic. Perhaps the author was playing one of his whimsical little games when he commented that the selection was divided into eight groups and that this grouping was "meant to be more or less significant." [11]

In the history of criticism, it is frequently the case that the critic catches the technique of a few poems and uses that quick apprehension to characterize an entire collection. P. N. Furbank's comment in *The Listener* illustrates this tendency: ". . . I thought the best poems in his recent collection *Solstices* were ones which played a curious trick of revolving upon themselves and swallowing their own tails, as if the thing that now really interested him in life was simply its power of repeating itself." [12]

The comment concerning repetition would be equally apropos to almost any of MacNeice's later poetry; the pattern of circle, cycle, and spiral, which seems always to have fascinated the poet, assumed special interest in his middle years. The very title of this collection[13] suggests the cyclical pattern of the planets; the solstice comes not once but twice annually, at June 21 and December 22 when the sun is at the greatest distance from the celestial equator. Perhaps in addition to the scientific reference of the title, it should be noted that astrology appealed to the poet's imagination, an interest which flowered posthumously in a large book on that subject.

It may be significant that June 21 is under the sign of Cancer, and December 22 under the sign of Capricorn; however, the poet has given no hint that the poems are to be grouped under the two dominant signs with their respective characteristics. The title poem merely asks "How did midsummer come so soon?"—another

example of the poet's surprised sense of youth suddenly superseded by middle age. But, as in *Autumn Sequel, Visitations,* and
Ten Burnt Offerings, MacNeice transforms the quickly passing
years from loss to gain, because they were unwittingly years of
waiting for the right person to come along. Now that she has
come, he asks wonderingly, "How can midsummer stay so long?"
As such, the poem expresses a hopeful interpretation of the passing of time—a theme which is descriptive of the largest group of
poems in the selection.

Furbank's rather clever simile of fish "swallowing their own
tails" can be illustrated at best by only about three items. "The
Riddle" follows the child-verse predilection of MacNeice in its
most dominant form—the naïve question and answer which do
not quite match—permitting the adult reader to fall through the
hiatus. In a boyhood home heated by a wood stove, the family
listens to the prowling sound of a wolf or a ghost circling the
house. Now, in a house unheated by an electric stove, he has lost
the dramatic dreams of childhood and retained only the fears. In
"Jericho," Joshua remembers Moses and the Decalogue brought
down from Sinai's height. As he recalls the breaking of the tablets
at the sight of the people's apostasy, he has a sense of the change-
lessness of time as he sees them broken today in the Passport
Office, the Law Courts, the Stock Exchange, St. Paul's Cathedral,
Notting Hill Gate, and the Ministry of Defence. The archetype
has been produced, the modern similitude noted, and the fish
swallow their own tails both indecisively and cyclically.

"Idle Talk," much like the clever pub talk of the earlier "Homage to Clichés," sniffs the wind which blows shoptalk, club talk,
cliché, and slang—letting some fall dead and making others
dance. Then the poet leaps back to the earliest dialogue of all.
When Adam says "I love you" to Eve, his words become the hoar-
iest of clichés; but, when Adam said it to the east of Eden after
the temptation and the fall, it was a different word than any
spoken in the serenity of the unsullied Garden. And the implication is that somehow the same old words manage to be different
because they are spoken each time for the first time. So new swallows old and first gobbles last, and the fish swallows its own tail.

There are a number of poems which suggest the "wit" of seven-
teenth-century metaphysical poetry. They are characterized by

one major image or figure, by their outrageous revelation of truth, and by their sheer dexterity of diction. A group of four such poems is entitled "Indoor Sports" including "Darts," "Shove Halfpenny," "*Vingt-et-Un*," and "Crossword Puzzles." All four poems follow the same form of five long lines, a short line, a shorter line beginning in the middle of the page, and a final short line. The poems are essentially trivial in meaning, but this triviality is at its coolest, brightest best. In "Darts" there is the opponent who wins easily, hardly looking at the target; "Shove Halfpenny" requires skill, luck, and the technique of the "glancing blow"; "*Vingt-et-Un*" is a game to play while asleep—all luck, no skill; "Crossword Puzzles" is a bit more substantial in its question about the "indefinite" personal pronoun, and its resolution that it is high time to leave puzzles and start to live.

"Nature Notes" is another series of "witty" poems on dandelions, cats, corncrakes, and the sea. The form is even more brilliantly involved and precarious than in "Indoor Sports." The first lines begin with "Incorrigible" and add only one other word; the first three of the second lines begin with "They"; the third lines begin alternately with "Unsubtle" or "Subtle"; the fourth lines alternate between "But" and "And"; the fifth lines of the first two poems begin with "Of" and the fifth lines of the last two poems with "Anywhere" and "Any time"; the sixth lines all begin with "Like"; all the second lines end with "childhood," and the fourth lines with "capable." In addition, the variety of line length in each stanza is repeated in the other stanzas.

Dandelions are the extrovert friends who can grow anywhere. We never come to love them, but they fill in the "primroseless . . . gaps." Cats are the women who are content with casual affairs, require no contracts, and pleasantly go their own way. The raucous voices of corncrakes somehow give us confidence and a sense of safety. The sea is the opposite of cats; it represents those persons to whom we must surrender completely if we are to find life and love at all.

Another group of "witty" poems is entitled "Sleeping Winds." The North wind is a tall young man, free, sure that he will never die. The East wind is the bringer of the monsoon to an Indian woman slumped in her sari at noon. The West wind suggests the legend of St. Brandan whose prayers for a homeward wind brought his becalmed ship to harbor. The South wind is a king cobra, uncoiling slowly, swaying rhythmically, ready to wreck or bless the world.

Four poems on Regency Park, London, are not held together by a group title, but follow each other consecutively in the volume. "The Park" begins with two biblical parodies: "Through a glass greenly men as trees walking" (I Corinthians 13:12; Mark 8:24). To the south, the great mass of yellow-stucco apartments lies; to the north, the Zoo, full of fossils of flesh. Children who have never been in the country think this park is it, but even men who know better use the park to force the city's lock open and let them through. The scriptural parody of the first line is further elaborated by the parody of the twenty-second: "Through a grill gaily men as music. . . ."

A lonely clerk sculls on "The Lake in the Park," where everything in Paris emphasizes his own loneliness. "Dogs in the Park" is a poem about atavistic memory: the dogs ignore their masters' whistles while they circle other dogs and remember dimly the running and baying of great packs. Guiltily, the dogs return, wag their tails, and attempt to communicate; but the attempt is a failure. Then both masters and dogs recall those legendary creatures of the prehistoric past which were doomed to die just as dogs were doomed to live. The recurrent word of "Sunday in the Park" is "irony." The strollers and mothers with prams are in the park, although there is a chill wind and no sun shines. On such a day, one forgets that on the seventh day of Creation God rested; one even forgets the Tree of Good and of Evil in the Garden; all is subsumed in irony.

"Old Masters Abroad" is an excellent example of the "witty" poem which is not part of a group. Shakespeare's codpiece "flaunted" at a dhoti, Pope conducting the dancers of Bali, a spurred Hampstead nightingale ripping the guts from a decadent bulbul—the poem ridicules the absurdity of the study of English literature everywhere the British flag is flown. The sharply absurd contrast—"wee sleekit courin' timorous warthog!"—leads the poet to suggest that the Old Masters now tyrannize past their time and place. "Icebergs" is a superbly witty complaint that if only icebergs were warm below the water line we could forgive their jagged tops. And, even in the life of man, can we congratulate ourselves on having had more than a mere ninth or tenth of our submerged life? "Variation on Heraclitus" brings the pre-Socratic Ephesian philosopher up to date; the modern understanding of physics suggests that not only do rivers flow, but walls, ceilings, and rooms. The poet suggests that even the slide rules of the physicists are inadequate to capture the rapidity of the earthly slide. Not only can we not put our feet twice in the same stream; we cannot live twice in the same room. "Reflections," the poem which won third place in the Guinness Poetry Contest for 1960, is a highly metaphysical conceit; the mirror above the fireplace reflects the room reflected in the window. With this play of reflections, the poet is able to disperse the secure comfort of being indoors and to leave the segmented room stranded outside in the street.

For a man to whom travel was always disillusioning yet somehow compulsive, it is to be expected that the selection would include some travel poems. Actually there are many more in this category than will be mentioned at this point, because about half of the poems which have their setting in foreign places proceed to say something essential about man's life and hope in this world; and they are, therefore, treated in another grouping. In "Invocation," a nursery-rhyme poem, the man stands still and invokes the familiar and unfamiliar from the plunge of the dolphin, the play of a fountain. "Indian Village" in four tetrameter sestets rhyming *abcadc*, portrays life as a sun which is already foundering as it rises. Each man has only a little part of this appearing-disappearing life, but it is his own and so he must "leap and shine." In a "Jungle Clearance, Ceylon," the travelers watch at dawn for elephants to come to drink. They never come, but a pelican brings to mind both the archaic and timeless world where nothing can happen—and the presumption of the West in attempting to slap the East on the back.

"Half Truth from Cape Town" shows life caught in the tension between opposite poles: between smoking fire and tolling bell, between Protestant Irish and Catholic Irish, between ants traveling north and ants traveling south, between the "Useful Plough" and the Southern Cross. "Solitary Travel" is a gemlike vignette of the traveler who finds the breakfasts, the hotels, and even the waiters just the same wherever he goes. He looks about in the lobbies at the "self-indulgent disenchanted old," and he longs desperately for an escape out of this neutrality of endless observation, where all the future must be faced alone. In almost a continuation of the same thought, and striking a note MacNeice had struck before in "Slow Movement" and "Conversation," the poet rides in a "Restaurant Car" where everything flows: past, present, scenery, waiters, food; and he wonders if, before the movement stops and they must all change trains, he will dare to risk catching the eye of the person sitting across the table.

A mark of the publication date of *Solstices* (1961) is the almost complete absence of war poetry. There are references to wartime experiences in many of the poems, but in most cases they are incidental, or the main point of the poem uses the war only as a simile. "Homage to Wren (a Memory of 1941)" portrays St. Paul's Cathedral as a ship sailing through the blazing seas of incendiary bombing. The poet, as fire warden, warms his hands at dawn by the heat of burning London, and then goes home from his duty. "Rites of War" points out that, although Hamlet's death may be greeted by "Alas" and accompanied by "a flight of angels," Fortinbras knows that war is more waste and gore than glory. This realization must be his special line, the realism of the warrior that restores the consideration of war to sanity.

The dream structure which has been a minor topic in all the collections is represented by four poems. "The Messiah (a Memory of 1940)" is an almost incomprehensible poem, not because of the inherent difficulty of its referents, but because of the telegraphese of the style. The images switch too fast from smelting to surgeons, Messiahs to refugees, hiccuping to a flashing light in a maternity ward. It is especially infuriating to read a poem which on the surface is written so clearly, in such simple diction, and with no convolutions of the progress of thought, and yet be totally unable to connect the images. The clue to the meaning of "The Messiah" is to be found, not in intensive explication of the poem, but in MacNeice's unfinished autobiography, *The Strings Are False:*

Then one day Wystan Auden was to come and see me, and the night before I lay on my back with the bed raised a little looking out of the window towards the Maternity Ward opposite where there was a window that periodically lit up brightly. Lit up, went dark, lit up, went dark. It was some time before I guessed what it was. It was a surgeon smelting metals. But oh so much more than a surgeon. He had wholly new methods of operating but he had also a new scheme of life, he held the panacea of history, Wystan knew all about him. I did not always trust Wystan's taste but this time there was no mistake; this surgeon of his was more than a mere great man: he was a human being but raised to the power of *n*, had had a mutation of some sort, could act as a midwife to others—a new mutation for all. But he had one drawback; a Central European refugee, he was somehow without a surname; whenever he was introduced to anyone he had to hiccough. A hiccough was his substitute for a name; I could hear him hiccoughing now, all the way over from the other building. Out of sympathy I got the hiccoughs too and the nightnurse came in, asked me what was wrong.

"Hold-Up" may be dream or parable, but at any rate it repeats the thing MacNeice does so well but which hardly anybody notices. It is a commonplace to talk about the rapid pace of his poetry, the lilting line of his melody, the breathlessness of his jazz lyrics. But he also has a special trick of reducing movement to stasis, in an instant of time, which both cuts the movie film to a single still shot, and produces a kind of dizzy terror in the reader. Traffic is stopped for miles, all the lights are red, a man in a telephone booth becomes a corpse pickled in a tall glass box—all because one conductress was "dark and lost" and "refused to change." The still-life technique is superb, but the hint of a human darkness and lostness which at any time could bring the whole mechanized civilization to a grinding halt is terrifying.

"Bad Dream" and "Good Dream" are set back-to-back in the volume. The former is a Surrealist horror about buzzing fly-sized bears, roaring bear-sized flies, and a young man who came to the weird house, like all young men, wanting food, drink, play, prayer, and love. He enters a room and finds a table laid for two, a crucifix on the wall flanked by a comic postcard, and a "tiny wisp of white" rising through a hole in the pockmarked floor. The wisp becomes the tiny arm of a girl who whispers "Wait till I grow." The arm grows and the voice, now of a woman, cries for help; but the youth is paralyzed, dreamlike, and cannot help. Everything buzzes, booms, hoots, breaks wind, and weeps. One shriek and the arm is gone.

The "Good Dream" is a charming parable of a young man who awakens in the middle of the night. He reaches for the light switch in order to read until he falls back to sleep, but the switch is gone and a warm hand takes away his book and a warm voice

speaks. He insists that he is not, as the voice claims, at the beginning of life and that he is in his own room and awake. The dim-
ming voice calls him to row in the dark to the island where she is.
He rows, feels a bump of landing, takes her hand, "And God said
Let there be light." The light reveals walls of blue sky, enclosing
green grass, and the girl now completely awake. This dream poem
joins the ranks of those other poems celebrating the great love
that came to the poet in middle life when he had accepted loneliness.

A biographical question may properly be raised about these
poems ("All Over Again," "Coda," "Deja Vu," "Good Dream,"
"The Introduction," "Selva Oscura") which stress the rejuvenating
power of a new love. Do they arise out of MacNeice's second
marriage which he celebrated in a number of poems and dedications as a continuing domestic idyll? Or, since the next volume
after *Solstices—The Burning Perch—*is reputedly dedicated to a
young B.B.C. actress, perhaps the rejuvenation of the middle-
aged poet came from a totally new and younger source? At any
rate, without being unduly intrusive concerning the poet's private
life, his poetry makes it perfectly clear that a transforming power
of renewal has been at work—a force which has the power to
make everything new in the present and to give MacNeice an
unusually hopeful and optimistic attitude toward the future.

MacNeice has often been celebrated as the completely honest
poet. This was the critics' affirmative way of saying that he did not
tack happy endings on his narrative poems, nor universal nos-
trums to his social problems. A wry sense of "this is the question
for which we have no adequate answer" has been pervasive in his
poetry. But *Solstices* contains twelve poems of hopefulness, if not
more. The title poem of the collection clearly moves from the
foreboding sense of middle life coming altogether too quickly, to
the fulfillment of hopes the poet hardly dared harbor; and it
reaches the exultant climax "How can midsummer stay so long?"
The "Good Dream" expresses precisely the same idea in parabolic
form. Just as "All Over Again" seemed to some critics to be a
weary theory of cycles and repetition, so it would be easy to mistake the meaning of "Apple Blossom." "All Over Again" referred
not to dreary repetition, but the constant power of human renewal; "Apple Blossom" states quite simply that first is first, second is first, and last is still first. When we emerge from our Eden

into the hostile outside world, the "morning after is the first day."

In "Windowscape" a lost soul lives at number one, The Grove. No one else lives on that suburban street, and all his life the occupant of number one has desired the gift of love that no one gave. After a long series of images of decline, senility and nonentity, the poet still manages to close the poem with hopefulness. Summer is seen in terms of bone, and the "metaphysical shudder" is dealt to the festive season. But "yet those bones are green." "Vistas" is a poem of emergence. Stanza one begins the first three lines with "Emerging," "The creature," and "Forest." Stanza two depicts a train emerging from a tunnel to the open plain. Stanza three shows the self, after years of loneliness, emerging into the freedom of love. In addition to the similarities of initial words, each stanza rhymes *abacdc*.

"The Wiper" reveals the same pattern of lengthy presentation of the problem and then the emergence of a final thought far better than one could have imagined possible. The driver crawls along the dark, unknown road in the rain, and his car is occasionally passed by the lights of vehicles moving in the opposite direction. There are dials on the dashboard to indicate speed and temperature, but no dials to tell where they are going or when the day will dawn. With all these data on the problem of living dangerously and alone in the dark, the poet closes with the reflection that, in spite of the overwhelming odds, we still somehow manage to hold the road.

The pattern is duplicated in "The Wall," a title which would normally symbolize ending, limitation, and imprisonment—as indeed the poem does at the outset. A window becomes a wall, and all the light is behind the bed-ridden figure. The man is old, the light fails, and the end is near. But from the other side of the wall comes the sound of singing, the wall opens, the light shines, a garden lies beyond. This hopeful poem is extraordinarily close to the usual Christian hope of personal immortality with its emphasis upon singing, light, and a garden. This poem is perhaps the most traditionally theological one of any poem Louis MacNeice had written up to this time.

"The Snow Man" treats the theme of hopefulness with a playful touch. A white dummy stands in a white waste. Yesterday it was a dance of snowflakes; today it is a dribbling lump. Or is there another way to look at the matter: Is it perhaps a dance of water-drops seeking to relive the dance of the flakes? With less of certainty and more of dubiety than some of the other poems of hopefulness, it yet presents an affirmative alternative. "The Truisms" is a parable which makes no specific mention of the Parable of the Prodigal Son, yet follows the same general outline. Father gives the boy a box of truisms and dies. Son goes out into the world and finds not only love but also war, sordidness, disappointment, defeat, and betrayal. Thoroughly disillusioned, he wanders back to the home he no longer recognizes; the truisms fly out and perch on his shoulder, and a tall tree sprouts out of the father's grave. Again this poem is a rather surprising one for a poet who has spent most of his writing career debunking conventionality and exposing public morals and mores as the croaking voice of a publicist parrot. In this poem, even truisms—truths so obvious that they are accepted without question—are shown as a valid inheritance and as a reliable guide for life.

"The Blasphemies" may be a semi-autobiographical explanation for the shift in the poet's attitudes. At age seven, the lad hears about the sin against the Holy Ghost as "the unforgivable sin." At seventeen, he lightheartedly parodies everything holy. At thirty, he is confident that there is no God; only humanism is left. At forty, he feels a surprising need for myth and the object which means more than it is. At fifty, humbly, he is asking, as did the little child, not "Is there a Holy Ghost?" but "The sin against the Holy Ghost—What is it?" Needless to say, MacNeice is fifty-four years of age.

"Selva Oscura" [14] is about the places a person has never been and about the life he has never lived. A house can be haunted by people who never visited it, if they are the people whose absence is missed. A life can be haunted by all the experiences it never had, if those experiences were glimpsed and dreamed about. Then out of this sad sense of lost places, lost persons, and lost lives, the light shines; bluebells are about the feet; the door swings open; and a hand invites the sad thinker to "all the life my days allow." It is notable in these poems of hopefulness that much of the apparatus of the mystic vision is included: light, flowers, emergence from the dark, the alien sense, the experience of merging, the beckoning hand, opening walls or skies, and the experience of a kind of beatitude which is a continuing possession.

The last poem in the book, "All Over Again," sounds like the needle stuck in the groove, the endless projection of the same old grade-B film, but the title gives the wrong impression. Instead of being about the experiences which are banal, trite, or repetitious, it insists that every time can be the first time, unique, rare, and timeless. Thus, the poet has escaped at last from the heavy hand of the "remembrance of things past" and from the fruitless longing for an uncertain future. In "All Over Again" the poet proclaims that he will never again ask for something more from the past or from the future; both, with all their possibilities, are now merged for him in the present perfect hour. "This," he cries, is "last and first sound sight on eyes and ears." The Between has finally become the All.

A group of rather heterogeneous poems may be gathered under the omnibus subject heading of man's life. Five brief poems are entitled "Notes for a Biography." The first poem relates the ups and downs of childhood. In the second, the boy graduates from college, goes through colonial service in India, and retires to a home of strangers where he keeps wondering about the morality of colonialism. The third shows the middle-aged man by the sea remembering an absent love, wondering if it were love at all, and taking comfort that later, when the blood cools, the memory will be like the sea, wave upon wave of reminder. The fourth concerns the elderly man who finds that the Lords of Convention who ruled his education are now outmoded. World War II and the bombing of Japanese cities have made him pray that, since love is clearly inoperative between nations, common sense may at least carry the day. The fifth poem presents the old man who examines the adage that it is never time to retire and comes to the conclusion that *now is never*. The lavender vendors in the street confront him with the image that he is now standing before Never, with a bunch of sweet-smelling youth-and-love in his hand.

The subject of "The Slow Starter" heard all his youth the counsel—don't be in a hurry. He heeded the advice and thus lost his main chance. Now ironically the boy who was not in a hurry has become the old man racing against a speeding clock. "*Il Piccolo Rifiuto*" [15] is a searing and yet oddly compassionate[16] picture of a reactionary temperament. He cannot stand cripples, foreigners, or children. But his birth certificate begins to fade, "wops" babble,

children go on a "spacelark," and God begins to limp. In madness
at the unpleasant and unsettling drift of the world, he screams
and curses at a Jewish waiter.

"The Atlantic Tunnel (a Memory of 1940)" is a striking epitome of a convoy trip across the wartime Atlantic. When the voy-
ager left New York, it was blazing with lights; eastward, the sea
was so black that the convoy route seemed to him "like entering a
zigzag tunnel." In the blackness, he muses that all human life is
thus: dark and parasitic; it is never entrusted with headphones,
signals, or codes but is steered unwittingly by forces beyond man's
reckoning. "Yours Next" is an ominous little ditty which recites the
old adage that someone always has to pay for the round, whether
it be a fruit-vending machine, pinballs, a contract or lease or marriage, a stake or faggot or gas chamber.

"Dark Age Glosses" is the work of the student of world literature. The Venerable Bede related the story of a bird's flight
through an Anglo-Saxon hall and then on out into the night as a
parable of the life of man, flight from darkness into darkness, with
but a brief moment of light and feasting and merriment. Mac-
Neice adds the not very searching questions: How could the
world inside the hall or the non-world outside the hall harbor the
life of a bird?

The Grettir Saga that MacNeice had used in "Eclogue from Iceland" reappears as he compares a British major who was refused
the Victoria Cross because he was a heavy drinker, with Grettir.
The Scandinavian hero was cursed by a foe; the major was
doomed and cursed by his age. A modern, tall blonde who is dab-
bing scent behind her ears before walking out on her lover reminds the poet of the Njal Saga and Gunnar's blonde wife who
would not give him a strand of her hair with which to string his
bow and thus save his life, because he had once slapped her. Yet
the very existence of that great saga reveals the nobler qualities of
men. Some consider the period of the Four Masters to be Ireland's
golden age. Yet it is necessary to recall that the destruction of the
great Irish abbeys was often the work of other greedy Irishmen
and not of the Norsemen at all. Even High King Brian looked
about and saw that the light, golden or otherwise, was just the
same in victory and in death.

"Country Week-End" starts with a poem about waiting for
coffee to perk: it always takes time, but we are always ready. The

second of the series is about the boots the poet wore in the Home Guard. Now, as he strides through the countryside, he remembers the blisters he wore on his heels on a hike through the Constable country on Easter Monday, 1944. It was a day full of cowslips, birds, and beer—and a night full of southbound bombers taking advantage of the full moon. The third poem arises out of a day spent confined in the cottage by rain. The man thinks of other rainy scenes: his fortune told in Tiree, a child watching a funeral through a streaming windowpane. Water was once man's native element. Now it is almost lost to him, but his mind retains the atavistic memory.

The fourth poem is written about night in a country cottage with oil lamps for reading. They call back memories for the poet of bustling women who were large and significant in his boyish life. Candles make the dark deeper and somehow evil; oil lamps confer the gift of peace, even upon a boy reading the *Lays of Ancient Rome*. The modern world is like electric light. Food, freedom, thought, life—whatever it may be—it is flicked on or off with a touch. Now in his middle life, back in the cottage of his youthful summers, he will read late at night by the light of an oil lamp—one good night in a naughty world.

III   The Burning Perch (*1963*)

One of the earliest notes of MacNeice's Muse was the blaring trumpet tone which heralds the end of everything. Back at the very beginning of his poetic career, in an innocent poem named "Laburnum," from the anthology of *Oxford Poetry*, a bell tolled the years, until, at a certain moment, there would come a "smack of the metal lip" and all would be ended. Just an omen in the anthology, it became a major theme in *Blind Fireworks*. At times in his poetry, the note became muted or quivered to silence, and then would flare out again superbly in such poems as "Black Panthers" and "Laredo."

The Burning Perch,[17] published posthumously on October 17, 1963, is appropriately the most eschatological of any collection of his occasional verse. The title phrase appears in a poem quite pleasantly entitled "Budgie." The poet is writing to one who may be presumed to be a small lad named Robert MacBryde. For a topic he ranges back to *Zoo* and a favorite bird, the budgerigar. In characteristic style, with the seemingly innocent central figure of a baby blue bird which likes to act for an audience and has no idea of the existence of a world out beyond his cage, the poet slips in the ominous note of a "burning perch." Quite abruptly the poem jerks from a small blue bundle in a cage, being described to a little boy, to the fate of the mortal ego, which shrilly cries "I Am" and insists *"Let me attitudinize,"* while his tiny perch is burning and the conflagration will soon swallow up bird, cage, world, and perhaps poet and little boy listener as well.

Universal doom to the cheerful peeping of a house pet is somehow quite the MacNeice manner of finding enormous meanings in the trivial and banal and of uttering the momentous with a deprecating drawl. The nightmare quality of this poem illuminates the Dedication of *The Burning Perch* to Mary. The poet asks to be forgiven for conjuring up a cinder path and a nightmare mount. Both path and steed will take him off the path to those "green improbable fields" where he may keep his appointment with Mary. The "mad-eyed" steed is much in evidence in the collection of poems; the green fields are, alas, "improbable" to the end.

"Soap Suds" follows the same pattern of the nightmare that shoulders the most secure domestic reality out of the mind and experience. As a boy of eight, the poet had visited a great country house, one full of joys for a young boy: a tower, a telescope, two globes of earth and stars, a stuffed dog, a walled garden humming with bees, a rabbit warren, and the sea. Now the man has returned for a visit; he washes his hands with the familiar-smelling soap; his bathroom window reveals the other guests playing croquet on the lawn. The mallet swings slowly; and, when it hits the ball, a crack of doom runs through the house, the grass is suddenly head-high, an angry voice demands that the game continue. But the ball is lost, and the mallet has slipped, and the soapy hands under the running water are no longer the hands of a child. Even so innocent-sounding a poem as "Spring Cleaning" becomes eschatological in the poet's hands. The spring returns to a weary world. In parody of the biblical reference,[18] the poet whispers that it is time for someone to make all things new. But the scene shifts from spring to desert, from the faint hope of renewal to Simeon Stylites crying from his pillar in the sand, "Repent." The sad recognition creeps into the poem that, instead of a time to make all things new, it is another kind of time—the end-time "to round things off."

MacNeice includes two poems about Egyptian tombs: "Réchauffé" and "This Is the Life." The first poem reheats the painted food, revealed on the walls of the tomb by the dragoman's torch to the inquisitive eyes of the tourists. There, in the same panel, appears the sun—with hands on the ends of its rays which might be the symbols of praise of a sun-worshiping king, or the emblems of something which he secretly dreads. Outside and above, the mad Nile lies dammed lest it be too empty or too full. Who knows when the now-docile and ringed bull might give a sudden surge and break down the dams that secure both the budget and the mind? "This Is the Life," like "Réchauffé," depicts elderly ladies wearing slacks in the tombs of the Kings on the Nile. As the women examine the hieroglyphics and see the food set out in imperishable granite, they consider the sarcophagus a kind of eternal hotel, always ready and made up for the night. Reluctant to leave such security, they muse regretfully that this was the life.

"Greyness Is All" is a whimsical little bit of logic in rhymed-couplet quatrains of tetrameter. If only there were any true black in the world, we might be able to believe in true white by the power of contrast. But everything we see is neither black, nor white, only gray. We wait for the final blackout of the world and ironically note that we will not be around to see if that also is only gray. "Star Gazer" is a more active version of the same theme. Traveling on a westbound train, the poet lurches back and forth from side to side to look out both windows at the stars. He considers that the light from some stars left its source before the poet was born. Then there comes the darker thought; light from some other stars, when it finally reaches the earth, will find no one left alive to see. "Off the Peg" is a play on haberdashery expressions that is only mildly eschatological. There are tunes that hang long upon the pegs of memory. Then some trial or difficulty comes, or even that final fall of Rockaby Baby's "coffinlike cradle pitched on the breaking bough." Whether it be purgatory, hell, or paradise, some tune can match the experience and the mood; and the chooser will be forced to confess that, in the shop of last things, "off the peg" really means "made to measure" in the end.

It is rather natural to expect that in a volume so strongly oriented toward last things, the first things of childhood would receive less attention than customary. *The Burning Perch* has only three witty poems about childhood. "Round the Corner" there is always the sea. Children returning from holiday tip sand from their shoes and know that there is more where it came from. We are all citizens of an anarchic democracy, an island realm rising out of the sea which is always there. A shell reminds, or the wind smells, and we are round that corner, and there, sooner or later, is the sea.

The first stanza of "Château Jackson" asks "Where is the Jack that built the house" and continues in the same singsong rhythm to narrate the story of a man who built a personal dynasty only to have it brought down by shipwreck, debts, unpaid loans. The second stanza answers that it was really the world that both made the dynast and brought him down. How far down? To a yew and a slab in the grass "that wears the words/That tell the truth that ends the quest:/Where is the Jack that built the house?"

The old instinct to play with words and rhythms in the cadence of the nursery rhyme is still strong in the sophisticated urban poet. "Children's Games" is an altogether engaging transformation of the first line—"Touch me not forget me not, touch me forget me" —through a running patter of deliberate misquotation of children's mottoes and rhymes, into the last line—"Touch me not forget me, touch me forget me not." Like many of his other witty childhood poems, "Children's Games" affects one emotionally with a sort of negative after-image. Through the running patter, and the bright insouciant lilting of words tossed about like rainbow bagatelles, there comes stealing a sense of loss, of unredeemable time, and of the pathos of nostalgia. Then the last line takes on poignant intellectual meaning, and life quivers between the childhood desire to be forgotten and untouched and the adult longing to be touched and unforgotten. Here is clearly that unified sensibility of the feeling mind and the thinking heart which should have pleased MacNeice's youthful model, T. S. Eliot.

If this collection has little about the beginning of life, it contains much about the end of life. The eschatological poems send out the burgeoning flames and shadows of the end of Western culture, and perhaps the end of all created things. The poems about death are the egoist's eschatology, for his personal ending seems to him to cancel out the universe. "The Suicide" is written with a rather remarkable collection of slant rhymes: *fact, stacked, packed, cracked, tract, lacked, act,* and *intact.* Although the poor chap jumped out of the window, he left something behind: his files, a doodle on a pad, a broken pencil, a shy smile, and something curiously still quite intact.

"The Grey Ones" returns to the sister Fates of earlier poems. In quatrains of rhymed couplets, the poet urges the youth to ask the way to Never Yet at about Once Upon a Time, the Golden Age, Kingdom Come, or Free for All. The stare of that one eye shared by all the sisters sees only fact; no fancies of what life might become enter there. The sisters chew their gums, pass the eye, and await the next client who may be struggling up a mountain, or taking dope in some Eastern town. "After the Crash" is the strange, cold vision of a man who has died in a motorcycle accident. He looks up into the sky and sees gigantic scales with both left and right pans empty, and he concludes that he arrived just "too late to die." "Charon" transforms a bus trip across London into a voyage on the river Styx. The familiar becomes symbolic, only to have its nightmare qualities finally reduced to the spare and unsentimental diction of the poet when Charon says coldly: "If you want to die you will have to pay for it."

"The Introduction" is an excellent witty trifle which plays MacNeice's familiar trick of the transformation of first lines into last lines. They were introduced in a "grave glade." She frightened him because she was too young; he frightened her because he was too old. A Greek chorus of caterpillar larvae cackles that the two should have met long ago or not at all. So the last line tolls the knell: "They were introduced in a green grave."

The poem "Birthright" has often been anthologized and reprinted in periodicals. With rapid pace and sophisticated simplicity, the poet retails the plight of man, born to a manhood he never requested, invited to ride a steed which will carry him to his death, missing all the best moments in terror of mounting, and at the end recognizing that now his "gift horse" is looking him in the mouth. "Tree Party" is another witty poem starting with childhood and ending with death. In tetrameter-pentameter triplets which rhyme *aaa*, with *you* concluding each third line, the poet proposes a series of toasts to the willow, oak, blackthorn, palm, pine, elm, hazel, holly, apple, redwood, banyan, Bo-Tree, and concludes with *Master Yew*. The poet's bones are few, and he fully admits that his rent is due; but he begs the yew not to be vexed—he will postdate his check.

"Sports Page" celebrates the interests of the "Ever Young" whose *Doppelgängers* toss the ball on the field, while they scream from the stands. But, amidst the vigor and mystic incantations of the sports page, there comes the sobering realization that the lines of print are all sidelines; these sports are all funeral games. "The Habits" is another witty life-death poem with an exceedingly difficult rhyme scheme: first lines of each stanza end with *habits;* second lines with *dressed;* third lines with *them, carried* (three times), and *nothing;* fifth lines end with *all for the best.* The poem revolves about a pun on the title in which *habit* is considered as both customary action and garb. In childhood, "he" has behaved and dressed appropriately; parents, masters, girls, and computers agree it has all been for the best. But as for the habits that outstay their welcome in old age, the old man says, if they will not go away from him, he will go away from them. And God says this, too, is all for the best.

To some degree, the "Coda" at the end of the book and the "Dedication" at the beginning fall into the relationship of question and answer. The latter made a rendezvous for the future in "green improbable fields"; the former muses that perhaps they knew each other better in the past when they were young. In the present, they find moments of knowledge "between heart-beats." The poet muses that perhaps they will know each other best of all when their tunnels meet beneath the mountain. There is the clinking sound of metal striking against rock and dirt in the darkness. While the dénouement is not very explicit, there is enough implication to suggest that the "green improbable fields" have been transformed into the macabre image of buried lovers tunneling toward each other beneath the mountain.

There are only two travel poems[19] from the poet who travels almost obsessively even when he knows that he catches mere surface textures. In the strange rhyme scheme *abcdbedfghijklmm,* the poet remembers "Ravenna" as a bad smell and a glory, the cold eyes of the Empress Theodora amidst the gold of mosaic. The other travel poem, "Constant," has equally odd rhyme: *abcbdaefgfghihjikjlml.* Constantinople is too full of history, rotten with age, and stagnant with hopelessness. It is full of the pathetic remnants of the abortive Fourth Crusade. Nevertheless, in that imperial city caught between Roman and Turk, men once dared to dream of the establishment of a universal church of Holy Wisdom (*Hagia Sophia*).

Although London has become for the poet more a place to work than to live in and to enjoy, there are five poems enumerating various aspects of the life of the city. "Another Cold May" describes the season in London when spring is frustrated by the cold and everything remains dormant: the tulips in their bulbs and the drinkers in the pubs. There is only the "False animation of failed levitation" in this chess game with time. The move is time's, but the loss is ours. "The Pale Panther" continues the theme of late spring. In two strong, tough images, the poet pictures the yellow teeth of the panther tearing the ribs of the roof, and the giraffe necks of lampposts are bent "to lick up turds and print." The second stanza introduces the ominous note of empty bottles piling up on the steps waiting to be collected by the milkman who does not come. It also contains an enigmatic reference to burns which cannot be healed. The third stanza about airmen, broken test tubes and shards, makes it clear that the poet is talking about both atomic and chemical warfare. The world is left like a stalled tractor, when the sun stops shining.

"October in Bloomsbury" is indebted to T. S. Eliot's *Waste Land* combination of culture coupled with sensitive nerves but only a threadbare capacity to feel. For MacNeice, Bloomsbury is essentially Edwardian in style. The Museum spreads "dead hands," a pigeon scores a direct hit on a scholarly collar, and Charles James Fox sits unconcerned with a bath towel "on his arse" while leaves plop gently into his sculptured hair.

"New Jerusalem" is one of MacNeice's most brilliant assessments of the losses involved in modern urban living. The new Jerusalem is London rebuilt after the Blitz but, instead of progress, the poet sees the rebuilding as the bulldozing of all memories and sanctuaries. A vertical, impersonal city emerges, with a horoscope of Stimulant in conjunction with Sleeping Pill. It is just the place for Lazarus risen from the dead; just a dab of rouge and he will look like everybody else. Or Ezekiel would be as much at home in the new London as in his biblical valley of dry bones. Daniel might go eternally searching from prison cell to cell in search of a man-eating lion. And so the bulldozers, modern mechanized dinosaurs, pinheaded Diplodocuses, go on rooting up old water pipes, now dry and forgotten.

The last of the London poems is appropriately entitled "Good-bye to London." A strange ballad combination of the tough manner with mean diction and a lovely lyric refrain: "Nevertheless let the petals fall/Fast from the flower of cities all." Now that he lives in the suburbs, MacNeice returns to London only to do his work. In valedictory manner, he reviews the meaning of London to a child, a youth, a young man, in wartime, and in rebuilding. The war time was the worst time, yet the crowding and terror produced a warm comradeship of the womb. But the rebuilding, after all the phoenix promises of politicians, is merely impersonal anticlimax where all men are strangers.

As in *Springboard*, MacNeice includes many vignettes of persons or types in *The Burning Perch*. Although he once disavowed any interest in Theophrastian character studies, he seems more and more to be producing them. In "Perspectives" he contrasts two points of view: the natural and the personal. Farther off people are smaller, he says; and he then gives examples of the truism. But through the myopia of egoism, one gazes far down the queue of the human race and about 2000 A.D. finds some infant who will straddle the world just as he did. "Pet Shop," in quintets rhyming *abcdb*, begins with exotic and dangerous birds and beasts; but it moves quickly to the kind of pet people can cuddle and imagine it returns their affection. People offer a home; the pets barter freedom; but the home might be worse than wilds or cage.

In sestets rhyming on *abcdbe*, "Flower Show" is a kind of Surrealistic nightmare about a man who pays his way in but forgets to leave at closing time. The unreal, fake-looking flowers form a firing squad to execute him. As he falls dead, the poet devoutly hopes that his bandaged eyes may show him an orchard, hedge, or garden where flowers still "speak a living language." A fierce disgust with all the substitutes of a dehumanized culture blazes forth from the poem "In Lieu." The lighthearted, sophisticated chit-chat of "The Taxis" is interspersed with "tra-la's" and describes man's illusion of being alone, when in fact each man carries about with him a growing company of ghosts out of his past, although they are invisible to all save the cabby (God?).

"As in Their Time" is a Theophrastian gallery of twelve vignettes, portrayed in vital, unsentimental style. The total impression is quite different from the delight of each corrosive portrait, for all twelve total such a sum of human frustrations, cul-de-sacs, doubtfulness, and Dead Sea fruit that the reader's mouth tastes dusty after the laughter. The first notes the difference between stingy tippers and extravagant tippers; then, having established the difference, abolishes it by pointing out that the cold computer averages the whole difference out in the long run. The second employs archeological references to polyglot texts, the Tower of Babel, clay tablets, and cuneiform writing; but it is a dead end in another sense when it points out that man, who knows so much about long-perished tongues, cannot read the grooves in his own brain.

Poem three destroys any simple belief in love. Did she believe in love, or was she playing a role? Was her affirmation simply a public profession, or the cumulative result of envy? And was it love really that she believed in? At this point in the discussion, the skeins are so twisted that it would be easier to cut all the knots than attempt to untwine them. The fourth poem is a riddle that disintegrates the human personality. He and I agreed on the image of me. But that image, so at home on land or sea, never was on land or sea for the simple reason that it does not exist. The fifth portrait is a double study in self-sacrificial futility. The old ladies saved year by year in order to give nice things to their nieces, and then their great-nieces, and then their "greater-nephews." But inflation left them nothing to leave in their wills to their heirs—who, as a matter of fact, were dead before them. The sixth etches the waste of great talent. He was born for the heights or the depths, but instead he always chose the comic role. It was a hoop of fire that he bowled around the arena, but he was dressed like a clown.

Poem seven is a sewer-play on words: she had her mind on the "main drain." She could always maintain that the point was the main, but the real point was that the drain was no more connected to the main than she was. Portrait eight depicts the futile rebel. He always made his protest; but it was a gesture, or a vindication, or an excuse. But what was it all worth? The ninth picture introduces the important man who so makes his presence felt as he enters a room that any room, by his entrance, becomes a morgue.

The tenth is a satirical study of the victim of a scientific age. Citizen of an expanding universe, he handled so many things wrapped in plastic that, when it came time to identify the body, he had no fingerprints left at all. The eleventh study is a slick photograph of the professional woman who knows all the statistics, keeps her skin creamy with skinfood, and is entirely camera-conscious when she goes on a safari. But for all of that, the cannibals ate her one day when they happened to have nothing else to do. The last is the bitterest, most futile picture of all. The child showed promise, and everyone said that there was no need to push him. But then there came a dry spell in his development and such a personal catastrophe on his twenty-first birthday that after that, everybody knew there was indeed no need to push him (cf. "The Slow Starter").

"Memoranda to Horace," in five cantos, is one of the longest and probably the most important poem in the volume. We have noted that the sense of death, so strong in this posthumous publication, is also related to the death of society and, indeed, to a blazing, eschatological end of all things. The tainted age, or the spoiled world, arouses in MacNeice the same bitter anguish expressed by Ezra Pound in his *Hugh Selwyn Mauberley*. Our day is epitomized by "funerary urns" purchased "from the supermarket." Our children have the bleak prospect of "one's life restricted to standing room only." All the poems of all the past will become a monument "weaker and of less note" than "a quick blurb for yesterday's detergent." Such is the biting analysis of the poet's fierce disgust.

But the "Memoranda" is not essentially a poem of social criticism. More significantly, it is the gesture of a modern poet looking back and choosing the poetic figure that most fits him, his genius, and his age. This Horatian self-identification is perhaps one of the most personal things MacNeice ever expressed about his thoughts of himself as poet. In *Modern Poetry*, he had argued for the definition that a poet is a man who happens to have a special gift for language, rather than first and foremost an artist, and only last or least a man. Now MacNeice speaks in a unique moment of self-analysis and reveals that self by identification with the Roman poet of the first century before Christ.

Horace is the author of the polished lyrics, the sophisticated satires, and the poetic essays of one who belonged to the court circle of Imperial Rome. His name has become an adjective to describe urbanity and wit. But, despite this societal identification, he fought quietly and constantly to retain his personal independence of thought. The points of reference to Louis MacNeice are unmistakable, and it is quite clear why the poet addressed to Horace what turned out to be his own last thoughts about his craft as a poet in a vulgar age for which his education had ill-prepared him.

In Canto I the poet asks why Horace and he bothered to polish their gems of language. Posterity will not even be able to read the language (no doubt the desperate verdict of a despairing Latin teacher). Poetry is of less value than Shakespeare's May flies or television's blurb for yesterday's detergent. Although Horace never sought fame, he believed that poetic images were more lasting than bronze. MacNeice—who (Canto II) has just returned from Ireland, a land Horace never saw—considers how far apart their realms of experience have been, and yet sees them as parallel lines separated by history but united by language. Both have lived in noisy and tumultuous days. The Roman poet offered no consolation to his contemporaries; he simply gave elegant descriptions of his works and days. Horace, like modern man (Canto III), had to bow the knee to Augustus; but then he slipped away to his villa, where he found the girl Lalage, love, laughter, and the warmth of peasant fables. The British poet reflects that he too, can find the same asylums in the country, in language, in love and laughter, and in his memories of peasant Ireland.

Although (Canto IV) the usual temptation of elderly poets is to profess to be Dionysian rather than Apollonian, MacNeice joins Horace in his "appetitive decorum." It is true that the age of Horace did not know our age's passionate sacrifice of quality to security, or our stress on unredeemable quantity. Yet both poets learned the hard lessons of non-recognition and pre-recognition: non-recognition of preconceptions which would make everything cyclic, expected, old; pre-recognition of the "unborn face" as absolutely unique among faces, the novel in the commonplace. These two lessons furnished them with an antidote to "the poison of time" and with a lever to pry compromises from the horribly glazed and jowly old fellows in authority—whom some day they themselves would resemble.

MacNeice (Canto V) even has something denied to the Roman —an addiction to the creatures of Gothic fantasy, to degenerate goblins and twilight monsters. To hobnob with the Gothic is a mortification, but no more of one than to be identified by the falsities of the day and the city, the very ones Horace escaped in his Sabine farmhouse. It is better to "opt out now" than to capitulate to the well-lighted and overadvertised "idols of the age." It is better to have bawdy exchanges with a goblin, or even to slip back into a second childhood entirely content to remember the first childhood, than the "blank posterity" of a world in which life will be "restricted to standing room only."

This last canto, is, of course, full of revelation. The reference to "opt out now" is well-nigh prophetic in the last poem of a last volume. The passage recommending second childhood rather than the maturity of today and tomorrow does much to explain the unabashed absorption with childhood and the vital role of memory. Perhaps it is well not to resist the temptation to read valedictory meanings into last volumes published posthumously—especially when they are so clearly there and so relevant.

IV   Varieties of Parable (1965)

Louis MacNeice delivered the Clark Lectures at Cambridge University[20] in the spring of 1963, just a few months before his death. They were published in 1965 largely as they were delivered, with only the necessary minimum of editorial revision. Professor E. R. Dodds of Oxford University saw the proofs through the press.

In the Introduction, MacNeice draws together the divergent theories of allegory, parable, and symbolism of Kingsley Amis, C. S. Lewis, George Wilson Knight, Janet Spens, Graham Hough, Martin Esslin, Northrop Frye, and Rosamond Tuve. He explains his reasons for using the word "parable" instead of allegory or symbolism and suggests that the area he explores in these lectures attracted him as a person who believes in dreams, as a poet who recognizes the necessity of symbolic language, and as a writer of radio dramas. We get a personal glimpse into his plans for the future when he confesses that "What I myself would now like to write, if I could, would be double-level poetry, of the type of Wordsworth's 'Resolution and Independence,' and, secondly, more overt parable poems in a line of descent both from folk ballads such as 'True Thomas' and some of George Herbert's allegories in miniature such as 'Redemption.' "

The last two lectures explore the contemporary literary scene in the areas of poetry and drama, and prose narrative, respectively.

Writers discussed include: Eliot and Auden, Francis Thompson, Dante Gabriel Rossetti, Housman, Ibsen, T. F. Powys, Samuel Beckett, Harold Pinter, and Edwin Muir. The final lecture takes its material from the writings of Kafka and the novels of Beckett and William Golding.

Perhaps the most significant partial shift to be found in the Clark Lectures, is the admission by the poet that his past obsession with the external world placed him in the danger of at times "becoming a journalist rather than a creative writer." He still thinks the poet should look at the world about him, feel for it, and ponder upon it, but his central job is less reporting its events and aspects than revealing those inner human conflicts which require some kind of metaphorical writing for adequate expression.

CHAPTER 6

Conclusion

IN *Solstices*, 1961, Louis MacNeice published a rather quiet little poem entitled "The Blasphemies." It had enough intrinsic interest to earn it a place in that volume, but the poem is important as well as interesting because it seems to reflect, to some oblique degree, the cyclic nature of the poet's own spiritual development. As Yeats was obsessed with gyres, so MacNeice seemed to have been attracted strongly in his later years by the symbolism of cycles representing the power of nature to repeat itself. It is only fair to point out that the cyclic movement often represented mere repetition with only infrequent suggestions of the cycle of renewal which becomes the spiral circling upward.

At the age of seven the protagonist of "The Blasphemies" wonders about the nature of the sin against the Holy Ghost, a sin so deadly that it alone among mortal transgressions is unforgivable (Matthew 12:31; Mark 3:29; Luke 12:10). For a child of the rectory, such haunting questions might seem natural and even inevitable. The next stage at age seventeen is perhaps natural but surely not inevitable: the adolescent parodies all things holy; but he recognizes the irony that, if one does not believe in the existence of God anyway, it is only a feeble joke to take His Name in vain.

At thirty he has dismissed God from his thoughts as well as from existence. The all and the only is humanity. Ten years later, feeling the need of something of greater meaning and value than mere facts, he dusts off the symbols and myths of his childhood. At fifty, he is simply a "walking question" murmuring "The sin/ Against the Holy Ghost—what is it?"

Whatever the doctrinal definitions involved, or the relevance to men generally (the poet says he is not "Tom Dick and Harry," nor is everyone Christ), it is safe to claim that the quest ended where it began; and the question of the boy also haunted the middle-aged man. The poet began his education in the Classic-haunted atmosphere of Oxford; he took a "first" in Classics and became a lecturer in Greek. Throughout his poetic career of intensive relevance to the modern world and its crises, he continued to feed upon the Classics and to share them with others in the classroom until 1939. In the cyclic pattern of the poem of 1961, this study of MacNeice's poetic career has been traced from the "bright young man" of the first in Classics to the recurring and final phase of the "classical humanist." Between the echo and the reecho of one haunting refrain, his life is strongly representative in the microcosm of all the macrocosmic trauma of European man through those same years.

The first publication of a few poems in *Oxford Poetry, 1929,* defined the continuing interest in sleep ("Cradle Song"), the passage of time and the imminence of death ("Laburnum"), as well as the philosophic structure of his mind and the wit of his expression ("Address From My Death-Bed to Dr. Bruno, the Concrete Universal"). In the same year, the first collection of his own poetry, *Blind Fireworks,* added the themes of childhood experience ("Child's Terror"), the search for identity and the early loss of faith ("Child's Unhappiness"), social criticism through biblical archetypes with personal reference ("Adam's Legacy"), and what was to be a lifelong interest in modern art ("Poussin"). With bright, light facility, and with macabre humor ("Corpse Carousal"), he writes about a moribund culture ("Neurotics") at the moment of its eschatological death throes, as if the total demise were a kind of witty shocker ("Middle Age").

The *Poems* of 1935 reveal the poet trapped by a sense of no place to escape and nothing to be done ("Eclogue for Christmas"). The philosophic mind begins to "toast the incidental things," to shift from large generalizations to concrete, material images. In the translation of Aeschylus' *Agamemnon* in 1937, the technique of the dialogue form, explored in the eclogues, is exploited and rehearsed for such radio dramas of the succeeding years as *Out of the Picture, Christopher Columbus, The Dark Tower, Sunbeams in His Hat, The Nosebag,* and the plays of the "March Hare Saga."

Letters from Iceland, 1937, introduces the interest of the "Thirties' poets" in Byron ("Letter to Byron" on the theme and in the rhythms of *Don Juan*). Auden's poetic parody in that volume is matched by MacNeice's prose parodies in *I Crossed the Minch* (1938) and by the poetic parodies of *Ten Burnt Offerings* (1952).

Autumn Journal (1939) represents the *agon* of Louis Mac-Neice and of all men who were reared on the dogmas of liberalism. The volume fails in depth, the poet confesses, because no great poetry will be written in our time until we have made sense of our world. The journal, which begins in amazement and shock, ends in an expression of that vague, diffuse good will that the poet has already admitted to have been outdated by the bombing of Barcelona December 7, 1937. There are many who renounce personal moral responsibility and simply take orders from the Italian or Germanic accents of the Mussolini-Hitler voice screaming out of the radio (Canto XVIII); but MacNeice is not one of these. He agrees with Aristotle that man-in-action is the essential and truly existent man (Canto XVI). But MacNeice's form of action is simply to write some very good modern love poetry (Canto IV) and to exhort the other liberals of his generation to sink their individualistic horror of politics in political action before they find they have no individual or political rights left (Canto XIV).

The poet himself describes *The Last Ditch* (1940) as odds and ends that lack heroics and belief—as "a thief/Bundled up in the last ditch" (Dedication). Some of the poems are embarrassingly juvenile both in theme and treatment; sixteen describe the coming of war. Amidst the frequent irrelevance and frivolity of the collection, the poet manages to say three things very expertly: this is how it was when I was a boy; the England I love is in that past; these broken fragments of that past are all that are left after the shattering impact of modern war. *Plant and Phantom* (1941) advances the philosophic poet's attack upon Monism ("Plurality"). Whenever the mind, he says, attempts to reduce plurality to genus, basic similarity, or universal form, it kills the many in order to produce the one ("Plain Speaking"). But the intellectual argument now has the emotional overtone of a despairing surrender of any attempt to reduce the world to order and a rather supine settling down with this item and this and this. . . .

Springboard (1945) marks the beginning of a profound change. The title poem deals candidly with the poet's problem of that paralysis which comes from unbelief. With equal frankness the poet describes the prewar Liberal as a kind of ethical "Bottleneck." He is so high-minded that he can fight only for a pure motive; but are there any pure motives in an impure world? His education and training have made him a constitutional noncombatant, with a soul too violent to kill anyone but himself. Thus the necessary compromises which make action possible in an imperfect world can never squeeze through the bottleneck of his idealism. However, the climax of the collection is not to be found in hopeless dilemma but in the saving exceptions of "The Kingdom." This kingdom is composed of rugged, individualistic souls, who— although molded by the same societal conditions as the paralyzed bottlenecks—have the courage to discover their own personal identity and to form a living kingdom of individuals beneath the hardening crust of bureaucracy. As such, they not only vindicate the human race but also give hope and courage to others.

The deep disillusionment with liberalism that could be plainly seen in *The Last Ditch, Plant and Phantom,* and *The Springboard* reaches its climax in *Holes in the Sky: Poems 1944–1947.* The poet, now middle-aged, is in the mood to analyze his own life as well as that of the world. He is still master of his own poetic idiom, but this technical mastery may also act as a straitjacket that confines the poet to the old themes expressed expertly in the old tunes. The old technique is quite inadequate to state new meanings and relationships, but is the poet himself ready to state these new meanings and relationships? *Springboard* gave a clue; *Holes in the Sky* was chiefly transitional; the dedicatory sestet "To Hedli" from *Collected Poems: 1925–1948* formed a developmental link; and *Ten Burnt Offerings* provides the answers.

Ten Burnt Offerings (1952) contains the best exhibits of the mature, reflective MacNeice. The poems are longer, more complex in structure, more substantial in theme, more religious in tone and topic, and more richly and deeply moving in diction and prosody than the old flippant ditties. There are not many final philosophic answers, but there is humility in the face of the imponderables and a refuge for the artist in the "Grecian Urn" theme of Keats—art need not explain; it need only capture the moment of fleeting love and make it immortal.

It would be pleasant to say that, once having achieved the note of high seriousness that the Victorians considered essential to true art, MacNeice remained consistently on that lofty eminence for the remainder of his poetic career. However, *Autumn Sequel*

(1954) not only has a retrospective ring but is downright regressive in style, social criticism, and the re-emergence of the old doubts and denials. But, amidst the catalogue of friends dead or dying, the poet reminds us that these references are neither primarily obituary nor esoteric; they comprise a list of members of that "Kingdom" first mentioned in *Springboard* and developed in *Ten Burnt Offerings* and in *The Burning Perch*—a kingdom which justifies humanity, asserts personal identity, and provides hope for the future. From this point of view, the *Sequel* is only antepenultimate, *Ten Burnt Offerings* is the penult, and the last three volumes (*Visitations, Solstices, The Burning Perch*) are ultimate.

Visitations (1958) has been well described as attempts at the "immediate experience of mystery." Much of the apparatus of the mystical vision—light, aloneness, apprehension, and unity—are to be found in these poems, particularly in the last seven which are entitled "Visitations." In many ways the volume seems the significant exploration of a path which the poet then rejects to return to one well trodden by his previous footsteps. *Solstices* (1961) implies in its very title the twin mechanisms of the collection. The solstice occurs twice annually, and this poetry is about life's infinite capacity for repeating itself. As such, it slides into the well-worn groove of MacNeice's cyclical thought. But the solstice occurs at the period when the sun is at the greatest distance from the celestial equator. This hints at both old and new: the old sense of aging, of cold doubts and paralytic denials, of shattering disillusionments without new and compensating illusions.

But in the actual context of the poems in this volume, the passing years, undoubtedly cold and unilluminated enough, are transformed from loss to gain because, unwittingly, they were spent waiting for the right person to come along. Now that she has come, the poet shakes off the *memento mori* shudder of "How can summer be so short?" and wonders comfortably "And now it is come, how can it last so long?" The oldest of old clichés—"I love you"—becomes not brutal denigrating repetition, meaningless because common and banal, but fresh each time it is used, newly minted and stamped with the wonder of the unique. The past, which, though dear, had been shattered, and the future so full of fears, are finally merged in the present perfect hour. The apparatus of the mystic vision is even more apparent in *Solstices* than in the preceding *Visitations*.

The Burning Perch, published posthumously in 1963, is from the title to the last stanza, by far the most eschatological of Mac-Neice's books. The budgerigar flutters on a burning perch, quite unaware of its imminent destruction, but with the mania of supreme egotism it calls the whole universe to regard its gyrations and all creatures everywhere to listen to its midget personal affirmation. Death is, of course, the egoist's eschatology—"If I die, how can the world survive?"; and it is tempting to interpret the burning of the perch as the dying of the "Budgie." But this interpretation would neglect one of the strong and insistent notes of universal doom heard in MacNeice's poetry from the earliest youthful beginnings and now full-throated and clarion after the very ending.

The collection is marred by the recital of some of the old frustrations, cul-de-sacs, and doubts; it is magnified by the final long poem "Memoranda to Horace." It is always significant when a modern poet reveals the name of a previous poet with whom he identifies himself. In MacNeice's case it is doubly significant because not only can an impressive list of similarities be noted, but also the modern poet was a reputable Classical scholar, quite capable of understanding his ancient counterpart's language, world, and personality. Like Horace, MacNeice was the poet of the polished style and the sophisticated satire. He, too, moved in "court circles"; but, like the Roman, he maintained his independence of thought. Each became in his own time a byword for urbane wit. Like MacNeice, Horace had no final answers. He bent the knee dutifully to Augustus, and then he slipped away to his rural villa and his real life of love and laughter. Both men appreciated and practiced appetitive decorum in times when it was not only unfashionable but a cause for the conjectural lifting of eyebrows. So far the poem moves in elevated strophes, elegant and mature and serene as MacNeice is seldom serene. But at the end the poem falls, the elevation drops, the MacNeice urbane wit slips through bathos into the silliness that occasionally marred his best work.

Having thoroughly established a remarkable number of identities with the ancient writer, the poet must go on to establish two differences. First, MacNeice has a Gothic fancy for the grotesque

which makes him cherish the company of trolls, elves, and leprechauns. Second, his retreat has been the curiously self-conscious
second childhood which had never quite lost touch with his first
childhood. At first, we are tempted to exasperation by the tasteless
imbecility of the marred close of a very good poem. The knee
bent formally to the established order, the real life elsewhere in
the recurrent renewal of the seasons and the laughter of friends
and lovers—and then the Irish jig and the childish lisp.

But perhaps even in bad taste the poet may be trusted to write
his own epitaph—urbane, witty, technically brilliant, the pro-
claimer of the real object rather than the philosophic definition,
the satirist of the social world of which he is a part, the cultus of
friendship and love, the long-sought and finally arriving fulfillment and peace—and then the sudden characteristic descent, lest
art should seem too serious and intention earnest, to consort with
trolls and leprechauns.

His old friend, W. H. Auden, gave a memorial address for
Louis MacNeice, at All Souls Church, Langham Place, October
17, 1963.[1] With urbane taste and ready wit he quoted at the close
exactly the sort of mordant but light understatement MacNeice
would have chosen—and from MacNeice's own works:

> . . . here is the jotter
> With his last doodle which might be his own digestive tract
> Ulcer and all or might be the flowery maze
> Through which he had wandered deliciously till he stumbled
> Suddenly finally conscious of all he lacked
> On a manhole under the hollyhocks. The pencil
> Point had obviously broken, yet, when he left this room
> By catdrop sleight-of-foot or simple vanishing act,
> To those who knew him . . .
> This man with the shy smile has left behind
> Something that was intact.[2]

Notes and References

Chapter One

1. Louis MacNeice and Stephen Spender, *Oxford Poetry: 1929* (New York, 1929), p. 24.
2. Louis MacNeice, *The Strings Are False*, ed., E. R. Dodds (New York, 1966), pp. 239ff.
3. *Time*, September 13, 1963, p. 105.
4. F. O. Matthiessen, "Louis MacNeice," *The Responsibilities of the Critic*, ed., John Rackliffe (New York, 1952), p. 106.
5. Louis MacNeice, Foreword, *Blind Fireworks*, London, 1929.
6. Matthiessen, p. 106.
7. "Know Thyself."
8. Geoffrey Grigson, ed., *The Arts Today* (London, 1935), p. 34.
9. Louis MacNeice, "Poetry Today," *The Arts Today*, ed., Geoffrey Grigson (London, 1935), p. 32.
10. *Ibid.*, p. 42.
11. Delmore Schwartz, "Adroitly Naïve," *Poetry*, LXVIII (May, 1936), 115.
12. Grigson, p. 30.
13. *Ibid.*, p. 43.
14. *Ibid.*, p. 26.
15. *The Strings Are False*, p. 143.
16. Louis Malone, pseudonym, *Roundabout Way* (London and New York, 1932), p. 45.
17. *Ibid.*, p. 226.
18. Louis MacNeice, *Poems*, London, 1935.
19. Acknowledgments, *Poems*, 1935.
20. Schwartz, 115.
21. Grigson, p. 43.
22. *Time*, September 13, 1963, p. 104.
23. Grigson, p. 28.
24. Louis MacNeice, *Modern Poetry: A Personal Essay* (London, 1938), pp. 174–75.

25. Aeschylus, *Agamemnon*, trans., Louis MacNeice, London, 1937.

26. *Ibid.*, Preface.

27. Aeschylus, *Agamemnon*, trans., Herbert Weir Smyth, Loeb Classical Library (Cambridge, Massachusetts, 1957), lines 1–7.

28. Aeschylus, *Agamemnon*, trans., Louis MacNeice, p. 13, lines 1–7.

29. Grigson, p. 51.

30. Louis MacNeice, *Out of the Picture*, New York, 1938.

31. *Ibid.*, p. 46.

32. *Ibid.*, p. 122.

33. *Ibid.*, p. 22.

34. *Ibid.*, p. 35.

35. *Ibid.*, p. 49.

36. *Ibid.*, p. 85.

37. *Ibid.*, p. 98.

38. *Ibid.*, p. 126.

39. *Ibid.*

40. Grigson, p. 67.

41. Samuel French Morse, "An End to the Abstract," *Poetry*, LI (November, 1937), 105.

42. Grigson, p. 59.

Chapter Two

1. Book Reviews, Section VII, New York *Times*, August 9, 1953, p. 7.

2. *Ibid.*

3. T. C. Wilson, "One of the Best" (Review of MacNeice, *Poems*), *Poetry*, LI (March, 1938), 339.

4. Section VII, New York *Times*, August 9, 1953, p. 7.

5. F. O. Matthiessen, *The Responsibilities of the Critic*, ed., John Rackliffe (New York, 1952), p. 106.

6. *Ibid.*, p. 111.

7. Louis MacNeice and W. H. Auden, *Letters from Iceland*, London, 1937.

8. *Ibid.*, p. 201.

9. Louis MacNeice, *Modern Poetry: A Personal Essay* (London, 1938), p. 189.

10. *Letters from Iceland*, p. 19.

11. *Ibid.*, p. 20.

12. *Ibid.*, p. 21.

13. "Letter to Graham and Anne Shepard."

14. *Letters from Iceland*, p. 44.

15. *Ibid.*, p. 57.

16. *Ibid.*, p. 237.

17. *Ibid.*
18. *Ibid.*
19. *Poems,* p. 18.
20. Louis MacNeice, I *Crossed the Minch* (London, 1938). The Minch is the body of water lying between the Outer Hebrides and the Western coast of Scotland.
21. *Ibid.,* p. 3.
22. *Ibid.*
23. *Ibid.,* p. 69.
24. *Ibid.,* p. 18.
25. *Ibid.,* p. 21.
26. *Ibid.,* p. 228.
27. *Ibid.,* p. 4.
28. *Ibid.,* p. 13.
29. *Ibid.,* p. 4.
30. *Ibid.,* p. 11.
31. *Ibid.,* p. 23.
32. *Ibid.,* p. 79.
33. *Ibid.,* p. 37.
34. *Ibid.,* p. 124.
35. *Ibid.,* p. 125.
36. *Ibid.,* p. 127.
37. *Ibid.,* p. 130.
38. *Ibid.,* p. 138.
39. *Ibid.,* p. 177.
40. *Ibid.,* p. 178.
41. *Ibid.,* p. 180.
42. *Ibid.,* p. 183.
43. *Ibid.,* p. 157.
44. *Letters from Iceland,* p. 124.
45. I *Crossed the Minch,* p. 156.
46. *Ibid.,* p. 106.
47. *Ibid.,* p. 159.
48. *Ibid.,* p. 175.
49. *Ibid.,* p. 245.
50. Louis MacNeice, *Zoo,* London, 1938.
51. I *Crossed the Minch,* p. 223.
52. Preface, *Zoo,* p. 9.
53. *Zoo,* p. 31.
54. *Ibid.* (Translation: W. D. Ross), p. 32.
55. *Zoo,* p. 66.
56. *Ibid.,* p. 227.
57. *Ibid.,* p. 239. "When they are in model zoological gardens, the animals, even though separated from the climate of their habitat, are

surrounded by comfort and attention. When they become accustomed to their situation, they prefer the peace and security of captivity to the freedom and terrors of wild life."

58. *Ibid.*, p. 239.
59. *Ibid.*, p. 78.
60. *Ibid.*, p. 84.
61. Louis MacNeice, *The Earth Compels* (London, 1938), p. 4.
62. *I Crossed the Minch*, p. 175.
63. "Sharp Winter Is Broken," Horace, *Odes*, Book I, Ode iv, line 1.
64. *The Responsibilities of the Critic*, p. 109.
65. *Modern Poetry*, p. 112.
66. *Ibid.*, p. 52.
67. *Ibid.*, p. 176.
68. *Ibid.*, pp. 176–77.
69. Preface, *Modern Poetry*.
70. *Ibid.*, p. 14.
71. *Ibid.*, p. 32.
72. *Ibid.*, p. 34.
73. *Ibid.*, p. 39.
74. *Ibid.*, p. 43.
75. *Ibid.*, p. 48.
76. *Ibid.*, pp. 88–89.
77. *Ibid.*, p. 111.
78. *Ibid.*, p. 135.
79. *Ibid.*, p. 151.
80. *Ibid.*, p. 152.
81. *Ibid.*, p. 157.
82. *Ibid.*, p. 162.
83. *Ibid.*, pp. 146, 166.
84. *Ibid.*, p. 178.
85. *Ibid.*, p. 198.

Chapter Three

1. Louis MacNeice, "The Poet in England Today," *New Republic*, CII (March 25, 1940), 4.
2. *Ibid.*
3. *Ibid.*
4. Louis MacNeice, *Autumn Journal*, London, 1939.
5. Julian Symons, "Louis MacNeice: The Artist as Everyman," *Poetry*, LVI (May, 1940), 92.
6. Note, *Autumn Journal*.
7. *Ibid.*
8. Symons, pp. 86–94.

9. David Daiches, "The Honest Man Alone," *Poetry*, LVII (November, 1940), 152–57.

10. *The Collected Essays of John Peale Bishop*, ed., Edmund Wilson (London, 1948), pp. 310ff.

11. James G. Southworth, *Sowing the Spring: Studies in British Poets from Hopkins to MacNeice* (London, 1940), pp. 165ff.

12. Stuart Gerry Brown, "Some Poems of Louis MacNeice," *Sewanee Review*, LI (January, 1943), 68.

13. Louis MacNeice, *Selected Poems*, London, 1940.

14. Louis MacNeice, *The Last Ditch*, Dublin, 1940.

15. New York *Times* (February 25, 1940), p. 28.

16. "Collected Criticism of Conrad Aiken from 1916 to the Present," *A Reviewer's ABC* (New York, 1958), pp. 285–88.

17. "The Coming of War" is the title of a group of four poems from *The Last Ditch:* "Dublin," "Cushendun," "Sligo and Mayo," and "Galway." In later collections these poems are called "The Closing Album."

18. Louis MacNeice, *Plant and Phantom* (London, 1941). Nietzsche, translated to fit MacNeice's use: "a division and a union of plant and phantom."

19. Richard Crowder, "Mr. MacNeice and Miss Sitwell," *Poetry*, LIII (January, 1949), 218–22.

20. Louis MacNeice, *The Poetry of W. B. Yeats*, New York, 1941.

21. F. O. Matthiessen, *The Responsibilities of the Critic*, ed., John Rackliffe (New York, 1952), pp. 25ff.

22. *The Poetry of W. B. Yeats*, p. 1.

23. Louis MacNeice, "Yeats's Epitaph," *New Republic*, CII (June 24, 1940), 862.

24. Preface, *The Poetry of W. B. Yeats*.

25. *The Poetry of W. B. Yeats*, p. 11.

26. *Ibid.*, p. 23.

27. *Ibid.*, p. 24.

28. *Ibid.*, p. 24.

29. *Ibid.*, p. 40.

30. *Ibid.*, p. 55.

31. *Ibid.*, p. 100.

32. *Ibid.*, p. 130.

33. *Ibid.*, p. 144.

34. *Ibid.*, p. 188.

35. Louis MacNeice, *The Strings Are False: An Unfinished Autobiography*, ed., E. R. Dodds, New York, 1966.

36. Louis MacNeice, *Christopher Columbus: A Radio Play* (London, 1944), p. 9.

37. *Ibid.*, p. 88.

38. *Ibid.*, p. 92.

39. Louis MacNeice, "The English Literary Scene Today," New York *Times*, Book Review, Section VII, September 28, 1947, p. 1.

40. *Ibid.*

41. Louis MacNeice, *Springboard,* New York, 1945.

42. Igor Stravinsky, "Memories of T. S. Eliot," *Esquire,* LXIV, 2 (August, 1965), 93.

43. Obituary, London *Times,* September 4, 1963, p. 14e.

44. *Springboard,* p. 48 (Dante: "I leave behind the bile and I go toward the sweet fruit").

45. F. W. Dupee, "Lewis and MacNeice," *The Nation,* CLXI (October 13, 1945), 380.

46. *Springboard,* p. 7.

47. Louis MacNeice, *The Dark Tower and Other Radio Scripts,* London, 1947.

48. *Ibid.,* p. 10.

49. *Ibid.,* p. 14.

50. *Ibid.,* p. 15.

51. *Ibid.,* p. 66.

52. *Ibid.,* p. 89.

53. *Ibid.,* p. 136.

Chapter Four

1. Louis MacNeice, "Poetry, the Public and the Critic," *New Statesman and Nation,* XXXVIII (October 8, 1949), 381.

2. Louis MacNeice, *Holes in the Sky: Poems 1944–1947,* New York, 1948.

3. William Van O'Connor, "Master of His Idiom," *Saturday Review of Literature,* XXXII, No. 5 (January 29, 1949), 27.

4. Denis Botterill, "Review of *Holes in the Sky,*" *Life and Letters Today,* LX (February, 1949), 111–13.

5. Horace Gregory, "The New January," *Poetry,* LXXIV (August, 1949), 301–4.

6. "Such a Dear Head."

7. Louis MacNeice, *Collected Poems, 1925–1948,* London, 1949.

8. *Goethe's "Faust,"* Parts I and II, trans., Louis MacNeice, New York, 1960.

9. Louis MacNeice, *Ten Burnt Offerings,* London, 1952.

10. D. Burnham, "Mind of a Man," *Commonweal,* LVIII (August 21, 1953), 495.

11. Louis MacNeice, *Autumn Sequel, a Rhetorical Poem in XXVI Cantos,* London, 1954.

12. "Personal Panorama" (Review of *Autumn Sequel*), London *Times,* November 20, 1954, p. 8.

13. "Mr. Louis MacNeice's 'Autumn Sequel,'" London *Times,* July 5, 1954, p. 11b.

Chapter Five

1. Obituary, London *Times,* September 4, 1963, p. 14e.
2. *Ibid.*
3. Stephen Spender, "Songs of an Unsung Classicist," *Saturday Review of Literature,* XLVI (September 7, 1963), 25, 33.
4. *Ibid.,* 25.
5. Louis MacNeice, *Visitations,* New York, 1958.
6. Janet Fiscalini, "Sympathetic Poet," *Commonweal,* LXVIII (July 4, 1958), 357.
7. Dudley Fitts, "With a Moralizing Public Tone," New York *Times,* Section VII, February 8, 1959, p. 10.
8. Fiscalini, 357.
9. *Ibid.*
10. Louis MacNeice, *Eighty-Five Poems, Selected by the Author,* New York, 1959.
11. *Ibid.,* p. 7.
12. P. N. Furbank, "New Poetry," *The Listener and B.B.C. Television Review,* September 19, 1963, p. 439.
13. Louis MacNeice, *Solstices,* London, 1961.
14. Dante: "The Dark Wood."
15. "The Little Refusal."
16. M. L. Rosenthal, "Everything Is Subject for Good Talk," New York *Times,* Section VII, November 12, 1961, p. 4.
17. Louis MacNeice, *The Burning Perch,* London, 1963.
18. Revelation 21:5.
19. In addition to "Réchauffé" and "This Is the Life," which are treated instead in the category of poems about death.
20. Louis MacNeice, *Varieties of Parable,* "Cambridge University Clark Lectures," Cambridge, 1965.

Chapter Six

1. W. H. Auden, "Louis MacNeice: 1907–1963," *The Listener,* October 24, 1963, p. 646.
2. W. H. Auden quoted only the last two lines from Louis Mac-Neice's "The Suicide," *The Burning Perch,* p. 14. I have taken the liberty of adding the obviously relevant lines which precede his quotation.

Selected Bibliography

PRIMARY SOURCES

1. POETRY

Autumn Journal. London: Faber and Faber Ltd., May 1939.
Autumn Sequel: A Rhetorical Poem in XXVI Cantos. London: Faber and Faber Ltd., 1954.
Blind Fireworks. London: Victor Gollancz Ltd., 1929.
The Burning Perch. London: Faber and Faber Ltd., 1963.
Collected Poems: 1925–1948. London: Faber and Faber Ltd., 1949.
Collected Poems. Edited by E. R. Dodds. London: Faber and Faber, 1966; New York: Oxford University Press, 1967.
The Earth Compels: Poems. London: Faber and Faber Limited, April 1938.
Eighty-Five Poems: Selected by the Author. New York: Oxford University Press, 1959.
Holes in the Sky: Poems 1944–1947. New York: Random House, 1949.
The Last Ditch. Dublin: The Cuala Press, 1940.
Oxford Poetry, 1929. Edited by Louis MacNeice and Stephen Spender. New York: D. Appleton and Company, 1929.
Plant and Phantom: Poems. London: Faber and Faber Ltd., April 1941.
Poems. London: Faber and Faber Ltd., September 1935.
Selected Poems. London: Faber and Faber Ltd., March 1940.
Solstices. London: Faber and Faber Ltd., 1961.
Springboard: Poems 1941–1944. New York: Random House, 1945.
Ten Burnt Offerings. London: Faber and Faber Ltd., 1952.
Visitations. New York: Oxford University Press, 1958.

Poems Not Reprinted in Collections

"Shopping," "Idealist," *New Statesman and Nation,* XVIII (December 9, 1939), 820.
"The Clock," "Interregnum," *New Statesman and Nation,* XIX (January 6, 1940), 11.
"Radio," *New Republic,* CII (May 20, 1940), 678.
"November Afternoon," *New Republic,* CII (June 3, 1940), 767.

"Ballade of England," *New Yorker,* XVI (November 30, 1940), 32.

"The Sense of Smell," *New Yorker,* XVI (January 25, 1941), 21.

"Straight Words to a Crooked Poet," *New Yorker,* XVIII (September 19, 1942), 34.

2. DRAMA AND DRAMATIC CRITICISM

The Agamemnon of Aeschylus. Translated by Louis MacNeice. New York: Harcourt, Brace and Company, May 24, 1937.

"The *Antigone* of Sophocles," review of the production at the Arts Theatre, Cambridge, *Spectator,* CLXII (March 10, 1939), 404.

"The Bradfield Greek Play, *Oedipus Tyrannus,*" review, *Spectator,* CLVIII (June 25, 1937), 1187.

Christopher Columbus; a Radio Play. London: Faber and Faber Ltd., 1944.

The Dark Tower and Other Radio Scripts. London: Faber and Faber Limited, 1947.

Goethe's "Faust," Parts I and II. An abridged version translated by Louis MacNeice. New York: Oxford University Press, 1952.

The Mad Islands; The Administrator. London: Faber and Faber, 1964.

Out of the Picture: A Play in Two Acts. New York: Harcourt, Brace and Company, 1938.

Unpublished Radio Dramas and Documentaries

(The Berg Collection of English and American Literature in the New York City Public Library includes a large selection of mimeographed radio dramas which were used for broadcasts, but never published. Some are marked with MacNeice's own penciled suggestions for production. A complete list can be obtained from the British Broadcasting Corporation.)

"*Trimalchio's Feast,*" transmitted December 22, 1940.

"Madame Tussaud's," June 2, 1941 (Series, "The Stones Cry Out").

"Salute to the Red Army," February 22, 1943 (Documentary).

""He had a Date," June 28, 1944.

"*The Golden Ass,*" November 3, 1944; December 31, 1956.

"Cupid and Psyche," November 7, 1944.

"Enter Caesar," September 20, 1946.

"The Careerist," October 22, 23, 1946.

"Enemy of Cant," December 3, 4, 1946.

"The Heartless Giant," December 13, 1946.

"The Death of Gunnar," March 11, 1947 (Icelandic Saga, number 1).

"Burning of Njal," March 12, 1947 (Icelandic Saga, number 2).

"Portrait of Rome," June 22, 1947 (Documentary).

"India at First Sight," March 13, 1948 (Documentary).

"India and Pakistan: The Road to Independence," May 23, 1948 (Documentary).
"The Two Wicked Sisters," July 19, 1948.
"Portrait of Athens," November 18, 1951 (Documentary).
"Twelve Days of Christmas," January 6, 1953 (Occasional).
"James Henry Selden Memorial Lecture," Connecticut College, New London. A recital of songs and verse readings by Hedli Anderson and Louis MacNeice, April 24, 1953.
"Return to a School," October 15, 1954 (Documentary).
"Also Among the Prophets," February 5, 1956.
"Spires and Gantries," July 29, 1956.
"Carpe Diem," October 8, 1956.
"From Bard to Busker," December 30, 1956.
"All Fools at Home," April 1, 1958.
"Scrums and Dreams," April 3, 1959.
"They Met on Good Friday," December 8, 1959.
"Another Part of the Sea," typescript produced and transmitted by B.B.C. TV, September 7, 1960.
"The Administrator," March 10, 1961.
"Persons from Porlock," September 19, 1963.

3. PROSE VOLUMES

Astrology. Garden City, New York: Doubleday and Company, 1964; London: Aldus Books Ltd., 1964.
I Crossed the Minch. London: Longmans, Green and Company, 1938.
Letters from Iceland. W. H. Auden and Louis MacNeice. London: Faber and Faber Ltd., July 1937.
Modern Poetry: A Personal Essay. London: Oxford University Press, 1938.
The Poetry of W. B. Yeats. New York: Oxford University Press, 1941.
Roundabout Way. Louis Malone, Pseud. London and New York: Putnam, 1932.
The Strings Are False: An Unfinished Autobiography. Edited by E. R. Dodds. New York: Oxford University Press, 1966.
Varieties of Parable. Cambridge: University Press, 1965.
Zoo. London: Michael Joseph Ltd., 1938.

Reviews and Literary Criticism in Periodicals and Collections

"Books in General," *New Statesman and Nation,* XLIV (September 13, 1952), 293.
"Eliot and the Adolescent," *T. S. Eliot: A Symposium.* Compiled by Richard March and Tambimuttu. London: PL Editions, 1948.

"The English Literary Scene Today," Book Review, New York *Times,* September 26, 1947, VII, 1.

"He Weeps by the Side of the Ocean," *New Statesman and Nation,* XLVI (December 5, 1953), 721.

"The Poet in England Today," Books in Review, *New Republic,* CII (March 25, 1940), I, 412.

"Poetry Needs to be Subtle and Tough," Book Review, New York *Times,* August 9, 1953, VII, 7.

"Poetry, the Public and the Critic," *New Statesman and Nation,* XXXVIII (October 8, 1949), 380–81.

"Poetry Today," *The Arts Today.* Edited by Geoffrey Grigson. London: John Lane, 1935, pp. 25–67.

"Sir Thomas Malory," *The English Novelists: A Survey of the Novel by Twenty Contemporary Novelists.* Edited by Derek Verschoyle. New York: Harcourt, Brace and Company, 1936, pp. 19–29.

"Subject in Modern Poetry," *Essays and Studies,* XXII. Oxford: Clarendon Press, 1937, pp. 144–58.

"Woods to Get Lost In (Pleasure in Reading)," London *Times,* August 17, 1961, 11b.

"Yeats's Epitaph," review, *New Republic,* CII (June 24, 1940), 102.

Articles on Sports

"Gael Force at Wembley," *New Statesman,* LXV (June 7, 1963), 876.

"Nine New Caps," *New Statesman,* LXIII (February 16, 1962), 239.

"Talking About Rugby," *New Statesman,* LVII (February 28, 1959), 286.

4. MISCELLANEOUS

"Great Summer Sale," *New Statesman,* LXVI (July 5, 1963), 10ff.

The Penny That Rolled Away. London and New York: B. P. Putnam's Sons, 1954 (*The Sixpence That Rolled Away.* London: Faber and Faber Ltd., 1956).

"Aragon: A Little Anthology," *Sewanee Review,* LIII (October, 1945), 611–29 (Contains translations by Louis MacNeice of three poems by Louis Aragon: "The Lilacs and the Roses," "The Unoccupied Zone," "Richard Coeur-de-Lion").

"That Chair of Poetry," *New Statesman,* LI (February 10, 1961), 210.

"Under the Sugar Loaf," *New Statesman,* LXIII (June 29, 1962), 948.

SECONDARY SOURCES

1. ANONYMOUS NEWS ITEMS AND REVIEWS

"*Autumn Sequel,*" London *Times,* July 5, 1954, 11b. The emphasis is less on public events than its predecessor, *Autumn Journal,* and more on those friends, living and dead, who are the life-giving antidote to the monotony of a machine age.

"Autumn Sequel," London *Times,* November 20, 1954, 8. The diction displays the old verbal dexterity, but the *Sequel* rings too familiarly; nostalgia not prophecy, memories rather than creativity.

"Candour, Clarity and Compassion in Modern Verse," London *Times,* September 28, 1961, 15e. The new collection (*Solstices*) easy, knowledgeable, with much verbal magic.

"Disturbing and Witty Play: Logic of Dreams," London *Times,* March 11, 1961, 3f. The radio drama, *The Administrator,* is disappointing because the careful analysis of all the factors that go into making a decision is shown to be curiously irrelevant to the decision itself.

"I Crossed the Minch," London *Times,* April 5, 1938, 10e. The brief imbedded poems are worth all the private jokes of sophisticated fun.

"Modern Poets in Search of a Public," London *Times,* August 15, 1957, 11e. *Visitations* is lit by an easy brilliance which seems on the verge of breaking into something important without ever quite doing so.

"Modern Poets Look Outside Themselves for a Theme," London *Times,* August 6, 1959, 11e. The critical reaction to *Eighty-Five Poems* indicates that Mr. MacNeice's extreme readability has probably hurt his reputation.

"Moonfolk and Mountainfolk in Some New Poetry," London *Times,* December 5, 1963, 17c. The locale of this posthumous volume (*The Burning Perch*) is a ghost-ridden London haunted by the unforgiving specters of failure.

"New Light on an Old Battle," London *Times,* December 9, 1959, 4g. A broadcast (*They Met on Good Friday*), full of clever but confusing mixture of early Irish lyrics, early English alliterative verse, the gruffness of saga, wisecracking colloquialisms, and caustic modern dialogue.

"Obituary," London *Times,* September 4, 1963, 14e. Louis MacNeice's drama had a sinewy quality actors loved; his poetry was marked by the sharp contemporary tang of his scholar-poet's idiom.

"Obituary," *Time,* LXXXII (September 13, 1963), 104. A handsome Irish-English scholar, he stood verse on its ear by mixing slang and sardonic wit, toff talk and tough thinking.

"Obituary," *Publishers' Weekly,* CLXXXIV (September 16, 1963), 88–89. One of the forgers of a new poetry which strongly asserted its concern for social and political issues.

"Out of the Picture, Louis MacNeice, with Music by Benjamin Britten," London *Times,* December 6, 1937, 18c. It tries to crowd

in more concrete and contemporary details than so loose a form can hold.

"Persons from Porlock," London *Times,* September 19, 1963, 16e. The drama has variety of character, mood, and pace, and MacNeice's happy playfulness with words.

"Poem in Seven Spaces," *National Review,* CXIV (April 1940), 514. Mr. MacNeice has something to say (*New Verse,* Ed., Geoffrey Grigson). But is it worth saying, and does he say it in poetry?

"Salute to the Red Army," London *Times,* February 22, 1943, 2c. The form is repetitious and the texture thin.

"Tale of Conflicting Loyalties: Strange Drama," London *Times,* September 7, 1960, 16e. Condensed and allusive dialogue which sets the scene, establishes the mood, and grips the listener (*Another Part of the Sea*).

"Ten Burnt Offerings," London *Times,* July 23, 1952, 8e. The collection has evidences of vitality and genuine experimentation, but is spoiled by technical sleight-of-hand.

"Ten Burnt Offerings," London *Times* Literary Supplement, August 8, 1952, 510. Amidst the superb poetic journalism, there is the development of a new, longer, more meditative, maturer poetry.

"Traitors in Our Way," London *Times,* March 26, 1957, 3c. The play depends on argument, but too much of it is off stage, and the remainder lacks weight and passion.

2. OTHER SECONDARY SOURCES

AIKEN, CONRAD. "Collected Criticism from 1916 to the Present," *A Reviewer's ABC.* New York: Meridian Books, Incorporated, 1958, pp. 285–88. *The Last Ditch* displays the author's speed, lightness, and intellectual range, but it is all topical, transitory, and reportorial.

ALLEN, WALTER. "London Literary Letter," Book Review, New York *Times,* September 22, 1963, VII, 38. A poet who looked like one, he was a player of games, a lover of sports, a gifted reporter of events, an effective writer for radio, a Classical scholar, and a pleasant companion.

AUDEN, WYSTAN HUGH. "Louis MacNeice: 1907–1963," *The Listener,* October 24, 1963, 646. His later poetry improved over his earlier poetry in sure craftsmanship and in power to move the reader.

BISHOP, JOHN PEALE. *The Collected Essays,* Ed. Edmund Wilson. London, New York: Charles Scribner's Sons, 1948. "The Hamlet of Louis MacNeice" is definitely post-Prufrock. He displays the tortured sensibility of his fellow poet Auden, but lacks his intensity.

BOGAN, LOUISE. *Selected Criticism: Prose, Poetry.* New York: Noonday Press, 1955. Consistently amusing and frequently brilliant, *Letters from Iceland,* in prose or in verse, also contains straight factual and historical information.

BOTTERILL, DENIS. "Review of *Holes in the Sky,*" *Life and Letters Today,* LX (February 1949), 111–13. *Holes in the Sky* represents that crisis moment in a poet's art when his past technical achievement is no longer adequate to his present needs.

BROWN, STUART GERRY. "Some Poems of Louis MacNeice," *Sewanee Review,* LI (January 1943), 62–72. Presents MacNeice as a writer of love poems, light-angry satires, and rugged and flexible blank verse.

BURNHAM, D. "Mind of a Man," *Commonweal,* LVIII (August 21, 1935), 495. In *Ten Burnt Offerings* the poems become more reflective and the technique of expression more mature.

CARRUTH, HAYDEN. "Uses of Typology," *Poetry,* CI (March 1963), 424–26. In *Solstices,* Mr. MacNeice has a decisive way of capturing the sensations of living in a crumbling empire.

CROWDER, RICHARD. "Mr. MacNeice and Miss Sitwell," *Poetry,* LXIII (January 1944), 218–22. Louis MacNeice shares Edith Sitwell's Peter-Panism, petulance at the approach of old age, and the use of nursery-rhyme principles of organization.

DAICHES, DAVID. "The Honest Man Alone," *Poetry,* LVII (November 5, 1940), 152–57. In *The Last Ditch,* the honest man stands alone at twilight; the poet marks time while he readjusts to the foreseen but shattering present.

DUPEE, F. W. "Lewis and MacNeice," *The Nation,* CLXI (October 13, 1945), 380. Witty, elegant, and a bit diffident, MacNeice has neither the ambiguities nor the inner contradictions essential to the production of great poetry.

ELIOT, THOMAS STEARNS. "Obituary," London *Times,* September 5, 1963, 14. In virtuosity a poet's poet, MacNeice also appealed to the larger body of poetry readers.

ELMAN, RICHARD M. "The Legacy of Louis MacNeice," *The New Republic,* CXLIX (October 26, 1963), 19–21. MacNeice's poetry is essayistic, discursive, but not incantatory.

FISCALINI, JANET. "Sympathetic Poet," *Commonweal,* LXVIII (July 4, 1958), 357. *Visitations* has high technical ability, pure music and mockery, and seven poems which are concerned with the immediate apprehension of mystery.

FITTS, DUDLEY. "With a Moralizing Public Tone," Book Reviews, New York *Times,* February 8, 1959, VII, 10. *Visitations* strikes the tedious attitude of "vaticism"—portentous public moralizing.

FURBANK, P. N. "New Poetry," *The Listener and B.B.C. Television Review,* September 19, 1963, 439. In *Eighty-Five Poems,* Mac-Neice said it was time to give the big answers or be silent—but he did neither.

GREGORY, HORACE. "The New January," *Poetry,* LXXIV (August 1949), 301–4. Is MacNeice torn between the old Auden manner and the liveliness of the younger, new Irish poets?

LARKIN, PHILIP. "Memoranda to Horace," *New Statesman,* LXVI (September 6, 1963), 294. *The Burning Perch* shows the human condition to be full of distress; the poet describes it not too solemnly so that it might be easier to bear.

MATTHIESSEN, F. O. "Louis MacNeice," *The Responsibilities of the Critic: Essays and Reviews by F. O. Matthiessen,* Selected by John Rackliffe. New York: Oxford University Press, 1952. Mac-Neice's poetic development has always been fairly independent of the young Oxford poets. For about five years (since 1938) he seems to have been standing still; but there are signs of progress in the architectural structure and complex harmonies of his new longer poems.

————. "Yeats: The Crooked Road," *The Responsibilities of the Critic.* New York: Oxford University Press, 1952. As a member of a very different school of poetry. MacNeice can point out what his generation learned from Yeats as well as what it rejected.

MORSE, SAMUEL FRENCH. "An End to the Abstract," *Poetry,* LI (November 1937), 104–7. In long-rhythmed, lithe verse, MacNeice writes the play, *Out of the Picture,* for which he had been long rehearsing in his eclogues; but all the honest poet can offer is his best wishes for good luck.

O'CONNOR, WILLIAM VAN. "Master of His Idiom," *Saturday Review of Literature,* XXXII, No. 5 (January 29, 1949), 27. Concentration of meaning is achieved in *Holes in the Sky* by use of a central "conceit"; MacNeice's old tone of satiric irony is replaced by a deeper feeling for England, childhood haunts, and the poet's craft.

ROSENTHAL, M. L. "Everything is Subject for Good Talk," New York *Times,* November 12, 1961, VII, 4. English verse (*Solstices*), to the American ear, has an articulateness close to glibness.

————. "Surrender to Despair," New York *Times,* December 22, 1963, VII, 4–5. *The Burning Perch* has plenty of the old vigor, sharp observation, and riddling wit; but the essential morale has turned moribund.

SALOMON, I. L. "Irish Oracle at Delphi," *Poetry,* LXXXIV (May 1954), 101–5. *Ten Burnt Offerings* is a series of quartets in a discursive opus that suffers from lack of unity and the footnotes that would clarify symbol and allusion.

SAVAGE, D. S. "The Poet's Perspectives," *Modern British Writing*, Ed. Denys Val Baker. New York: Vanguard Press, 1947. Also *Poetry*, LXIV (June 1944), 148–58. MacNeice's poetry provides a study in disintegration as topics become miscellaneous and the poet's concern moves from center to periphery.

SCHWARTZ, DELMORE. "Adroitly Naïve," *Poetry*, XLVIII (May 1936), 115–17. MacNeice is too emphatically contemporary; the center of the poem may be personal, but the circumference is always social.

SOUTHWORTH, JAMES G. *Sowing the Spring: Studies in British Poets from Hopkins to MacNeice.* Oxford: Basil Blackwell, 1940. Mr. MacNeice's distinction lies in his personal independence, his experimental attitude toward prosodic forms, and his great wealth of imagery and allusion.

SPENDER, STEPHEN. "Songs of an Unsung Classicist," *Saturday Review*, XLVI (September 7, 1963), 25–33. Louis MacNeice is one of the best poets of the present century, and one of the most neglected. The neglect stems from his clarity, his honesty, and the quiet milieu of his Classical humanism.

SYMONS, JULIAN. "Louis MacNeice: The Artist as Everyman," *Poetry*, LVI (May 1940), 86–94. MacNeice's poetry is the simple autobiography of the ordinary man. It is his lack of belief in any external force that keeps him from being a very fine poet.

WILSON, T. C. "One of the Best," *Poetry*, LI (March 1938), 339–44. Intelligence, sympathy, imagination, sensitivity, wit—MacNeice possesses them all. His lack of impact and inevitability comes from his unwillingness to decide and take sides.

3. DISSERTATIONS

ARMITAGE, CHRISTOPHER MEAD. Louis MacNeice: "A Biographical Account and a Study of His Prose Works". Durham, North Carolina: Duke University, 1967. Dr. Armitage is invaluable for biographical dating and the identification of persons from pseudonyms in the poetry. His analysis of MacNeice's prose is kept carefully in account with his poetic development.

POVEY, JOHN FREDERICK. "The Oxford Group: A Study of the Poetry of W. H. Auden, Stephen Spender, C. Day Lewis, and Louis MacNeice." Michigan State University, 1964. Dr. Povey argues that these poets must be considered as a group because, after representing a proletarian position in the 1930's, their voices have become less certain and their poetry less significant.

STAFFORD, MRS. OTTILIE. "A Critical Appraisal of the Works of Louis

MacNeice." Boston University, 1960. Dr. Stafford claims that MacNeice was never properly a member of the Auden group and proceeds to show how MacNeice's work developed after 1940.

Index

(Note: The number in parenthesis following a poem title indicates the number of poems included under that title.)

225